SCULPTURE IN THE ANCIENT MAYA PLAZA

Sculpture in the Ancient Maya Plaza

The Early Classic Period

Flora Simmons Clancy

UNIVERSITY OF NEW MEXICO PRESS
ALBUQUERQUE

LIBRARY OF CONGRESS CATALOGING-IN-PUBLICATION DATA

Clancy, Flora S.
    Sculpture in the ancient Maya plaza : the early classic period /
Flora Simmons Clancy, — 1st ed.
      p.   cm.
    Includes bibliographical references.
    ISBN 0-8263-1787-1 (cloth)
    1. Maya sculpture. 2. Inscriptions, Mayan. 3. Mayas—
Antiquities. 4. Mexico—Antiquities. 5. Central America—
Antiquities. I. Title.
F1435.3.S34C53   1999
730´.97281—dc21   98-46528
                                      CIP

Contents

Figures

Preface

The freestanding monuments placed in the Early Classic plazas of ancient Maya cities are the subject of this book. These monuments were carved in relief to display richly dressed figures and glyphs. They have been studied, almost without exception, by iconographers concerned with the content of their images and by epigraphers poring over their texts. This book is devoted to the artistry of the monuments and to the decisions made at the time of carving that were concerned with a monument's composition, its carving techniques, and its imagery and text: decisions predicated on that monument's eventual erection in the context of a civic plaza. I have tried to reconstruct these ancient decisions by following their traces in the artistic work that went into the making of the freestanding monuments.

The remarkable and recent advances in reading the ancient glyphs carved on the monuments have been essential to my ability to draw social and historical contexts for the plaza monuments. However, no matter how abundant and available, primary texts are never the sole concern of the art historian. Ancient, primary texts have yet to reveal much about the knowledge and skills of a sculptor, how the artist and patron worked together, and why they chose (and just as importantly, did not choose) certain compositional schemata and images. As with most art histories, these issues are best approached by looking at the works of art themselves. However, looking at works of art is a subjective enterprise with relative results, and this is so whether looking at imagery created in our own time and place or long ago and in distant lands.

One of the things that has consistently fascinated me about the discipline of art history is that it works with objects that, in substantial ways, defy history. A work of art, no matter when it was made, if it is still around, has presence and can be effective and potent in times and places very different from its making. This continuing potency subverts its authentic connections to a particular history or originating culture. (One of the traces of this subversion occurs in this book: a problematic mixture of tenses in describing an ancient monument as it exists now.) I have therefore tried, first, to acknowledge the paradoxical presence-pastness of the ancient monuments and, then, to find acceptable ways to link these two conditions.

My interpretation of what I see arises from who I am, and I know I am not seeing or thinking as an ancient Maya did coming into a plaza. Nevertheless, we do share certain conditions: we both have a human body, our eyes are in the same place in our head, and if we stumble on a path we fall down. Starting with these sorts of conditions—big/small, in/out, up/down—for my descriptions of plaza monuments, my hope is that at least I have begun this history within authentic boundaries. From that point on, however, my interpretations and many speculations must enter, like all others, into the ongoing discourse about ancient Maya history.

This project has taken so long that some of the precepts I held at its beginnings have been crumbled and retempered, especially my thoughts and understanding of structuralism. I found I was not able responsibly to manipulate the objects of this study according to my structural ideals (and I really tried). In the end, I found myself in a discourse with them, and as many authors say of writing, my "characters took on lives of their own." This is, of course, only what it *felt* like, but the ancient Maya sculptors who carved the monuments begin my list of grateful acknowledgments.

In its beginnings, this project was generously supported by an American Philosophical Society Grant from the Johnson Fund for travel in Mexico during the summer of 1982. In the following academic year, 1982–83, I was given a National Endowment for the Humanities Fellowship at the School of American Research in Santa Fe, which enabled me to start writing, and while this turned out to be a most tentative beginning, the intellectual benefits of the fellowship were substantial. In 1986–87, I received a Dumbarton Oaks Robert Woods Bliss Fellowship, again to write the manuscript. This was a productive year. I wrote about the Preclassic beginnings of Classic Maya sculpture (Clancy 1990), and I completed (unpublished) monographs on the ancient Late Classic sculptures of Yaxchilan, Piedras Negras, Caracol, Altar de Sacrificios, and Uaxactun. It was as if I were encircling, thus defining, what became the actual project—a history of Early Classic plaza sculpture. The University of New Mexico generously supported my work with Research Allocations Committee Awards in 1985 and 1990, but after 1990 I was fairly certain I had used up all available support for this everlasting project, and I did not again apply for assistance.

There are many friends and colleagues who have significantly and positively assisted my efforts to complete this project. Some I know only through their published works: Rudolf Arnheim, Roland Barthes, Gregory Bateson, John Gardner, Mark Johnson, C. S. Lewis, Alfredo Lopez Austin, Erwin Panofsky, and Meyer Schapiro. While I cite some, but not all, of these "companions" in my text, their perceptions and their ideas about the forms and events of history have corrected as well as inspired my perceptions and ideas. I am especially grateful to those friends and colleagues who are implicated in this project through correspondence and conversations as well as publications: Anthony Aveni, Janet Berlo, Elizabeth Boone, Clemency Coggins, Charles Gallenkamp, David Grove, Peter Harrison, Jeff Kowalski, Arthur Miller, Sheldon Nodelman, Jacinto Quirarte, Linda Schele, Mary Elizabeth Smith, Andrea Stone, and Richard Townsend.

Jeremy Sabloff has continually supported my efforts to understand an ancient artistry visible to us through and from archaeological contexts. I have tried to emulate his disciplinary rigor, and, certainly, I have been instructed by the large and generous intelligence he always brings to bear in his work. Tatiana Proskouriakoff was an enthusiastic supporter of this project in its beginnings, and I regret that I will never know whether she could approve of the result. I do know, however, that without her seminal contributions to Maya studies, this book would never have been written. Ian Graham has allowed me free access to his considerable files of photographs and drawings of the ancient monuments, held in the Peabody Museum of Harvard University. His resources were achieved through a lifetime of effort and an almost mythical persistence, and they sustain my work as they have sustained, for the last twenty-five years, the efforts of the entire field of scholarship focused on the ancient Maya.

Finally, because there is no other way I can characterize the importance of his contributions, I dedicate this book to George Kubler. He introduced me to the dubious pleasures of the art historical enterprise, its large and labyrinthine arena, its pitfalls, and its equivocal results. The paradoxical brilliance and humility of his scholarship gave shape to my goals and will always serve as my guides.

SCULPTURE IN THE ANCIENT MAYA PLAZA

CHAPTER ONE
An Introduction

First published in 1946, Sylvanus Morley's *The Ancient Maya* set a standard for representing a descriptive history of the ancient Maya peoples. Beginning with a description of the modern lands and peoples, he then turned to a description of the ancient religion and the remarkable calendar for which the ancient Maya are famous. The more particular aspects of ancient life were then treated, organized by categories—architecture, sculpture, and crafts—reflecting in their order academic valuations. Morley's data were derived from archaeological information and from chronicled accounts of Maya life in the sixteenth and seventeenth centuries.

The Ancient Maya has been updated and revised (Morley and Brainerd 1956; Morley, Brainerd and Sharer 1983), but its basic organization and, indeed, many of Morley's original passages remain the same in the 1983 book.[1] However, the differences in the revised versions illustrate that the original 1946 volume was written at a major cusp in our efforts to understand the ancient Maya. While the calendrical data given in the ancient inscriptions have been understood since the turn of the century, between 1946 and 1983 scholars began actually to translate the Maya glyphs carved on monuments and painted on pottery and books, and the field changed from a discipline concerned with the material traces of prehistoric events to one that had to include the more ideological perspectives of history.

Since 1946, there have been several good historical overviews of the ancient Maya written by archaeologists for general audiences that follow Morley's great work in spirit and in organization (Ruz Lhuillier 1963; M. Coe 1987; Henderson 1981; Hammond 1982b; Sabloff 1989). Since the mid-fifties (see Knorosov 1956, 1958; Berlin 1958), these accounts have had to discuss at least the prospect that primary historical data could be read from the ancient glyphs. Then, following Tatiana Proskouriakoff's (1960) reasoned analysis of the pattern of dates carved on the monuments of Piedras Negras that reflected a lifetime of events for an individual, the general histories began to reflect that the old paradigm for ancient Maya life—theocratic and peaceful, and basically ahistorical—had changed to the more usual one with stories of birth and death, marriage and alliance, war and power. *A Forest of Kings* (1990) by Linda Schele and David Freidel, also written for a general audience, forcefully incorporates these paradigmatic changes in their represented history for the ancient Maya. It is ironic that J. Eric S. Thompson, whose categorical work with hieroglyphs (1950, 1962) so greatly facilitated (and still does) efforts at translation, could never accept the, now unimpeachable, fact that the glyphs represent syllabic signs. His historical overviews (1966, 1970) are erudite, but his descriptions of ancient Maya life are infused with the old theocratic paradigm.

Important to the formation of this book is a group of more specialized and topical histories that use ancient Maya images as an important source for data with which to document ancient historical and ideological matters. Herbert Spinden published *A Study of Maya Art* in 1913, when only the calendrical dates written in the glyphic texts were fairly well understood, and he had relatively little archaeological information on which to base his representation of art historical sequences. These were achieved through stylistic and formal evaluations of the ancient monuments, which, when combined with calendrical data, produced a remarkably clear picture of ancient Maya history and ideology, still worth consulting today. However, it was not until Tatiana Proskouriakoff's publication of *A Study of Classic Maya Sculpture* (1950) and George Kubler's effort to represent ancient Maya iconographic systems in *Studies in Classic Maya Iconography* (1969), that an art historical point of view fully joined with the archaeological one in an effort to reconstruct the ancient histories (see Culbert 1973, 1991; Coggins 1975; Marcus 1976; Adams 1977; Hammond and Willey 1979; Willey and Mathews 1985; Parsons 1986).

For over thirty years now, all efforts to represent ancient Maya life have had to account for these basic paradigmatic changes in ancient Maya studies. This change has not been, and is not being, accomplished easily or smoothly, because it requires dealing with the profound problems of interpreting and gauging the accuracies of the primary, authentic texts. There are disagreements in how to translate the texts and dates, about how much historical "truth" one can expect from the glyphic texts, and how to match archaeological facts with written texts and dates.[2]

There seems to be little disagreement, however, that the "themes" of ancient Maya history are similar to those that distinguish our own (modern and western) history. The ancient Maya are now represented as having suffered a predictable and political history of dynastic intrigue, violent warfare, power-elitism, women as marriage-pawns, and economic power controlling cultural energies. Ancient images that had once been used to illustrate the old paradigm of a peaceful theocratic intelligencia are now used to illustrate that of a wealthy and fractious elite sponsoring wars and public ceremonies dedicated to torture and sacrifice.[3]

When works of art are used to illustrate a reconstructed history, as is often the case for ancient cultures, their images are treated as artifacts of that culture. This can only be done by focusing on the "pastness" and "otherness" of the work of art, not on its "presentness."

Few histories about the ancient Maya peoples have looked at their art for those qualities that do not serve as factual data about the past, qualities that are not facts *per se* but belong to those perceptual and potent factors that "put constraints on what we experience, leading us to take the experienced item in one way or another."[4] These qualities are found in the orientations of images, their scale and form, their carving techniques, and the ways in which they are composed. For example, monument size in relation to human size is a common, perhaps unavoidable, gauge of hierarchic scale. What can be held in the hand was not imbued with the same intention for its images as something thirty feet high, even though both are inscribed with the image of an honored person. Such qualities are not "lost" in the same way scriptural or iconographic meanings can be lost through a forgetting or ignorance. They remain effective in the present.

To work with what is presently potent carries different dangers for distortion and misrepresentation than those encountered in interpretations of epigraphy or iconography. The challenge lies in forming a link between a work of art's effective qualities as they are experienced now and as they were experienced in the past. How far can empirical and existential perceptions reach? If, as is commonly implied in various cultural critiques today, one's intelligence and imagination are limited to one's own culture and time, then historical studies, and this must include archaeology, are truly defunct and, in fact, have always been specious enterprises.[5] On the other hand, it cannot be denied that images and music, like improbable bumble bees, manage somehow effectively to fly across whatever cultural and historical borders are constructed. The link exists and it is a sensual, physical, and bodily one.

Mark Johnson (1987) demonstrates how the spatial and existential conditions of being in-out, up-down, near-far, big-small, and so on, are, what he calls, image schemata based in a preconceptual awareness of the world that arises within an experiencing body interacting with that world (31). If this is a basic link between the ancient Maya body and my body, then I can assume that when I use the descriptive term "big," there will be, and there would have been, general agreement about "bigness." However, as soon as the question, "how big?" is asked, my particular answer may no longer solicit any general agreement. The answers to this question would require what Johnson calls metaphorical projections from the basic image scheme of big-small (65ff.), and these may not transcend the barriers of language and culture (37–38). Nonetheless, image schemata "constrain" (42) the range of possible metaphoric projections that may arise from them, and since these constraints are inherent in the basic schemata, the constraining shape they give to meaning is the same today as it was in the past.

There is a positive relationship between Johnson's image schemata and my descriptive analysis, given in chapter 2, of compositions as patterned and repeated artistic traits that establish a very general range or field of meaning within which the composed imagery must be understood. The efforts reported in chapter 2 deal with those aspects of ancient Maya artistry used in monument making that are non-mimetic, to use Meyer Schapiro's (1969) useful term, by starting with the medium of relief carving and working through the artistic traits of composition to monumental programs and then to the plaza in which the monuments were placed.

Chapter 3 presents a general iconographic survey of what images could have been seen in the Early Classic plaza. The icons are first categorized by their position within the limited compositional schemata and then characterized by comparative and contextual analyses that work between descriptive similarities and differences. While the interpretations offered for certain icons are carefully framed within the perceived constraints of compositions, they are just that: interpretations.

Chapters 4 through 9 represent the Early Classic plaza monuments in chronological sequences determined by perceived changes in, or differences between, the compositional schemata and the use of certain icons for the main image depicted on the monument. The Early Classic begins with carvings of a generic but honored person being entered into the plaza (chapter 4), and this figure is quickly followed by a pair of warriors and foreign imagery (chapter 5). Chapter 6 describes the monumental images carved in response to the turning of the baktun, a millennial event in the ancient Maya calendar (see below), while the monuments carved in its wake are the subject of chapter 7. Chapter 8 accounts for the appearance of insignia instead of persons on plaza monu-

ments, and chapter 9 describes the last monuments carved during the Early Classic period. In a sense, chapters 2 and 3 establish a vocabulary with which to talk about the monuments presented in chapters 4 through 9. Finally, chapter 10 attempts to draw an historical overview for the plaza, its monuments, and their images.

The reader should understand this history makes no pretense to a scientific method or results. It was conceived to allow the art work to be the object and the investigator to be the subject/subjective. Its discipline is closer to philosophy than science.

One major caveat exists. Paint and color, given the few traces extant on plaza monuments, probably comprise a fairly common visual feature for which we are unable to account. I do not think, however, that the potential value of this history is undone by this lack of information. Applied thinly over the relief-carved forms, the traces of paint found on plaza monuments suggest that one color was applied overall, as was the case for Stela 26 of Uaxactun.[6] Nonetheless, the reader will have to imaginatively color the monument, as I have had to do, when and where there are any traces left to see.

THE SETTING IN SPACE

Early Classic activities that centered around erecting freestanding monuments in the plaza spaces of the ancient cities first took place, as best we know now, in the central regions of the Classic Maya realm: the modern Peten District of Guatemala, and to the east, into modern Belize (fig. 1). Ecologically, this region was, and is today, a low-lying, humid rain forest, lush in its abundance of plants, flowers, and animals. Seen from atop the great and massive Preclassic or Late Classic platforms constructed to rise above the jungle canopy, the visible horizon is relatively flat and monotonous. Experienced from within, that is on foot, the differences in the elevations of bajos (swamps) and higher and dryer lands with their different flora and fauna seem endlessly various. During the Early Classic period, the Maya seldom built structures that achieved any great elevation, and it is the latter, more existential and subjective experience within the landscape that may more authentically describe an Early Classic "point of view."

The plaza was the spatial context for the objects of this history, the stelae and pedestals carved with reliefs and erected as freestanding monuments (fig. 2). Ancient cit-

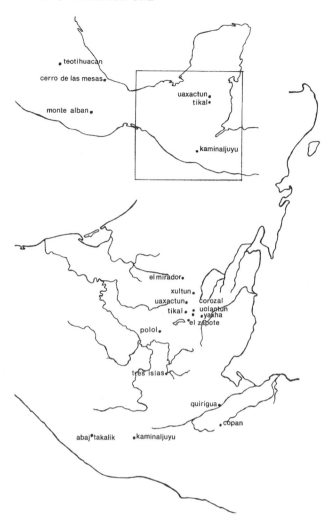

Fig. 1.   Map of the Maya Area with Sites Discussed in the Text. (Map design by Flora Clancy.)

Fig. 2.   View of the Great Plaza of Tikal. (Photo courtesy Patrick Clancy.)

ies generally had several plazas ranging from grand, civic spaces to small and private openings within residential compounds, and the size and accessibility of these open spaces have been taken as indexes of social functions and organization (Awe, Campbell, and Conlon 1991). In plan, public accessibility can be seen as a positive factor in the size of plazas, and it was the larger, more accessible plazas that were inhabited by the freestanding monuments (see G. Andrews 1975, 37; Adams and Jones 1981). Furthermore, there is a general perception that Early Classic plazas were more easily accessible than their Late Classic counterparts, that the civic "flow patterns" allowed greater public involvement in their designed spaces, and that these spaces were "open" as well in terms of the social ranks of the peoples coming to them (Awe,

Campbell, and Conlon 1991, 28; Pendergast 1992, 62–63; Potter 1985, 142). The freestanding monuments erected in these spaces would have been looked at by a great many and various people.

Stelae are vertically oriented slabs of stone set upright in the plaza floor or in the low terraces surrounding the plaza.[7] There are four sides to a stela, two broad faces and two narrow side faces. The stela would be set so one broad face carved with an image would be its front (fig. 52). During the Early Classic period, stelae were approximately as tall as an adult human, and the most common image was an honored or, at least, a very well-dressed person. The sides and the back could be carved with images and/or glyphs, or left plain. Occasionally, monuments recognizable as stelae by their form bear no evidence of carving and are referred to as "plain" stelae. The plain stelae may have had painted images rather than carved ones, but there is also reason to believe that the monument shape itself, regardless of whether it bore images, carried important messages (see Hammond 1982a; Clancy 1990, 27).

Pedestals are differently shaped and differently oriented. They are cylindrical, rectangular, or square blocks set so that one broad surface, the top, is parallel to the plaza floor, that is, like a pedestal (fig. 47). The top is usually carved, and the peripheries may or may not contain imagery. Like plain stelae, there are plain pedestals, recognizable by their shape and orientation.

Pedestals are commonly called "altars" in the literature of Maya studies. Years ago (1976) I argued that the term "altar," traditional as it was, evoked a religious function not easily confirmed when the contexts, compositions, and images of these monuments were studied. I suggested that instead they functioned as pedestals or daises for royal display—as places for the sitting or standing of elite persons. The wearing away of imagery carved on the tops of many pedestals is an index of such a function (fig. 47). Their subject matter differs from that of stelae, and, by comparison, it looks to be metaphoric and emblematic.

The normal setting for the stela and pedestal was at the edge of a plaza or on a low terrace that sometimes framed the plaza. Often the monuments would be axially aligned with the stairs of a pyramidal platform rising at the edge of the plaza, stairs that would give access to the small temple at the top of the pyramid. These monuments are usually assumed to mark the structure that functioned as the place for ceremonies performed for or by the person "portrayed" on the monument, and it is a normal expectation that this person's burial would be found within the structure fronted by his stela. The best evidence for this reconstruction comes from Tikal (Coggins 1975, 138).

The plaza as a context for the stelae and pedestals evokes connections with nature and that which is natural—the sky, rain, sun, wind, fog. The plaza was not so much a natural setting, as its design could hardly be called natural, but it was conditioned by, and subject to, natural events and forces (Clancy 1985). The possibility exists, and is reinforced in this study, that the plaza-as-nature confers this impression to the stelae and pedestals—that these too originated naturally.[8]

Stelae and pedestals functioned as freestanding plaza monuments throughout the Classic period, but in the lowland Maya regions, their use was dramatically limited during the enframing Preclassic and Postclassic periods. These periods characteristically produced architectural sculpture.

As monuments, architectural sculpture is usually classed by the functional name of the architectural part they inhabit: lintels, columns, jambs, and wall panels are the major monuments of architectural sculpture.[9] Given an important function of plaza monuments—accessible to a general public—only some exterior wall panels and columns could have functioned as public art, but whether architectural sculpture was visible from the plaza or not, it was almost always conceived and designed very differently than the freestanding monuments. Imagery carved as architectural sculpture is either monumental (larger than life), or small (about one-third the size of the figures on stelae). The small-scaled compositions tend to represent dynamic and active figures in a narrative context, while the monumental images are composed in isotropic symmetry. Figures on stelae are human-scaled and stationary in their composition.

The "natural" context of the plaza monument differs from the cultural, human-made context provided by architecture for its relief carvings, and the viewing possibilities for most architectural sculpture are considerably limited in comparison with those for the plaza monuments. Few people would have been invited or have had reason to ascend the steps of a temple or a palace to view its lintels and wall panels, and while this last statement is an assumption, it is supported by architectural designs that cannot physically accommodate many people: the rooms are small with little available light, terraces narrow, and stairs steep. Still, I think it is better to consider architectural sculpture as recondite, "put away and esoteric," than to pose the usual complements of public versus private. I am not certain how the ancient Maya conceived of privacy, but it is formally evident that the monuments placed in the plazas differ in kind from those found in the less accessible spaces of architecture.

THE SETTING OF TIME AND HISTORY

Most histories of the ancient Maya contain introductory explanations of their truly remarkable calendar. I refer the interested reader to Anthony Aveni's *Sky Watchers of Ancient America* (1980, 133ff.) for a careful and understandable account. For my purposes, it is necessary to

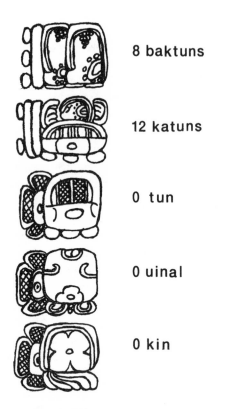

8 baktuns

12 katuns

0 tun

0 uinal

0 kin

Fig. 3.   Maya Long Count Date: 8.12.0.0.0.
(Drawing by Flora Clancy.)

Mesoamerican cycle of time, 260 days. While there are twenty nouns denoting the days there are only thirteen day numbers and the intercycling of the two represents 260 permutations. The Mesoamerican day/month statement, known to Mayanists as the Short Count, defines a 52-year cycle because it takes 18,980 days, or fifty-two years, to intercycle the days and the months ($260 \times 73 = 18,980 = 365 \times 52$). The date expressed by the Short Count, 11 Ahau 3 Pax, will occur again in fifty-two years.

A Long Count was also used by the ancient Maya and is a hallmark of their culture as few other peoples of ancient Mesoamerica chose to use it. It expresses a much longer cycle of time than the Short Count, and the usual explanatory simile is an interlocking system of gears representing time periods that mesh together on individual days.

Mesoamerican and Maya numerical calculations used a twenty-count, or a vigesimal system.[11] Numerical placement in order of twenties was usually written vertically (unlike our horizontal placement of numbers) and a symbol for zero or naught was used to signal no value in a particular place. When we write Maya numbers, we place them horizontally, such as the date, 8.12.0.0.0, where the highest value is at the left. We place a point between the numbers for the practical reason that when translating Maya numbers into our notations, two digits often must be used to express the value of one place.

The date given above for the beginning of the Early Classic Period can also provide an example for the difference between calendrical and numerical notation. (Actually, we have no clear examples of ancient Maya numerical calculations, only examples of calendrical ones.) The date 8.12.0.0.0 is a Maya Long Count date expressed by a five-place notation. Figure 3 shows how the Maya would have written this date. Bars hold the value of five, dots hold the value of one, and the flower-like shapes signal naught. The bar and three dots attached to the left-hand side of the top and first glyph signals the value of eight to this highest of places called the *baktun* glyph. The next glyph down is called the *katun* with its value of twelve, which is followed by glyphs for the *tun*, the *uinal*, and the *kin*, each with the zero or naught sign in front of it. For calendrical calculations, the Maya altered the value of the third position so that it more nearly approximated the Mesoamerican calendar and the solar year. (I think of this as an elegant "fudging" of the conceptual numerical structure to more clearly reflect the experienced reality of a solar year.) The kin position expresses the value of one, or days; the uinal, the value of

describe those aspects of ancient Maya calendrical notation, concepts, and terminology that are used consistently throughout this book, such as *Katun Cycle, baktun, katun, Ahau,* Long Count, Short Count, and so on.

The Maya date given in this history as the beginning of the Early Classic is 8.12.0.0.0 11 Ahau 3 Pax (March 27, A.D. 278).[10] The ending clause, 11 Ahau 3 Pax, expresses the more common Mesoamerican calendrical system of giving a day (11 Ahau) and its position in a month (3 Pax), which can be restated, "it is the day, 11 Ahau, which is the 3rd day in the month of Pax." There are eighteen months of twenty days ($18 \times 20 = 360$) plus a short month of five days, the *Uayeb,* a period of liminal, in-between times best spent at home. Day names consist of both a noun and a number and in themselves represent a basic and ancient twenty days, or months. The next place, the tun or year, holds the value of 360 (not 400) because there are only eighteen months in the Mesoamerican solar year. Continuing from this shift in value, the next place, the katun, holds the value of 7,200 (not 8,000), and the baktun is valued at 144,000.

Given these values, the number expressed by 8.12.0.0.0 is 0 kin, 0 uinal, 0 tun, 12 katun or 12 × 7,200 (151,200 days), and 8 baktun or 8 × 144,000 (1,152,000 days). This date, the Long Count, then expresses the number of days that have passed since the beginning of the ancient calendar and the present great cycle, that is 151,200 + 1,152,000 = 1,303,200 days have passed since August 8, 3114 B.C., the date we know the be the base date for the Maya calendar but not the reasons why. The ancient Maya seem to have calculated only thirteen, rather than twenty, baktuns for the great Long Count cycle, but this is long enough. It takes over five thousand years to move through a great cycle.

During the Early Classic, the baktun count changes from the value of eight to nine, known to have been a very significant event in the mind of the Maya (Coggins 1990). It is referred to as the "turning of the baktun." One more turning of the baktun occurred during the Classic history of the ancient Maya at 10.0.0.0.0 (A.D. 830). We have more information about the turning of the katun every twenty years, because it obviously happened more often, and because it occasioned the dedication of plaza monuments.

Within the Long Count, the katun moved in its cycles of twenty, but as a separate cycle not expressed in Long Count dates, it too was involved in a cycle of thirteen. The ancient records for this cycle are not clearly understood, but few scholars deny the importance of the duration of approximately 260 years this cycle expresses (a katun or 20 years × 13 = 260 years) (see Hammond 1982b, 290; Coggins 1975, 444; 1979a, 45; Puleston 1979; Farriss 1987; Taube 1988). In Colonial times this cycle of 260 years was all important to the Mayan people as they underwent profound cultural upheavals. In native Colonial accounts, such as the *Chilam Balam of Chumayel* (see Roys 1960, 1967; Edmonson 1986), prophesy was an important event for the rituals associated with the turning of the katun—predicting which historical themes would be major events and which would play minor roles during the katun. A shaman, or priest, would orate his prophesy, and in Colonial times, at least, the most famous orations were written down.

Katuns were named for the days on which they ended, which in the structure of the calendar was always the day *Ahau* coupled with its number. The Colonial Katun Cycle, or Katun Wheel as it is also called, began with Katun 11 Ahau, proceeded to Katun 9 Ahau, 7 Ahau, 5, 3, 1, 12, 10, 8, 6, 4, 2, and ended with Katun 13 Ahau. Because of the continual cultural disaster experienced by the Maya during the Colonial period, it is difficult to extrapolate what historical themes had been expected in more coherent and ancient times (Roys 1960, 32), but it is clear that specific themes were associated with particular katuns. Each twenty-year period was defined or colored by a major historical theme, or themes, which would be manifested again in some way when the katun, designated by its numbered Ahau, came around again (see Roys 1967, 184; Puleston 1979; Taube 1988).

In Colonial times all katuns save Katun 12 Ahau were given disastrous predictions.[12] Why Katun 12 Ahau escaped the general tenor of tragedy is not known, but it is described as a time of plenty, unity, and righteousness (Edmonson 1986, 218–19). Roys (1967, 184) observes that "surprisingly large proportions of important upheavals in Maya history appear to have occurred in some katun named either 4 Ahau or 8 Ahau." Extrapolating from the katun prophesies in the *Chilam Balam of Chumayel*, a few other katuns can be given possible themes: Katun 9 Ahau, a time for the tribute of food; Katun 7 Ahau, a time of no teachings, crazy times. Other major historical themes, not easily associated with a particular katun, are natural disasters, such as famine, drought, and storm; the human disasters of war, conspiracy, and injustice; and more subtle themes that can be called beginnings, endings, and accountings.

The date I assign to be the beginning of the Early Classic, 8.12.0.0.0 11 Ahau 3 Pax, is the beginning of a Katun Cycle at Katun 11 Ahau (A.D. 278). This date has the potential of having been more significant to the ancient Maya historians and prophets than the traditional beginning we have given for the Early Classic, ca. A.D. 250, if, and it is a big if, the ancient Maya started their Katun Cycle as we know it from the Colonial period. The end of the Katun Cycle occurred at 9.4.0.0.0 13 Ahau 18 Yax (October 14, A.D. 514). Again, this more specific date can be seen to match archaeological interpretations that posit a Middle Classic period (Parsons 1978; Coggins 1979a; Pasztory 1978). As the reader may expect, it also accords well with the art history of plaza monuments presented in this volume.

It is obviously speculation that such specific dates actually marked an authentic beginning and ending of the Early Classic period; such precision does not represent the haphazard happenings of history as we understand them. Using specific dates, however, is based in the idea of ancient Maya historical "themes" and comes from an effort to understand the Early Classic plaza monuments as happenings within a cycle of time rather than sequentially attached to a "time line" of history.

Time and history need not be, and perhaps seldom are, conceived as equivalent things.[13] Time must account for natural events, while history accounts for cultural ones. As ideas, they are surely rooted together, but where and how distinctions (if any) were made between nature and culture (B. Tedlock 1982, 1983) and how their interweavings were understood are important questions (Farriss 1987, 572–75). The ancient Maya worked with, what appears to us, complex conceptions about history and time as means of explaining and manipulating their reality. To understand or reconstruct Maya conceptions of history, time, or space, we must first of all acknowledge that their basic perception of time was a cyclical one. It has recently been suggested, however, that the Classic Maya, uniquely in ancient Mesoamerica, had a conception of linear time. Arthur Miller (1986, 24–29) considers a linear conception of time evident in the Maya use of the Long Count because of what he believes is its concern for marking the quantity (as opposed to the quality) of time. Others describe the "linear aspect" (Houston 1989, 48), or the "historical element" (Aveni 1989, 250–51), of Maya texts as existing within a more profound cyclical sense of time (Schele and Freidel 1990, 82).

Perhaps the argument for linearity comes from our relatively recent perception of the ancient Maya as *having* a history; in the texts carved on monuments they made careful note of important people's lives and deeds within time. This surely is history, but the apparent corollary, history is linear, need not follow, and indeed an insistence on the linearity of history denies a major difference that makes the ancient Maya contribution to human thought so intriguing and potentially important. What the ancient Maya show us is that historical thought can be rooted in a cyclical reality as well. It is not necessary to postulate a special linear sense of time to explain their obvious historical concerns, rather to reconsider the proposal that the philosophies of history are confined to linear thought structures.[14]

How might history be defined and function within a cyclical sense of time? The idea of progress, which so colors our sense of history, would be quite differently expressed by an ancient Maya, who would expect the present and future to contain familiar things and events. The Maya, however, did not seem to expect to have exactly the same characters, words spoken, or events repeated as time moved through its cycles (Farriss 1987, 583ff.). A good analogy is drama: the play would be the same, but the roles would be taken up by different actors; the staging, while recognizable, might be different; and the interpretation of the play's meanings could be stressed differently. Historical themes were limited, but differences—matters for prediction and debate—occurred in the relative potency of the various plots that could be carried within a theme. Historical explanation could rely on the expected return or constancy of historical themes associated with certain cycles of time; what may have been difficult for the Maya was how to predict whether the theme, say of famine, would be a major or minor plot or force in the present cycle. For the ancient Maya, then, the events and things of history could be explained by their predictable repetition. Not so easily predicted was how these themes would "play," or how the characters would interpret their parts.

On the surface, this does not seem all that different from our understanding of history based in a linear sense of time. We search history for explanations of the present and predictions for the future. However, our explanations and predictions come from the precept of cause and effect (one thing leads to another), and are linear in essential form. Perhaps, it would be more correct to say dendritic in form, but despite the possibility of enormous complexities in interweaving causes and effects, the structure is linear and its movement through time is described as evolving—a progression—for good or ill.

The great themes of Maya history do not change through progress: they are; they exist. Each katun could carry several possible and potential historical themes, and not all would be expected to be "played out" in the present in any affective way, although they were known to exist. The ancient Maya spent a fair amount of effort trying to evoke latent histories they thought might be important for the present, there to be experienced if these themes could be brought to the fore, so to speak. Rituals and individual actions described in the primary texts, as we have interpreted them so far, were often based on timed and meaningful connections with (past) known themes and on predictable, astronomical events (see Lounsbury 1980; Schele and Freidel 1990, 84; Aveni 1989, 250–51).

These efforts have been described as the Maya "using" history to rationalize their actions (Marcus 1992, 235–37). However, there is an important difference between the way an ancient Maya might "use history" and what we mean by that phrase. Our use of history to rationalize or explain action requires an objective relationship to history where an individual can think of himself or herself as somehow outside of history: history forms behind us as we walk into the future. For the Maya, who understood history as already formed within the present and the future, being outside of history would be impossible. In a sense, an individual was an object of history, was *within* history. Perhaps individual action was understood as the creation of a subjective difference within history, like a perturbation, but not as a begetting or a changing of history.[15]

A concept of history as progress, imbued with moral character (at least since the Enlightenment), would be foreign to the ancient Maya (Aveni 1989, 332–33). The events and things of the present were the same events and things of the past—albeit with different qualities determined by the relative potencies of interpretation and characters. Within such percepts, history may have been perceived in terms of the different inter-relationships of expected themes, but not in terms of cause and effect giving rise to the new. In other words, the Maya would have perceived historical change as difference, not as evolution or progress. This is important when trying to reconstruct Maya history.

THE EARLY CLASSIC PERIOD

The Maya placed the base date for their calendar (3114 B.C.) in a time we believe most Mesoamerican peoples were still living as hunters and gatherers. Material evidence for the actual use of the Long Count, as far as we know now, begins some time around the beginning of our own era (M. Coe 1957, 1977), and only when it is regularly carved on plaza monuments, around A.D. 250, do we consider the Early Classic Period as beginning to take form. This conjunction took place in "interesting times" as defined by archaeologists.

In the duration of time between A.D. 278 and 514, the Mayan-speaking peoples living in the lowlands of the Yucatan peninsula experienced, along with the rest of Mesoamerica, a time of growth and expansion. Archaeological evidence shows that in general it was a time of prosperity, as represented by the growth and expansion of cities, long-distance trade, and efficient agricultural strategies for feeding not only the growing numbers of people, but the growing classes of people working in non-agrarian jobs, such as merchants, civic laborers, teachers, scientists, artisans, and, of course, the elite.

What is different in these times from what had been before is growth and expansion, not the social or cultural structures that supported this magnification of Early Classic life. The Preclassic peoples did not lack merchants, cities, or teachers, and there were rich and deep legacies from the Preclassic period for the monumental arts, the arts of writing and painting, and the sciences of mathematics and astronomy. The physical signs required for archaeological perception, therefore, do not define the Early Classic culture as originating any particular material invention (Culbert 1991, 130, 312). The Early Classic, then, is archaeologically defined by a relatively sudden burgeoning of cultural artifacts.

Our perception that "something happened" making the Early Classic a specific social and cultural entity is correct, nonetheless, and it is not just based on the quantity of artifacts that begin to appear in the archaeological record of Mesoamerica. There is a perceivable difference between a Preclassic monument (using a pertinent example) and an Early Classic monument. It is not that the stela monument is new—it is not—but its appearance, its use of imagery, and its contexts are different. The changes that took place, then, are signaled by differences in both the quantity and the quality of the archaeological artifacts.

By focussing on the differences traceable in the material expressions of the Early Classic plaza and its monuments, it is suggested that these positively mark changes in the ceremonies and events held in plaza spaces. In the Early Classic, then, these were popular events, and civic life was an engaging activity for the sponsoring elite and for the responsible community. Within the Early Classic civic context of the plaza, it is likely that some kind of general literacy was necessary to sustain participation in public life.[16]

Embedded in these differences are other more particular events marking the Early Classic that can be traced through the plaza monument, its images, texts, and archaeological contests: the rising power of dynasts and polities (city-state is the usual analogy) and the clear evidence for cultural and economic interactions with the other peoples of Mesoamerica on an interregional scale. These things certainly shaped Early Classic life in general but the evidence for them comes more specifically from the contents of elite burials and from the icons displayed on the plaza monuments, icons more telling about the concerns of the elite classes.[17]

CHAPTER TWO

The Contexts and Compositions
of Plaza Monuments

THIS CHAPTER EXAMINES HOW IMAGES ARE REPRE-
sented on the plaza monuments through descriptive and
critical analyses of their form, style, and context. In order to do this, some pertinent terms are suggested for
discussing the stylistic and graphic qualities of ancient
Maya art.

By the time art historians began to look at the art
works of ancient Mesoamerica the discipline's concern
for form and aesthetics was being replaced by iconographic and structural analyses and a greater interest in
content.[1] The arts of ancient Mesoamerica, therefore,
never received the careful (some would say fulsome)
formal and stylistic analyses that were the focus of art
historical studies in the 19th century. Scholarly attention
to ancient Maya art has been almost entirely centered on
the image and its iconography. Sylvanus Morley's great
work, *The Inscriptions of Peten* (1937–38), is unusual in
this regard: in as much as he discussed the artistry of the
monuments, he did so through stylistic assessment and
comparison. Tatiana Proskouriakoff's *A Study of Classic
Maya Sculpture* (1950), however, stands out as a major
exception to the hermeneutic endeavors that have characterized modern scholarship in ancient Maya art. She
studied changes in the graphic renderings of images, and
her discussion of "The Classic Monuments" (102ff.) is
decidedly formal and contextual.[2]

NON-MIMETIC ASPECTS OF THE MONUMENTS[3]

There are certain qualities about Early Classic relief-
carved monuments that make them easily recognizable
as such to every student of the ancient Maya. Tatiana
Proskouriakoff's (1950) enduring work laid the ground-
work for describing qualities that pertain to the graphic
style of delineation and its history of change. One of the
clues in our quick recognition of an Early Classic monument is the way the human figure is rendered. Proskouriakoff charted the changes in the figure's delineation
and pose and demonstrated that the Early Classic figure
is "distinguished from similar positions of later periods
by the placing of the legs, which *never overlap at the level
of the knee*" (ibid., 19, Proskouriakoff's emphasis). The
correctness and usefulness of Proskouriakoff's observations have continually been borne out in the forty-some
years since she published her *Study*.

To account for the student's ability almost instantly to
recognize the difference between Early and Late monuments, other formal characteristics besides delineation
can be defined: characteristics that are as perceptible as
the image itself, but perhaps are not as consciously acknowledged. Julian Hochberg's (1972, 60) distinction between line and edge is instructive, wherein "line and edge
reflect two different tasks that can be pursued by the

13

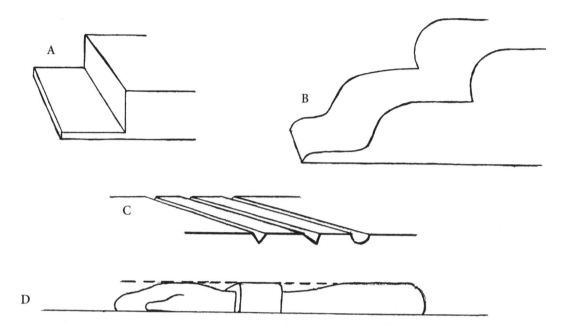

Fig. 4.   Types of Relief: A) Square-cut, B) Abraded, C) Engraved, and D) Cushioning. (Drawing by Flora Clancy.)

perceptual system." According to Hochberg, line is expressive and connotative, while edge is descriptive and denotative. Because edge and line each name the same physical entity in a given work, we can explore how the same image might function as an icon (edge) and serve as an index of aesthetic effort (line).

The Techniques of Relief Carving

The art of relief is an ambiguous medium existing somewhere between the second and third dimension. It generally requires the perspectival techniques used in two-dimensional representation for creating spatial logic among its images, such as overlapping and foreshortening (Grieder 1964), and at the same time it partakes in three dimensions by manipulating actual spatial recessions from the foreground to the background. It establishes image by cutting away some, but not all, material that is non-image, non-mimetic: background and often a plain frame remain as "neutral" contexts for the positive imagery.

A distinctive attribute of relief carving is the use of light and shadow to enhance the material definition of its imagery and to create expressive, dramatic qualities. Like edge and line, the light-catching, shadow-making effects of relief-carved images are both denotative and connotative. These effects were achieved by the ancient Maya sculptor using a variety of cutting techniques to define

the edge/line (fig. 4). A *square cut* describes an edge that turns almost ninety degrees from the image plane and establishes an abrupt, dramatic change between light and shadow. An *abraded cut* describes an edge that is rounded in its turn. Its use creates a less abrupt change in "color" and allows for a more plastic and dimensional definition of a form by a modulation of light to shadow. *Engraving*, a term taken from the printing process, describes a cut that creates a channeled line in the surface of the stone. It does not work between foreground and background as the square and abraded cuts do, but by controlling the angles of its channeled sides or by varying its width, the artist can create denotative effects of texture or expressive effects of a moving line. *Cushioning* is an intriguing, and perhaps unique, method of relief cutting employed by ancient Maya carvers (fig. 4). Overlapping forms (say, an arm overlapped by a bracelet) would not actually be on different planes, but the surface of the form to be "overlapped" would be cut or shaved in a very slow angle, that is "cushioned," so that it met the overlapping form with a visible planar difference (Robertson 1974, 105; Clancy 1992).

Modeling is different from the above techniques in that it represents the more subtle qualities of dimension not possible to achieve with abraded cuts or with planar distinction (see below). It can render such actualities as the sculptural differences between the projection of the nose and the curve of the cheek. Faces, human or grotesque, and the disc-like jewelry called earflares, were often modeled by the artist, even when all other imagery was defined by square or abraded cuts.

To create a relief-carved image, the artist would (must) work from the surface of the quarried stone towards a background to be established during the process of carving. The background, therefore, is part of the artist's work, while the foreground, as a spatial plane, is a given. The surface of the stone may or may not be smoothed by the artist but its spatial definition will always be as the foremost plane. This may seem so obvious as to be not worth mentioning, but it establishes the artistic purview of the relief carver. In Early Classic monumental relief carving, the place and definition of the background changes, reflecting certain decisions made by the artists, probably in response to patron desires about how the monument's imagery should be represented.

Ancient Maya artists usually relied on two-dimensional drafting techniques to denote spatial logic, and so the various ways they manipulated the actual spatial features of their relief was as expressive as it was denotative. Although there are many varieties, there were two main ways of handling the relief from foreground to background. *Planar recession* positively represents the logical overlapping of forms—costume over body, body in front of cape—as a series of planar levels.[4] *Silhouetting* relies on the two spatial planes of foreground and background, and defines the distance between them only at the outside edges of the image, thus creating a silhouette by highlight and shadow. Costume details within the silhouette may be created as thin planes or by such cutting techniques as engraving and cushioning, but they are not visually logical in relationship to the established background. With silhouetting, objects that are known to be farthest away from the viewer are often carved in the deepest relief, and those closest to viewer, in the shallowest relief (fig. 48).[5]

The depth of relief is another perceptual factor that can be denotative or expressive. The deeper the relief, the more the Maya artist would rely on modeling techniques rather that planar recession and angled cuts. To the Western eye, deep relief and modeling are a sign of artistic attainment because they create an image that is closer to sculpture in the round and to optical reality.[6] For Early Classic plaza art, the relief carved on stelae and pedestals was handled in many ways, but it was never deep.

The 8th Baktun

Eighth-baktun stelae are irregular and asymmetrical in shape, evoking the impression that the stone from which they were carved was untouched and in a natural state (fig. 15). When quarried, limestone slabs are naturally four-sided with irregular edges and surfaces. The varying qualities of limestone—its composition or hardness—create different kinds of irregularities, but all limestone shafts, as quarried, would need planing and dressing to achieve the regularity of monumental form common for the Late Classic monument. In the 8th baktun, the relief-carved images flow over an uneven, sometimes deeply pitted, surface. While the 8th-baktun stone shafts give the impression of being in a "natural" state, the sculptors nevertheless worked their surfaces—but just enough to achieve a desired coherence between the image and its bearing stone.

No clear visual distinction is made between the image and the area of non-imagery or background; neither is unified into a simple plane. The relationship between the monumental figure and its field is not presented by the spatial logic of figure and field, or background and foreground. The figural image is actually *in* the field, not in front of it. Even when it is easier to pick out the figure, as with Stela 5 of Uaxactun (fig. 20), the irregular, "natural" condition of the monument shape and its surface imparts the same texture and visual vitality to both figure and background and negates reading the image as clearly distinct or separate from its background or its monument. (This certainly contributes to the common classroom complaint of how difficult it is to see the images.)

During the Early Classic period, and especially the 8th baktun, the relationship between the monumental images and the stones that bear them is an intimate and reflexive one. The interplay between stone and image is one of revelation—a revealing of synthesis, of coincident, of coevent. Thus, the 8th-baktun monuments formally attest to the meaningfulness, perhaps the sacredness, of the stone "naturally" revealing an image. This attitude toward the stone and its function may derive from an older tradition concerning stone carving established during the Middle Preclassic (Quirarte 1977, 282). Given the monument shape and the lack of a figure-field relationship, it appears that the greater concern was in the processes of carving the monument than in its actual image.

Nonetheless, even during Preclassic times, the ritual and mythical powers attributed to certain stones would have been co-opted by elite patrons for the practical purposes of extending and maintaining elite power. The patron could "collaborate" his vision with that of the sculptor so that certain pragmatic images were "seen" in the stone. However, even with the realities of power and patronage, the evidence, in the 8th baktun at least, indicates that the innate powers of the stone were strong forces in the way the imagery was produced, and that each stone to be carved was still understood as requiring certain unique responses according to its own nature. This would better account for the various compositions and styles that are characteristic of 8th-baktun monuments, than the usual description of unformed, hesitant beginnings where, even at one site, the differences between contemporary monument compositions and images vary greatly (Marcus 1976, 32, 34).

To be an 8th-baktun sculptor required a mystical attunement to one's material, a carving skill of great artistry, and a patient diplomacy to be able to act between the demands of the stone and the demands of the patron.

The Turn of the Baktun

Experimentation and innovation in composition, carving styles, and iconography characterize the last forty or fifty years of the 8th baktun as well as the first two katuns (forty years) of the 9th baktun. For about a hundred years, spanning the turn of the baktun, a remarkable corpus of plaza monuments was produced that, in my estimation, is not equaled in its aesthetic and stylistic qualities until Late Classic times, if then.

The experimentation, especially in composition, evident in the plaza monuments of the late 8th baktun becomes a coherent artistic genre during the early 9th baktun. The sculptors start to make use of a more regular monument shape: limestone shafts are prepared with carefully planed faces, parallel sides, and rounded tops (although often irregularly rounded). Pedestals become more common at this time as a plaza monument and are cut into the geometric shapes of the cylinder and the rectangular block.

Along with the more regular monument shape, a subtle and important formal change occurs that distinguishes the monuments of the early 9th baktun from those of the 8th baktun. The image is now envisioned as separate from the monument that bears it, and a formal *distinction* between the figure and its field is established; the background is visually passive, a carefully leveled plane from which the image is projected to the foreground (fig. 35). Such a distinction can be detected on some of the late-8th-baktun monuments, but only ten-

tatively, for example, Stela 12 of Xultun (fig. 19). In the 9th baktun, the figural image is no longer within the body of the stone; it is foregrounded and distinct, separated by a real and spatial demarcation of a foreground and a background (fig. 48).

The almost ubiquitous use of a plain frame now plays a notable role in objectifying the image apart from its bearing stone by physically marking the limits of the image, both at the edges of the image's field and in the limits of its spatial depth. The plain frame proclaims the edge of imagery and illusion at the same time that it reifies the reality of the stone's form and edge (Uspensky 1973, 151, 165; Clancy 1990, 30).

The construction of an independent image signals a change in the function of the monument. The (mystical) powers of the stone become latent in favor of the image expressing what we assume to be the more political requirements of dynastic power. Certainly, this very latency was *used* to evoke a sense of ancient validity, the old signs of religious function and social tradition, but the traditionally inherent traits of the monument become picked out and translated into conventional signs themselves.

The End of the Early Classic

The 3rd katun (A.D. 495–513) is defined by a marked reduction of plaza imagery, as well as formal and iconographic changes. Only two sites, Uaxactun and Tikal, are surely known to have produced plaza images, and at Tikal these are radically different kinds of presentations (Clancy 1992). Rather than displaying the exuberant, complex imagery of the preceding years, the plaza monument at Tikal is reduced in size, its imagery is uncomplicated, and only the simplest compositional field—the framed panel—is used (fig. 49). At Uaxactun, the opposite is true. Here, the compositions and imagery become more inclusive and complex—in comparison with Tikal's plaza monuments, seemingly to the point of obsession (fig. 56).

After the turn of the baktun, the geographic distribution of sites erecting monuments expands beyond the central area that focused on Tikal and Uaxactun: in the south along the Pasion River (Tres Islas and Altar de Sacrificios), and in the southeast along the Motagua River (Copan and Quirigua). However, during the 3rd katun these sites experience something akin to iconoclasm. The archaeological record presently suggests that no site outside of Tikal or Uaxactun produced plaza imagery, and while Altar de Sacrificios erects plaza monuments (Stela 13 and Pedestal 3), they display only glyphs, no image.

There is a relationship between the stark events charted in 3rd-katun imagery and a change in the focus of meaning within the plaza monument. When process was the focus and the image was the result of "negotiations" with the stone shaft, this seems to have produced a vitality, an excitement that can still be detected in the early monuments. When image was the reason for production, the monument necessarily acquired a predictable and repeatable kind of rhetoric.

COMPOSITION AND THEME

In 1939 Erwin Panofsky (1962, 5–17) suggested that the artistic trait of composition was connected to theme. Taken more concretely than Panofsky's use of it, this connection becomes critical when literary themes are unknown or only to be guessed at (see Kubler 1969; Clancy 1985). Describing and analyzing compositions by their formal construction discloses certain features that guide viewers towards particular points of view: features that signal *where* to stand to look at the composition and *how* to look at the images it contains. While these compositional features are schematic, abstract, and various, in order to perform their signaling tasks properly, they must be positively related to the actual theme being represented.

The themes that can be deduced from compositional schemata are very general ones and have more to do with the qualitative conditions of the theme—time, space, and mood—than with its specific literary and iconographic identifications. These conditions, however, limit the possibilities of thematic identification: certain compositional schemata can only support certain kinds of themes.

Two very general but definitely related traits in a work of art begin the description of compositional schemata: the *field* within which the image is placed and the *mode* by which the image is arranged within the field. Four compositional fields and three modes of composition were used by the ancient Maya sculptors of plaza monuments, but during the Early Classic period some fields and modes appear only as exceptions at certain times and places.

Compositional Fields

The compositional fields are as follows: the panel, the wraparound field, the recto-verso field, and the multi-panel (fig. 5). The paneled field is most commonly used by Maya sculptors, whether for plaza sculpture or the more recondite architectural reliefs.

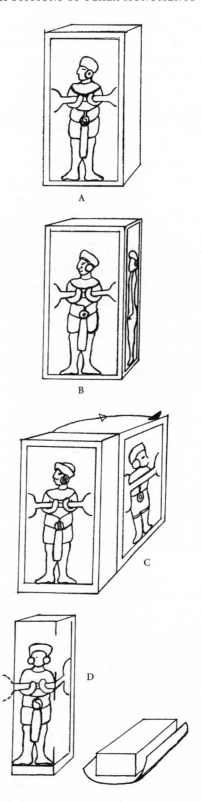

Fig. 5. Compositional Fields: A) Panel, B) Multi-panel, C) Recto-verso, and D) Wraparound. (Drawing by Flory Clancy.)

The *panel* presents its imagery on only one flat surface of a monument, and, as the basic and most common field, represents a broad and general scheme for display. It does this in a very straightforward manner: the viewer can see all there is to see by simply standing in front of the panel of imagery, which is generally defined by a plain frame. The frame actually specifies where the viewer should stand in order to see the display properly.

What is displayed, of course, varies rather widely. Stelae generally (but not exclusively) display images that refer to people, things, or events in ways and (compositional) modes that intermix the denotative and connotative, and realistic and unrealistic images. Panel imagery on pedestals generally displays insignia that allegorically refer to content or meaning. The basic panel scheme for display underlies the schemata evoked by the other compositional fields, but with real qualifications because the different physical definitions of the wraparound, recto-verso, and multi-paneled fields use the actual dimensions and shape of a monument to display imagery on more than one of its planar surfaces, and the viewer must walk around the monument to see it all. This takes movement and time, and requires the use of memory as the imagery unfolds on the different planes. The panel's display is thus conditioned by the fact that imagery is revealed sequentially to a viewer who is physically active.[7]

The *wraparound* field displays an image across several faces of the monument; no frames separate the image as it extends from face to face (fig. 37). The image is made to partake in the actual dimension of the stone, but with visually peculiar results. The normal drafting techniques used to achieve spatial logic for a basically two-dimensional image are not altered when used with the wraparound field, and a tension is created between the spatial illusions within the image and the actual dimensions of the stone. Where are we to "place" the image? Does the image partake in the actual dimensions of the stone, or does the rendered illusory space define its place? The revelation of the image that is provided by the wraparound field is conditioned by this tension, this ambiguity of place.

The wraparound field is an ancient compositional strategy found on monuments dating back to the Middle Preclassic period and used to display the narratives of the Preclassic (Clancy 1990). Its use was eclipsed during the Late Preclassic, perhaps because of its inherent ambiguities. During the Early Classic it is revived, or reinvented, for the purposes of publicly representing an honored figure—a strange choice of field for a plaza monument because one would normally assume that public arts would avoid ambiguous compositions. Not surprisingly, its use is restricted during the Early Classic period, and after the Early Classic, almost non-existent. Still, the Early Classic use of the wraparound field, in conjunction with the other ambiguous fields of recto-verso and multi-paneled imagery, makes ambiguity in the evocation of meaning in the plaza monument something to acknowledge. It specifies something about the ancient ideals for the plaza's function.

The *recto-verso* field defines the condition where two opposing faces of the monument are carved with images, thus representing a pair of images that are physically but not visually connected. During the Early Classic period, reversed but like images of an honored figure are the most common pairing (fig. 31). To be clearer about this, the iconography of costume and regalia are similar for the two figures represented, as are their poses. The poses, however, are represented as reversed; if one figure's left hand is raised, the right hand of the other is raised. If the recto-verso figures are shown as profiled (Tikal, Stela 31, for example [fig. 33]), the impression is that one sees the right and left side of the same figure: the stone of the monument becoming conceptually transparent. As a kind of polemic, the other kind of recto-verso pairing used during the Early Classic is that of opposites, specifically in the recto-verso portrayal of a man and a woman who wear different costumes and hold different regalia while maintaining a similarity of pose.[8]

The experience of looking at a monument composed by a recto-verso field displaying reversed images is a complex one. The two images were never *intended* to be seen together at one time, but their physical bond to the same stone seems to require a connectedness in their meaning and intent—especially when the paired images are contrived by similar costumes, regalia, or poses. Perception of recto-verso imagery is an interplay between memory (of one side) and vision (of the side being looked at): two points of view each being conditioned by the memory of the other. Meaning is not presented to the viewer as in the panel, but is achieved by the viewer's personal experience and interaction with the composition. Unlike the wraparound field where one image is revealed as spatially distributed over two or more contiguous planes of the monument, the recto-verso field reveals two physically disjunct images as meaningfully connected. The scheme of revelation conditioned by the recto-verso field requires active interpretation as well as interaction on the part of the viewer. With the wraparound field, the viewer must walk around the monument and physically interact with the image if the whole image is to be seen, but despite the planar shifts from one face to the other the connections between the parts of the imagery are graphically rendered. With the recto-verso pairs, such a connection must be supplied, that is, interpreted, by the viewer. It is not a given.

It cannot be claimed that all ancient monuments carved front and back are examples of an intentional use of the recto-verso field. There are only a few examples of this field known to have been carved before the Early Classic period, and these can be questioned as to their authentic intentions because the two carved faces are carved in different styles. Reuse and recarving may leave a monument with what looks like recto-verso intentions.[9] For the Early Classic plaza monument, however, there is little doubt about the intentionality behind the use of the field. Recto-verso pairs are too closely allied by costume, pose, and carving techniques to suggest that their paired connection was arbitrary. What is surprising is how vulnerable this connection is and how much interpretive leeway a viewer was (and is) allowed.

In "roll-out" illustrations, recto-verso pairs of the Early Classic look very much like examples of reflected or mirrored symmetry. Given the particular dimensionality of the recto-verso field, the "point of reflection" would be within the stone of the monument. Like the wraparound field, then, the recto-verso field is interlinked to the stone that bears it in an intimate and dynamic manner.

The compositional field of *multi-panels* is different from the wraparound field because frames separate the images into discrete panels. Most commonly, the framed panels take up one whole face of the monument, as with Stela 20 of Uaxactun (fig. 52), and so the planar shifts of the monument are positively reinforced by the frames. The effect of viewing a multi-paneled composition is like seeing single panels connected in a potentially meaningful sequence.

As with the wraparound and recto-verso fields, multi-paneled fields require an active viewer to see all the imagery. This field is also a scheme for revelation but with a difference established by frames that separate and sequence the images. They more fully control the possibilities of perception by providing limits, by showing the

beginning and ending of each paneled image, and by establishing what might be the optimal points of view. Thus, the use of the multi-paneled field allows the sculptor more carefully to establish what is to be revealed and how. The two other dimensional fields permit greater ambiguity for interpreting their images.

Multi-paneled fields are not common in the Early Classic. Only two examples are known, Stela 20 of Uaxactun and Stela 40 of Tikal.[10] Two examples are known from the Terminal Preclassic period—Stelae 2 and 5 from Abaj Takalik (J. Graham, Heizer, and Shook 1978). Like the recto-verso field, however, the multi-paneled field is a compositional scheme best associated with Classic monumental traditions because only faint traces can be established for its use in earlier times.

Display of proper imagery is basic to the schemata represented by the four compositional fields. The paneled field places the fewest conditions upon what could be displayed or what might be referred to, but limits the ways in which to view it. For the other three fields, the additional schemata for revelation are physically conditioned by the different spatial strategies. This limits the possible thematic ingredients, but it opens up, or allows, different ways of viewing by requiring active participation on the part of the viewer. In brief, and with some distortion because of generalizing, wraparound fields make revelations about the image's space or place; multi-paneled fields reveal the image in an ordered sequence or time; and recto-verso fields do both, but in being able to do so, both revelations about space and time may "cancel" each other, leaving the suggestion that the two images occupy the same space at the same time.[11]

Compositional Modes

A compositional mode diagrammatically charts the formal means by which an image is displayed within its field. Three modes have been identified in ancient Maya art—isotropic, stational, and narrative—that interact in various ways with the broad schemata elicited from the compositional fields. In a previous effort (1985) to understand compositional modes, I discussed them as hieratic (here termed isotropic), iconic (now stational), and narrative, and called them styles rather than modes. While the words "style" and "mode" can be used synonymously, mode has the additional connotation of "schema," with which I hope to maintain a greater consistency in the following discussion.[12]

Isotropic compositions organize imagery symmetrically within a given field. Because the main object of Maya plaza imagery is the human figure, bilateral symmetry is the most common system for isotropic compositions. The figure is represented in a full-frontal pose whereby the axis of symmetry is the vertical centerline of the body, and the arms and legs are positioned to reflect or mirror each other (fig. 42).

The isotropic mode may have been a Classic restatement or translation of sculpture in the round. Only a few Preclassic examples of full-frontal figures carved in relief can be found as possible prototypes (Stelae 1 and 2 from La Venta and Monument 2 of Izapa, for example), and the greater number of sculptures carved in full-round is more likely to have been known to the Early Classic patrons and sculptors. The few Classic Maya examples of isotropic compositions are usually carved in relatively deep relief, and while this may suggest sculpture in the round as a prototype or inspiration, the exigencies of maintaining spatial logic when carving a full-frontal figure in relief requires deep cutting, if only to keep the head on the shoulders of the figure where it belongs. Only three examples of the isotropic mode—one from Quirigua (Monument 26 [fig. 42]) and two from Uaxactun (Stelae 20 and 26 [figs. 52 and 32])—are known to have been carved during the Early Classic period.[13]

The schematic possibilities for using symmetry as a compositional mode are twofold. The first, seldom associated with the arts of the ancient Maya, may be found in certain abstract systems of proportion or structure, such as the Golden Mean or optical perspective. While these systems can be applied to, and will affect, the composition and meaning of an image, they seldom result in an actual isotropic picture (see Panofsky 1991). This situation may have an analogy in ancient Maya art, wherein an asymmetrical composition is unified by a geometrical structure based on the Integral Right Triangle (Clancy 1994c).[14]

Second, and more importantly in this discussion, two-dimensional representations of symmetry must be defined within the context of a given field; otherwise, we would not know that symmetry was the condition. The defining field with its imagery is divided into symmetric parts and is comprehended through the patterned repetition of these parts. The symmetrical image, then, is reflexive, self-contained, and self-referential.

Isotropic compositions utilizing bilateral symmetry do not imply movement or time as part of their meaning. By their symmetry, however, they can represent conditions of stasis and timelessness, or as easily, everywhere and all-time. Bilateral symmetry is a compositional mode that can project such thematic conditions or qualities as eternal, god-like, achronic, atemporal, spiritual, ethereal. The ancient Maya translated the self-referential, self-defining forms of isotropic symmetry into a proper condition for representing the plaza image of an honored person, but not often. Even less often, however, are the Classic Maya deities, as we now recognize them, represented by the isotropic mode.[15]

Many two-dimensional representations come very close to being isotropic but "break" the symmetry with spots of asymmetry. Everything is bilaterally symmetrical except the face of the figure which is turned in profile, or the arms are not symmetrically positioned (fig. 14). These places or insertions of asymmetry are important for the identity of the figure and its "story." Many Byzantine and Medieval depictions of holy figures are represented as almost symmetrical except for their hand gestures. One hand may hold a palm frond, identifying the figure as a martyr; one hand presents a paten with two eyes on it, identifying the figure as Saint Lucy and alluding to the story or narrative of her martyrdom. When asymmetry appears, actual characters, deeds, and action can be identified.

An asymmetrical organization of imagery within a given field is identified below as the narrative mode. Its conditions are many and various and can range from "almost" symmetrical to "almost" chaos. For purposes of analysis, however, not all asymmetrical images are classed as examples of the narrative mode. A middle ground is identified as the stational mode.

The *stational* mode is a particular kind of asymmetry. It represents a balanced and stationary image that draws near the isotropic in composition and appearance. It is the most common choice for organizing the imagery on a stela where one human figure is identified by costume, regalia, and gesture, and understood to be a "portrait" of an honored person, usually considered a ruler. There are relatively few dynamic outlines used in the portrayal of the individual on the stela; however, asymmetrical gestures and profiled faces with headgear imply direction and movement. The stational mode does not illustrate narrative, but through its use of asymmetry invokes narrative and may identify it. An asymmetrical gesture refers to action, and this action implies a particular set of circumstances or narrative. The profiled face and headgear indicate direction and imply a spatial relativity or dimension in which the figure stands.

The stational mode in two-dimensional compositions appears as a convincing, or intentional, compositional choice during the Late Preclassic period. Relief carvings of a single figure rendered in the stational mode are nonetheless rare at this time and often associated with small, apparently, provincial sites (Clancy 1990). It was adopted by the Early Classic Maya for plaza imagery almost to the exclusion of the isotropic or the narrative image. It is meaningful to note that since the plaza images of the Preclassic were generally composed in the narrative mode, one gets the impression that the Early Classic patrons and sculptors actively rejected narrative as proper plaza imagery.

The *narrative* mode, defining an asymmetrical, representational image, cannot be self-referential in the same way that symmetry is, because the outlines of its images are unique forms not matched or reflected within the given field. Representational asymmetry is the schematic condition necessary for illustrating narrative, story, or history. Asymmetry represents imagery as having direction, making a distinct gesture, and therefore implies movement and time. Things that are asymmetrically arranged are associated with dynamic states—things that move and are alive. As Heinz Herrmann states, "asymmetry is a requirement for the maintenance of the living state."[16]

The narrative mode is often recognized in ancient Maya art because two or more figures are shown interacting. Two figures are not necessary, however, if a single figure is depicted by an especially dynamic pose, as if running, swimming, dancing, playing ball, or flying.

The narrative mode never becomes the composition of choice for the main images of plaza sculpture, but beginning in the Middle Classic period it is commonly used in architectural sculpture—for wall panels and lintels especially. Also, use of the narrative mode is concentrated in the western Maya area, found in sites ranging along the Usumacinta River drainage. On the rare occasion when the narrative mode is used for plaza imagery, that is on stelae, it is predictable that the stela was carved in one of these western sites.

MONUMENTAL PROGRAMS

When a patron had erected more than one plaza monument, the possibility of an intentional monumental program can be raised. Reconstructing possible programmatic plaza displays is made difficult by the common ancient practice of resetting or redepositing old monuments. Not one of the 8th-baktun plaza monuments at Tikal, for example, has assuredly been found in its original position (W. Coe 1965, 34). The deprivations of ancient and recent looting and an incomplete archaeological record for the Early Classic also limit the discussion of monumental plaza programs.

Stela/Pedestal Pair

The best known monument program is the pairing of stela with pedestal. How this programmatic pairing was practiced during the Early Classic is, again, difficult to assess because of resetting. Several monuments found by archaeologists were paired, such as Stela 4 with Pedestal 1 at Tikal, but as Stela 4 was found set upside down in front of Structure 5D-34 of the North Acropolis, and Pedestal 1 was sawed in half and off to one side (see Satterthwaite 1958), it is difficult to insist that the original intention for placement is manifest in the pairing found by archaeologists.

An Early Classic intention behind the pairing of stelae and pedestals is likely, however, because the practice seems to have been fairly common in the Preclassic (Lowe, Lee, and Martínez 1982; Parsons 1988; J. Graham, Heizer, and Shook 1978), suggesting that the simple program of pairing stela and pedestal had a long history. Classic pedestals, however, were more commonly carved after the turn of the baktun.

What seems formally or schematically important in such a program are the differences in orientation: the stela is vertically upright, reflecting human stance and gravity, while the pedestal is oriented horizontally, perhaps reflecting its more earthly context: to look at a pedestal is to look down.[17] The emblematic content of pedestal imagery can be taken up by a basal panel when it is part of the stela image, but in either case it is used as a pedestal, actually or figuratively supporting the figural imagery of the stela (see Clancy 1976).

Pairs and Triads of Monuments

Certain programmatic concepts, elicited not just from context but from the monuments themselves, have to do with the representation of pairs and triads. It is possible to discuss programmatic pairs with some confidence. Triadic programs, however, are made from paired monuments (or images) flanking a central one, and as such are more difficult confidently to identify separately from a program of pairs.

The pair can be represented either as two figures together on one face of the monument, as a pair carved recto-verso on the two broad faces of the stela, or as two stelae set up together, each representing one figure of the pair. As a programmatic theme for public monuments, the pair can be found throughout the Maya Classic period, and following the 8th baktun it is usually represented on paired stelae. Monumental triads appear just after the turn of the baktun.

There is a clear reference in the imagery of Polol "Altar" 1 (fig. 7) to the Preclassic stelae compositions of Abaj Takalik (Pahl 1982), which may be an important source for the programmatic theme of pair as it was expressed in the lowlands. The pair, presented on the same face of the monument, however, is a Preclassic strategy, and Polol "Altar" 1 represents the only known example from the Preclassic lowlands. (I will argue later that Altar 1 of Polol was originally a stela, now a fragment that looks like an pedestal.) Presented together on the same face of a monument, the pair maintains, albeit minimally, the Preclassic penchant for narrative as proper plaza display. It is, therefore, not surprising that there are so few Early Classic examples of this type of pairing on plaza monuments in the lowlands.

The pair presented on one monument by the recto-verso compositional field is used first at Uaxactun (Stelae 10 and 5), where figural similarity is as important as the reversed poses of the represented pair (figs. 10 and 20). This is the more common Early Classic use of the recto-verso field. When differences are represented, such as the male paired with the female on Stela 5 of El Zapote (fig. 35), there is always some expression of similarity in the pose or costume.

Pairs carved on two separate monuments may or may not have been part of 8th-baktun monumental programs. The two possible examples put forward in chapters 4 and 5 are tentative: Stelae 18 and 19 of Uaxactun, and Stelae 4 and 7 of El Zapote. Stelae 18 and 19 (fig. 17) were found together associated with the Commemorative Astronomical Complex (Group E) in front of Structure E-2, each apparently inscribed with the same Long Count date of 8.16.0.0.0 (A.D. 357). Both are panel compositions with the main figure facing to the viewer's right. This, of course, is the normal way in which the figure is displayed. Usually, however, pairs of monuments show one figure facing right and one facing left, as if recto-verso images were split apart to form two monuments. This would be the main reason to doubt the pro-

grammatic pairing of Stelae 18 and 19, even though they share proximity and date. Stelae 4 (fig. 24) and 7 of El Zapote could have "faced one another," and while there are stylistic affinities in terms of composition and carving techniques between the two images, archaeological information and the decipherment of their inscriptions are not as complete as the Uaxactun examples.

The Early Classic warrior, when its iconography first appears on plaza monuments, is always represented in like but reversed pairs, either as recto-verso pairs, as on Stela 5 of Uaxactun (fig. 20), or as paneled pairs on separate stelae, as found at Tres Islas Stelae 1 and 3 (figs. 39 and 41).[18] The consistent compositional pairing of the warrior affects how he should be understood, and is an important aspect of his iconographic attributes.

Stelae 1 and 2 of Tikal, carved after the turn of the baktun, were found together as a pair of monuments in the small court in front of Structure 5D-26 of the North Acropolis (figs. 36 and 37). This location is probably a secondary setting for both stelae (W. Coe 1990, 786; Jones and Satterthwaite 1982, 9–11), but there is little doubt that they were originally conceived as a pair. The similarly costumed figures hold fancy ceremonial bars and are positioned to "face" one another, and both are composed by the wraparound field. However a third monument, Stela 28 (fig. 38), belongs with Stelae 1 and 2 because of its strong similarities of wraparound field, style of carving, and iconography of the fancy ceremonial bar. Even though Stela 28 was found in a dump to the west of the Main Plaza (Jones and Satterthwaite 1982, 60), the possibility that Stelae 1, 28, and 2 originally formed a triad of monuments is strong.

The triad is usually represented on three separate monuments. When three figures appear on the same monument, they tend to be composed in a narrative rather than a stational mode. A case, however, can be made that the three stational figures carved onto the three sides of Stela 31 of Tikal represent a triad or Trinity (fig. 33). If so, it is the first identifiable use of the triadic program. Stela 31 is an extraordinary monument and eludes easy categorization.

In summary, a pair comprises two things somehow joined together by reasons of formal similarity (a pair of gloves) or because of conventional or conceptual links (a wedded pair, a pair of opposites). The intention for pairing is easily discerned when formal similarity is the bond, or when the recto-verso field is used, whereby the pair, whether they look alike or not, has a concrete connection. It is out of these convincing circumstances that a description of ancient monumental pairing begins.

The Early Classic Maya sculptors created pairs by interplaying formal similarities with conceptual links. Formal similarities clearly exist between the recto-verso faces of Stela 35 of Copan (fig. 31), or between the two wraparound Stelae 1 and 2 of Tikal (figs. 36 and 37). They look alike and only close inspection reveals what appear to be potent differences. On Stela 5 of El Zapote (fig. 35), difference is the beginning point—male/female, simple/complex, and old/new imagery—but the intention of pairing is a given because of the "yoke" of the recto-verso field.

Represented in the Early Classic program of monuments, the pair is like a balanced equation: a proposition about a complementary reflexiveness between apparent similarities and differences, calling to mind the Mayan linguistic penchant for semantic parallelism or *diafrasmo* (Léon-Portilla 1963, 76–77; Edmonson 1973; Hunt 1977; Neuenswander 1987). The import of the paired image is expanded and more precisely characterized through repetition, reflection, and in the details of similarities and differences existing between the pair.

As mentioned above, within the Early Classic plaza a pair can be used to flank a third and central image, creating a triad. Such a triad illustrates a particular kind of sequence in which the beginning and ending are paired and represent either a more complete illustration of what was already implied by pairs or an elaboration of the dualistic concept behind pairing. The central figure is an insertion and may be understood as representing the point of mediation, or reflexion, between paired images. In triadic programs of the Late Classic period, the central monument portrays the historical, honored person flanked by a pair of conceptually conceived (mythological?) figures.[19]

PLAZA AND PATRON

Plazas in ancient Maya cities were civic areas receptive to general public activity. Anyone from the city, or coming into the city, had easy access to many of its plazas used for public gatherings and ceremonies (G. Andrews 1975, 37; C. Jones 1969; Becker 1979; Adams and Jones 1981), and a greater public access is more evident in Early Classic plaza designs than in the Late Classic period (Awe, Campbell, and Conlon 1991).

Freestanding plaza monuments do not suddenly appear in the Early Classic period. They have a long history dating back to the Middle Preclassic (Clancy 1990). However, it is not until close to the end of the 8th baktun

that the freestanding monuments, the stela and pedestal, become a ceremonial and civic necessity in the lowlands, and the increased production of these monuments is a definite signal that a major change occurred in lowland plaza life and ceremony.

In the lowlands, during the Late Preclassic period, the architectural forms surrounding and defining a plaza were decorated with panels of stucco relief sculpture. The careful study of the great stucco masks of Cerros (in Belize) by Freidel and Schele (1988) represents them as cosmic entities—the Sun and Venus, specifically—important to the rituals celebrating significant durations in the cycles of the Sun and Venus. Schele and Freidel (1990, 103ff.) suggest that the "invention" of kingship was justified, and the person of the king deified, through his ritual use of a plaza platform on which these cosmic events were represented by the large stucco masks.

At Cerros, the masks are placed and painted to positively embrace the cycles they represent; important to their interpretation is how the masks were composed in paired relation to one another, expressing iconographic qualities for right/east/red, left/west/black, and up/down (Freidel 1985b, 17–27). For the stucco masks of Tikal found on platforms of the North Acropolis, Arthur Miller (1986) also finds cosmic meanings. He too understands the movements and directions of the sun to be associated with, and indicative of, divine kingship.

The advent of the stela placed in the plaza seems to be related to an apparent decrease in the production of the great stucco panels (Proskouriakoff 1950, 103; Schele and Miller 1986, 106–9). Freidel and Schele (1988, 85) understand the stucco masks on plaza structures as the prototypes for the headdress and hand-held regalia of the honored figures portrayed on the newly popular stela. While there is a certain economy in the perception that the public or plaza function of the stucco panels was reiterated by the new freestanding monuments of stela and pedestal, the only actual connections between the two are iconographic details. The stucco panels and the stelae are very different in terms of context, medium, scale, composition, and form. The symmetrical images of anthropomorphic and zoomorphic faces or masks modeled in stucco are of such a disparate, often enormous, scale and compositional order from the stationally composed stela, that it is difficult to imagine how they could have performed similar functions within the plaza. Ostensibly, then, the plaza function of the stucco masks was not, or could not have been, taken up or continued by the stelae, and Freidel and Schele (ibid., 93) suggest the masks became more passive, "cosmic frames" for the honored figures depicted on stelae.

The freestanding plaza monuments represent a different characterization for the function of the plaza space, one that belongs to the other perceivable differences between Preclassic and Classic traits. As tokens of how Classic period public life was conceived and structured by the plaza, stelae differ from the stucco masks by being closer to human in scale, by taking up public space within the plaza and the low-lying terraces framing the plaza, and by representing their messages through the human image and by glyphic inscription. The large, isotropic masks of the lowland Preclassic, identified as deities, support the proposition of a divine ruler, but the stational images of humans on the stelae that are human-scaled emphasize the humanity of the portrayed figure, not its divinity.[20]

Active Subjects

Compositional fields displaying imagery on more than one side of the monument require an active viewer to walk around the monument, and viewer participation was called for by the compositions and imagery of the new public monuments now inhabiting the open spaces of the plaza. Stela 35 of Copan (fig. 31), for example, cannot be fully comprehended by taking one optimal position in front of it. Furthermore, since its two faces are carved with like but reversed images, it is unlikely one image was "public" while the other was more esoteric.[21] The full meaning and power of the wraparound or recto-verso fields are predicated on an active viewer.

The stelae and pedestals were placed where they would directly confront people walking or gathering in the plaza. The use of compositional fields and modes requiring an active subject/viewer therefore opens up the possibility that the new plaza monuments were intentionally conceived to support multiple points of view and allow the different meanings each individual viewer could/would achieve.[22] The new monument, composed to illicit personal interaction and placed into the plaza itself, suggests a strategic change caused the formal changes that distinguish the Early Classic plaza.

The Early Classic patrons and sculptors did not produce plaza monuments to carry only one political message to a passive public. Through the monuments set into the plazas we can perceive a different idea about public life and public participation that sets the Early Classic period apart from what went before and after.[23] As a general description, the Early Classic period can be defined as a time when the general public was asked to assume a more active and participatory role in the plaza and its ceremonies.

Speculations on Patronage and the Sculptor

The changes perceived in the use of plaza space and in the style and composition of the monuments lead to speculations about patronage. Undoubtedly the ancient Maya sculptor worked with both the demands of his worldly patron and the more technical and spiritual demands of his art and trade. That the Preclassic emphasis on mytho-narrative and ritual changed during the Early Classic to the formation of more ceremonial, and perhaps secular, public experiences, certainly points to differences in the demands and agendas of patrons.

At the beginning of the Early Classic, the making of a plaza monument was more process-oriented, the image arising from a "proper" handling of the stone. Towards the end of the Early Classic, the process was more image-oriented with the finished image fully preconceived and, perhaps, even traced on a prepared stone, a stone that was no longer in itself so demanding. The reasoning behind this observation has to do with differences in the way the stone was prepared for carving. The earlier monuments are only partially dressed or shaped and their imagery is carved over and with the natural irregularities left in the stone. The visual force of the stone is as strong (sometimes stronger) as the image it carries. This interaction between image and stone is lost some time after the turn of the baktun. The monument becomes more carefully planed and smoothed, and the imagery is foregrounded, while the stoniness of the monument has been subdued.

These particular changes suggest that the relationship between the patron and the sculptor changed from a kind of partnership to a more hierarchical one, such as that between employer and employee. When the process of making a monument was the focus, the imagery was an outcome. Both the patron and sculptor worked with the "demands" of the stone, which had to do with its physical properties and its imagistic possibilities—that is, what imagery it "held" had to be revealed by the sculptor's and patron's vision. In the 8th baktun, the patron certainly had a vested interest in what kind of image would result from the stone, but does not seem to have ordered the vision all that precisely for his or her own ends. The notable differences in the contemporary 8th-baktun images of Tikal, Uaxactun, Xultun, Yaxha—or even in the contemporary monuments of one site, such as Tikal's Stelae 4 and 18 and Stela 39 (see figs. 21, 22, and 18)—intimate that a prescribed ritualized process from which an image arose was primary.

When the focus turns to the image, which may have been inevitable, given the viewer's proper interactive roles with monuments within the newly and differently defined plaza, the relationship between patron and sculptor changes. The image motivates the making of a monument and, presumably, the patron dictated more fully what that image would be, maintaining, of course, the stela monument for the very reason that it would suggest traditional expectations for meaning. By 9.2.0.0.0 (A.D. 475) this more political and secular function, signaled by the primacy of the image, is successfully grafted to the ancient monument form.

We have access to historical information about patrons gleaned from the glyphic texts if, indeed, the patron is the subject of the monument's imagery. This is the usual assumption, but there is one last speculation to put forward before leaving the topic of sculptor and patron. Plaza monuments could have been commissioned by a group of people—elites, officers, members of religious-civic groups—whose concern or purpose was the overseeing of public ceremony and plaza activities. This suggestion, while not currently considered in reconstructions for ancient Maya patronage of stelae and pedestals, is closer to modern Mayan community organizations, such as *parcialidades* and *cofradias*, and to Mayan ideals about the expression of individuality within the community (Hendrickson 1989, 132; Farriss 1984, 320–43; Hill and Monagham 1987). Classic Maya stelae are not really portraits, even though they are always referred to as such, but conventional representations of an honored figure placed, usually, in an historical context by a glyphic text. The text, naming a ruler with his titles, genealogy, and deeds, also connotes historic themes of the time—such as "in the time of Lincoln, the liberator of slaves." The honored figure may have stood for the ruler, but equally it could have represented the personification of a dynasty or clan, a city or polity.

CHAPTER THREE

Plaza Imagery

MAIN IMAGES

THE ICONOGRAPHY OFFERED HERE IS CATEGORICAL and general. The effort is to determine the meaningful range of contexts within which a particular icon or image operated. Icons are grouped by descriptive categories, which take into account their basic graphic configuration and their contexts within a compositional field. While description has revealed some new iconic categories, attention to context reveals the multiple levels of meaning, beyond denotation, with which icons were sometimes invested, such as metaphoric, emblematic, and allegoric. Within the general themes represented by the three compositional modes—isotropic, stational, and narrative—described in chapter 2, sub-themes or plots with more specific meaning are supplied by the iconographic content of the plaza monuments. While the main image of stelae was most often defined by the stational mode, the sculptor could, and often did, interweave secondary images that contrasted with the main image in mode, carving methods, and scale. Therefore, the clearest way to begin a description of Early Classic use of iconography on plaza monuments is to divide it by these two kinds of imagery: the main image and secondary image.

Main images take up the greatest amount of space in a given field, and it is a good assumption that such an image was considered important and was invested with great meaning. The main image is usually composed by the stational mode and represents an elaborately dressed human figure qualified by context, pose, gesture, and costume. The display of an anthropomorphic being rather than a human is a rare but intriguing main image found on Early Classic plaza monuments, as are the few insignia that were carved as main images on stelae.

Figures

The *honored human*, the main image of plaza stelae, is distinguished by a fancy costume and body type (fig. 18). While the parts of the costume most often referred to in the following chapters are here mentioned and described, the reader can get detailed iconographic accounts of royal costuming in Proskouriakoff (1950, 46ff.), Coggins (1985, 47–57), and Schele and Miller (1986, chap. 1).

The normal features of the headdress are a headband, sometimes beaded, topped by a helmet or large hat often shaped like an animal or deity head (fig. 6). Wing-like elements are commonly appended to the sides of the hat just behind the ears, and emblematic signs rise from its top. An

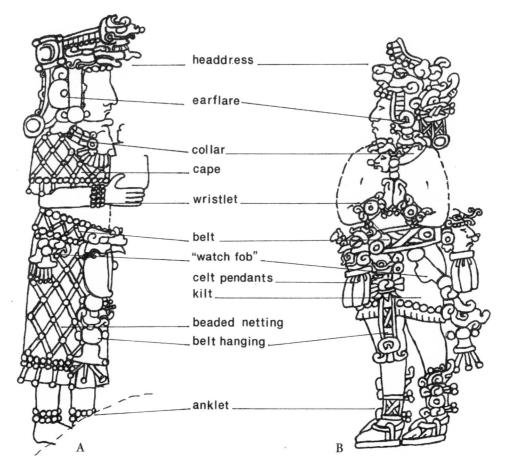

headdress

earflare

collar

cape

wristlet

belt

"watch fob"

celt pendants

kilt

beaded netting

belt hanging

anklet

A

B

Fig. 6.   Costume Elements: A) Female, Drawn from El Zapote, Stela 5, B) Male, Drawn from Leiden Plaque. (Drawing by Flory Clancy.)

arching panache is sometimes attached to the back of the hat, but feathers are more commonly portrayed on headdresses in the Middle and Late Classic periods (Proskouriakoff 1950, 46, 50–51). The emblems rising from the top of the helmet or hat sometimes include glyphs representing the actual name of the figure (see Stela 31 of Tikal [fig. 33]). Because of this and the many iconographic variations within the headdress's particular features, as described, the headdress may be understood as an item of costuming that admits personal insignia.

The fancy belts are as various as headdresses but lack identifiable personal insignia. They are thick and wide and often support two or four masquettes of humans or deities, from whose chins depend celt-like objects and other pendent forms. An item called the "watch fob" is

sometimes attached to the belt and is a long, chain-like affair that hangs diagonally from the side of the belt to below and behind the figure's knees.

Other items of elite costume are perhaps more symptomatic of the traditional community status and role inherited or achieved by the individual. Beaded collars and necklaces, presumably of precious jade, are depicted with fewer variations than headdresses or belts, and the articles themselves could have been bequeathed from one generation to the next, or acquired through participation in rituals associated with, for example, heir-apparency and battle victories. The same case could be made for the large earflares, kilts, skirts, anklets and wristlets.

Netted capes and skirts, usually shown as overgarments, were constructed out of tubular and round beads (fig. 6). These are thought to be the dress of royal women (Proskouriakoff 1961; Marcus 1976) or evoke the connotation of the feminine (Schele 1979). Lately, the netted costume has been understood as signifying an image of the male/female creator god (Freidel, Schele and Parker 1993, 272–73) where the male aspect is also associated with the maize god (see Taube 1985).

For the most part, body type seems to be a function of local style or a particular school of carvers. One particular body type, however, is found widely distributed in the Early Classic period: a wasp-waisted figure, an early example of which is the main figure of the small Seattle Stela (fig. 16). Wasp-waisted figures have proportionately small diameters at their waists, but "normal" proportions for shoulders and hips. Their outlines have a feminine or soft quality.

The wasp-waisted figure may have been inspired by the ceremonial-bar holders as they were depicted on the Late Preclassic Stelae 1 and 5 of Abaj Takalik (fig. 8) to the south. When they occur in the lowlands, they are shown supporting ceremonial bars, disembodied heads, and using an extroverted gesture. No warriors are known to be so outlined. What this figural type means is unknown, but it ranges throughout the lowlands from the beginnings of the Early Classic period until the 3rd katun of the 9th baktun (Stela 3 of Uaxactun [fig. 56]).[1]

The representation of an *anthropomorph* as the main image is rare, and may be understood as an ancient Maya conception of the "other" (Clancy 1994a). "Others" can be recognized when they are represented as anthropomorphs and/or when canons of normal human scale and proportions are altered. The use of the anthropomorph occurs at the turn of the baktun, a millenial moment, of which there were only two in the history of the Classic Maya, and so this figure is designated the baktun-other. It may be that the anthropomorph was a human wearing a mask, but I think this is unlikely. At least in the Late Classic period, the Maya artist was careful to render the use of masks by clearly showing the human face beneath the outer one (see for example, the well-known Stela 11 from Yaxchilan). Why the baktun-other was chosen for plaza imagery at these rare and potent moments in cyclical history, cannot be fully explained, but Clemency Coggins' (1990) observation that few, if any, monuments are known to have been specifically erected in honor of the baktun may be an initial clue. Coggins (ibid.) demonstrates that the turn of the baktun as it is known at Tikal (the first) and Ceibal (the later and second turning)

can each be associated with rituals defined by the cycles of the planet Venus and its rich mythical and religious meanings for the Maya. The baktun-others identified here may or may not be expressions of Venus iconography, but they are certainly rendered as other than a "normal" human figure.

The main figure of Stela 1 from El Zapote (fig. 29) is rendered as an anthropomorph with a feline face and an old man's body, pot-bellied and bent-kneed. Stela 20 of Xultun (fig. 30) and the anthropomorphic figure carved on Pedestal 19 of Tikal (fig. 34) also belong to this small group of anthropomorphs as main figures. Associated with Stela 31, Pedestal 19 displays the anthropomorph in a full-frontal view, seated cross-legged, and like the main figure on Stela 20 of Xultun, it has large, bulging eyes with high cheek bones, a broad flat nose, and curls coming from the corners of its mouth. More speculatively, because the actual faces are lost from the extant monument, it is argued that Stela 35 of Copan (fig. 33), for contextual reasons, may have also represented the baktun-other. One other fairly sure example of the baktun-other dating from the Classic period is Stela 2 of Ceibal, most likely carved near the turn of the next baktun at 10.0.0.0.0 (A.D. 830). These monuments, then, represent public imagery thought to be appropriate to the millenial turning of the baktun.[2]

Pose

The main figure is a *standing* figure. Because of its ubiquity and assumed naturalness, the fact of standing, as opposed to other possible positions a body could take, seems to hold little iconographic meaning in itself. The standing figure is taken as a more-or-less neutral support for the more meaningful costuming. However, this is an assumption. Gesture, which is certainly meaningful, is discussed below.

For the Early Classic period, two types of profile poses are distinguishable: articulated and broad. The articulated-profile pose shows a figure, like the main figure in Stela 1 of Tikal (fig. 36), with shoulders and torso displayed frontally, hips and legs in three-quarter view, and head and feet in profile. The turning of body parts from profile, to frontal, to three-quarter views is nicely described as articulation, and omits any suggestion that the ancient artists were unable to create true three-quarter-profile projections, which is implied by the term, quasi-three-quarter profile (Proskouriakoff 1950, 19). With the broad-profile stance, the body parts are only somewhat articulated. The face, legs, and feet are profiled, while the torso region is shown in a three-quarter view. The sculptors have "broadened" the profile body mass to create a better display of costume and regalia. The main figure on Stela 5 of Uaxactun (fig. 20) and the lateral figures on Stela 31 of Tikal (fig. 33) are so posed. The broad profile is more commonly used. The articulated profile is often, but not always, associated with the horizontal display of the ceremonial bar (see below).

Representations of a main figure in an actual profile pose are rare, as such poses are seemingly reserved for the depiction of secondary figures. Profile poses depict the near shoulder and upper arm of the main figure as overlapping the torso, rather than being drawn back from the torso as it is in the broad profile. While the body is not articulated or broadened, its costuming can be "articulated" (fig. 48).

A *seated* figure distinguishes Tikal's 8th-baktun stelae. Because it is different from the normal standing pose, its meaningfulness seems more apparent. There is an evocation of a narrative theme in the more visually active presentation of a seated figure, angled at the hips and the knees. For Stela 4 of Tikal (fig. 21), and perhaps Stela 18, the full-frontal rendering of the face, however, suggests that the stational mode is the proper way of describing these seated figures. The physical requirements of depicting a seated pose, with its expanded width for the angled legs, led the Tikal sculptors to choose a monument shaped very like a pedestal, that is, almost as wide as it is tall.

The representation of a figure seated on a throne had few prototypes in the medium of relief carving.[3] The Late Preclassic Stela 8 of Izapa depicts, as part of a larger narrative composition, a profile figure seated cross-legged upon a pedestal or throne and set off from the rest of the imagery by a quatrefoil frame. A quatrefoil also frames the famous rock relief of Chalcatzingo (Relief 1) depicting a figure seated on a block-like throne (Grove 1984, fig. 5, pl. 4). The quatrefoil frame, as depicted at Chalcatzingo, is a great, open-jawed monster within which the figure sits as if in the mouth and/or a cave (Grove 1968; Angulo V. 1987, 135–41). The association of an enthroned figure with the cave has a long history dating back to the famous Olmec monuments (altars) that depict a seated figure in a niche, interpreted as a figure emerging from a cave (Grove 1973). As suggested by Grove (ibid., 1970), the altars themselves are best understood as pedestals or thrones upon which actual figures sat. The comparison of these pedestals with the Olmec painting at the cave of Oxtotitlan, Guerrero, where a figure is seated on a throne depicted very like the Olmec pedestals, strengthens the symbolic associations of cave, seated figure, and throne (Grove 1970).

The quatrefoil frame, as it has been iconographically interpreted, is a shape capable of carrying multiple connotations. By its shape, it is commonly linked to the flower-like emblem for the *tzolkin*, or the sacred calendar of 260 days, and is understood as a sign meaning "completion" (Thompson 1950, 137–38). It is also associated, as it is in the Preclassic, with caves and chthonic regions (Grove 1973; Heyden 1975; Taylor 1979; Schavelzon 1980; Tate 1980, 1982). Bassie-Sweet (1991, 95–109) gives a careful review of quatrefoil-as-cave associations, detailing how the flower-like aspects of the quatrefoil can be related to glyphs for the planet Venus as Evening Star, the Moon, and to the iconographies of bees and rain deities. She outlines how quatrefoil frames, with their connotation of cave and tomb, can house depictions of ancestors and connote birth by the cave's metaphoric association to the womb (ibid.). Freidel, Schele, and Parker (1993, 215) characterize the quatrefoil as a "portal" to another world. Implicated by all of these associations, the quatrefoil may be understood as indicating that what it enframes is of a different time and place from that which is without it.

As a frame, it is used with the Early Classic representations of an insigne on pedestals (see below), which, by their horizontal orientation, reinforce the chthonic and earthly connotations of the quatrefoil. It is *not* used to frame the seated figure carved as the main image on stelae.

It seems unlikely that the Preclassic monuments cited above were the direct inspiration for the use of the seated pose when it first appeared on the monuments of Tikal. It is more likely that these meaningful associations were preserved by other means, such as narrative lore, than through a direct succession of carved images. Thus, the sculptors and patrons of Tikal revitalize an ancient tradition that associated seated figures on thrones with caves and their metaphoric connotations, but represent this ancient narrative within a stational composition. The subtlety of altering the monument shape of the stela to approximate that of a pedestal or throne should not be overlooked. When the seated figure was displayed on the plaza stelae of Tikal, there would have been, at this time, an evocative interplay with insignia used as main images on pedestals, where the "aura" of the emblematic would be acquired by the honored figure represented in a seated pose.

Gesture

The number of different gestures used to display hand-held regalia as depicted on Early Classic plaza monuments is intriguingly small and implies conventions for gestural meaning that go beyond the pragmatic requirements of holding something. We are unable at this time to determine what these meanings are, beyond their repeated use in a particular context or by a psychological reading of gesture in the hope that such a reading is properly applied to the Classic Maya. One thing is clear, however: during the Early Classic period the main figures' gestures change from supporting, cradling, or bearing regalia to holding or grasping them.

The *flat-hand gesture* shows the arm bent ninety degrees at the elbow with the hand continuing the horizontal line of the lower arm by displaying an open palm with extended fingers. Impossibly, this hand supports an object by "balancing" it on the top edge (fig. 12). Despite its illogical appearance, such a gesture is in line with the Early Classic conventions of supporting and balancing objects of regalia rather than grasping them. The flat-hand gesture is used fairly consistently during the Early Classic, on a few occasions in the Middle Classic, and rarely in the Late Classic period, where its configuration is altered just enough to suggest a more reasonable holding of the regalia (see the secondary figure on Stela 2 of Machaquila [I. Graham 1967, fig. 44]). The flat hand is used to "support" disembodied heads, one end of a ceremonial bar (as in the Seattle Stela [fig. 16]), and glyphs (as on Stela 5 of El Zapote [fig. 35]).

In her analysis of the Seattle Stela, Linda Schele (1985b) likens the flat-hand gesture to the scattering gesture (the offering gesture) associated in the Late Classic with autosacrifice and blood. Easby and Scott (1970, 214) discuss the gesture as it appears on the verso side of Stela 5 of El Zapote and suggest it was used to hold "unreal" objects. Given the impossibility of the gesture as actually rendered, this last interpretation has a positive resonance.

The *cupped-hand gesture* is always shown as in front of the body mass with the fingers curling around or over the thumb. During the Early Classic period, this gesture makes a distinctive compositional curve as the arm is bent at the elbow and the cupped hand is raised towards the center of the chest. The outline of the lower arm is gently curved, and this line continues around the slightly bent wrist to the tops of the curved fingers. If the honored person is holding a disembodied head, it rests in the crook of the arm, framed within the curve (fig. 15). If he

uses this gesture to display the ceremonial bar, the bar is oriented diagonally, resting within the bent elbow and pressed to the body by the cupped hand (fig. 12). This gesture is posed asymmetrically, with the other arm and hand hanging down more-or-less naturally or bent at the elbow to display regalia with the flat-hand gesture. When the ceremonial bar is held diagonally, as is usual for the 8th baktun, its diagonal line together with the asymmetry of the gesture create a sense of movement and a suggestion of narrative content.

The cupped-hand gesture symmetrically repeated by the other arm and hand becomes the better known *ceremonial-bar gesture*. This gesture is specifically associated with the ceremonial bar oriented in a horizontal position (fig. 52). With the ceremonial-bar gesture, the bar rests in the crooks of both elbows and is pressed at the center of the chest by the two cupped hands rendered back to back. The symmetry of the gesture presents a more formalized, and perhaps a more ideal, representation of the honored person. The gesture requires that the bar be presented horizontally and symmetrically and generates a visual stability that approaches the isotropic. In fact, the first depiction of the ceremonial bar in the 9th baktun, Stela 26 of Uaxactun (9.0.10.0.0 [A.D. 446]) (fig. 32), shows it held by a full-frontal figure in true isotropic composition.

In plaza imagery the ceremonial-bar gesture plays a greater role in the image of the honored figure after the turn of baktun. During the 8th baktun, only the main figures depicted on the Preclassic Stela 5 from Abaj Takalik and the well-known, but non-monumental, Leiden Plaque use this gesture to hold the ceremonial bar. Importantly, however, the secondary figures pictured on the Leiden Plaque (fig. 14) and Tikal's Stela 39 (fig. 18) have their hands bound in this gesture. In this they compare with small jade carvings and ceramic pieces where an "empty" ceremonial-bar gesture may be taken by dwarfish dancers (Clancy 1994b).

The ceremonial-bar gesture is related to an ancient Olmec gesture with a long history (ibid.). In Olmec representations, the figure's elbows are bent, and the forearms extend forward from the body; the palms are turned up, and the fingers curl. Whatever is being held rests atop the forearms cradled by the upward curling fingers. Although not always the case, the most famous thing held by this Olmec gesture is a "baby" or were-jaguar baby.[4] The Early Classic Maya maintained the symmetry of gesture, but drew the arms up to the chest and used the gesture with the ceremonial bar, which is usually rendered as a double-headed serpent.

The history of serpent iconography connects the ceremonial-bar gesture to the *extroverted gesture*. This is a gesture that evokes a sense of emotive action. One arm is raised at the shoulder projecting the hand above the head of the figure (fig. 19). During the Early Classic, it is used first to support a disembodied head and then later to grasp it. The gesture is very like an ancient pose first seen on the basaltic columns from La Venta (Monument 63) and San Lorenzo (Monument 56), where it is used in narrative scenes depicting a human wrestling an enormous serpent (de la Fuente 1973, 234–35, 264–65; Milbrath 1979, 39; Clancy 1990, 22). At some point, probably near the beginning of the Late Preclassic, the gesture was used in two apparently different narrative contexts: the original one (a human wrestling with a serpent) appeared in the southern Maya area on monuments carved at Izapa (Stela 3) and Kaminaljuyu (Stelae 4 and 19); the new context shows a bellicose figure using the extroverted gesture in the presence of a bound, secondary figure. This new narrative combination was employed, interestingly enough, in the Veracruz region of the Olmec, exemplified by the Alvarado Stela and Monument 2 from El Mesón. The use of the same extroverted gesture attests to an early conceptual link between the undulating serpent and a bound figure. The undulating serpent is discussed further with the ceremonial bar, and the bound figure is taken up again under "Secondary Images."

In all probability, the extroverted gesture's associated meanings would have been modified from its earliest use. For its Early Classic depictions, the extroverted gesture is dynamic, thus carrying traces of its origin in narrative scenes, but it appears as a synecdochic device—one that reduces whatever narrative traces it may hold to one evocative gesture appropriate to stational displays.

The extroverted gesture first appears in the lowlands around 8.17.0.0.0 (A.D. 376), and can be associated with specific costume details: a long, angled necklace made of large cylindrical beads that hangs to or below the main figure's waist, and an emblematic device in the shape of a jaguar paw usually worn on, or as, the loincloth. The jaguar paw, generally considered an emblem belonging to the early Jaguar Paw clan of Tikal (Coggins 1975, 146–47; Laporte and Fialko 1990), is first evident on Stela 39 of Tikal (fig. 18).

Only one Early Classic monument displays the *offering gesture*, Stela 4 of El Zapote (fig. 24). In ancient Maya imag-

ery, it becomes an important gesture only in the Late Classic. The gesture is commonly termed "scattering," and refers to the same gesture identified by Teobert Maler (1903, 2(2): 126) as the beneficent gesture. The offering gesture shows the hand slightly bent back at the wrist and angled toward the ground. From the hand various things appear to fall: beads, seeds, droplets, or a fall of liquid. Although the stuff issuing from the offering hand has recently been identified as kernels of corn (Love 1987) or cornmeal balls (Taube 1985), the most common interpretation is blood (Stuart 1984, 1988). Whatever falls from the hand does not alter the fact that the gesture is one of offering and that what is offered was precious.

The contextual, associated iconography belonging to the offering gesture is rich and complicated. During the Early Classic period at Teotihuacan in Central Mexico, the gesture is used by attendant figures rendered in profile (Kubler 1967; Pasztory 1974) and dressed in costumes that are iconographically similar to the costume of a warrior pair that appears throughout Mesoamerica towards the end of the 4th century (ca. 8.17.0.0.0 [A.D. 376]).[5] The warrior's costume will be discussed with the regalia of the warrior below, but here it is important to note that the two—the warrior and the offering gesture—appear about the same time on Maya monuments, but do not appear together; the offering gesture is first associated with the regalia of the staff and bag on Stela 4 of El Zapote. It has been argued, however, that the staff and bag are "translations" of weapons (Clancy 1980, 45–46), so the "Mexican" connection between costume and gesture probably was known by the Early Classic Maya, even though they chose not to bring them together in plaza imagery.

Holding gestures do not appear meaningful beyond their pragmatic function of holding by the hand items such as weapons or staffs (fig. 49). There may have been deeper meaning to these grasping gestures, undetectable at this time, because the Early Classic Maya *did* distinguish between the more apparently symbolic gestures that supported or balanced or displayed regalia, and those that grasped or held regalia like a tool.

Regalia

Along with elaborate costuming, Early Classic regalia consists of disembodied heads, ceremonial bars, weapons, bags, and staffs held in the hands of the honored figures. It is assumed that each kind of hand-held regalia signals the different occupation or role attributed to the figure holding it. Thus, plaza images classed by their hand-held regalia would be bearers of heads, ceremonial bars, and glyphs, and holders of staffs, bags, and weapons. All hand-held regalia surely signaled ceremonial aspects within the office of rulership, but the understandable connections between weapons and war, whether they be of a ceremonial nature or not, cannot be as easily drawn between, say, the ceremonial bar and the particular ceremonial aspects of office it may have signaled.

Disembodied heads were major items of regalia for 8th-baktun plaza imagery. They become less frequent after the turn of the baktun and are rarely depicted in the Late Classic period. There was an equivalence of some kind between disembodied heads and the ceremonial bar, because they are displayed by the same cupped-hand and flat-hand gestures, and because the ceremonial bar exhibits disembodied heads within the open jaws of its two serpent heads. Disembodied heads are anthropomorphic entities, never human, wearing hats made from graphemes or actual glyphs, and are usually considered to be representations of deities. There is actually a fair amount of variation in the iconography of these heads, but at Tikal, the jaguar-eared, cruller-eyed head (hereafter the JC head, for convenience) is repeated with some frequency, often with the Tikal emblem glyph worn like a hat (Stelae 36, 4, and 31 [figs. 11, 21, and 33]).[6] The JC head is thought to be associated with the "night-sun" or the "jaguar god of the underworld" (Schele and Miller 1986, 50), and thus an aspect of God III of the famous Palenque Triad of deities (Berlin 1963; Kelley 1965; Schele 1979). Freidel and Schele (1988, 67–72) demonstrate how its iconographic features are similar to, and may be derived from, certain stucco masks modeled on Late Preclassic plaza architecture.

The specifics of the cruller and the jaguar ear also define an anthropomorphic head important for ancient Oaxacan (Zapotec) images identified as God 5-F (Caso and Bernal 1952, 187 and figs. 317–21) portrayed on ceramic urns placed in burials dating to the third and fourth centuries, that is, the transition between the ceramic phases, Monte Alban II and IIIa. The JC head, therefore, may have been "imported" into the Maya lowlands (Clancy 1980, 28–29) when plaza imagery was being redefined at the beginning of the Early Classic.

As well as being cradled as regalia, disembodied heads appear in other compositional contexts: as supernal and basal images, and as supplementary images placed at the feet of the main figure. In these contexts they also wear glyphs as headdresses or hats. Since they can inhabit all areas of a composition, they are an excellent example for arguing the importance of contextual placement and associations in the study of iconography. As a supernal image, it has long been thought to depict an ancestor of the main figure; placed at or below the feet of the main figure, it is now thought to be a place-name.[7]

Disembodied heads as hand-held regalia are not common in Preclassic narrative contexts. In the south, Monument 1 from Chalchuapa is a Late Preclassic monument depicting a crouching figure holding out a head with bird or jaguar features. Its ruinous condition precludes much analysis (see Anderson 1978, figs. 2 and 3). Stela 1 of Chocola, also from the south, displays an honored figure holding two disembodied heads by the cupped-hand and flat-hand gestures. As Christopher Jones (1988) points out, however, its stylistic and iconographic traits suggest an Early Classic date rather than the Late Preclassic date that has commonly been assumed for its carving. If this is true, and I think it is, then the disembodied head, as hand-held regalia, has an almost imperceptible presence in the Preclassic. Its presence on Early Classic monuments is innovative for its use as a qualifier of personal, polity, and place-names.

Not often, but occasionally, the main figure will display *glyphs* supported by the flat-hand gesture. Unfortunately, these glyphs are for the most part unreadable due the poor condition of their monuments. In the Early Classic period these hand-held glyphs are accompanied by bar and dot numbers (fig. 35). Because disembodied heads are sometimes accompanied by a number, as on Stela 1 of El Zapote (fig. 29), it is possible to assume that hand-held glyphs represent a similar kind of meaning to that of the head, that is, a name of some kind.[8]

The *ceremonial bar* is usually represented as a bar designed with conventional references to a segmented serpent body, and with open-jawed serpent heads attached to either end. Small anthropomorphic heads or manikins are depicted within the open jaws. This is the basic and most common form of the ceremonial bar, even though all bars vary in their details (see Clancy 1994b). "Fancy" bars are made by the addition of pendants attached at the joining of the serpent heads with the body/bar shape. The fanciest pendants have been termed "serpent poles" by Joyce Bailey (1972, 56) and are displayed by the wraparound stelae of Tikal (figs. 36 and 37). The bar is held either diagonally with the cupped-hand and flat-hand gesture or horizontally with the symmetrical ceremonial-bar gesture.

Introduced into the lowlands by the portrayal of the figure on Stela 29 of Tikal (fig. 12), the ceremonial bar is maintained as an important and evocative piece of regalia throughout the Classic era. As Proskouriakoff (1950, 88–89) states, "By the time the typical Classic style emerges, one of the most common motifs presented is the figure holding a ceremonial bar ."

Proskouriakoff (ibid.) identified two kinds of bars: a rigid bar, and a curved "flaccid" bar connecting the two serpent heads (fig. 14). Although she thought the flaccid bar was an early type, it really is more indicative of locale, that is, the eastern and south-eastern Maya regions where it is portrayed, for the most part, during the Late Classic period, on the monuments of Copan. However, the flaccid body refers more graphically than the rigid bar to the older undulating type of ceremonial bar, as seen on Stela 5 of Abaj Takalik (fig. 8).

The pictorial history of the hand-held serpent is a complex one and is related to those of the extroverted gesture and the ceremonial-bar gesture (see above). On Monument 63 from La Venta and Monument 53 from San Lorenzo, both Middle Preclassic relief-carved basalt columns, the serpent-like creatures held in part by the extroverted gesture are enormous and powerful. Later, during the Late Preclassic, a similar narrative and gesture are portrayed on Stela 19 of Kaminaljuyu (Parsons 1986, 30, fig. 55), where a coiling serpent, not so imposing in size as the Middle Preclassic image, is wrestled by an anthropomorphic figure with human hands and claws for feet. Also dating from the Late Preclassic, Stela 3 of Izapa narratively displays an anthropomorphic figure raising an axe or club before a relatively large serpent monster. Stela 5 from Abaj Takalik (fig. 8) presents a pair of figures separated by a double column of glyphs. The figure on the (viewer's) right presses a long and sinuous serpent to his body by the ceremonial-bar gesture. This serpent is not as active and it has been reduced in size relative to the figure that now appears to display it rather than interacting with it. Similarly, the Seattle Stela (fig. 16), carved just before or after the beginning of the Early Classic period, shows a masked human with a cupped hand pressing, and flat hand supporting, a long sinuous serpent that coils in controlled curves over his shoulder and across his chest, rising to become the supernal image of a disembodied head within the serpent's open jaws.

The serpents rendered on the Abaj Takalik Stela and the Seattle Stela are related not only by reference, but by the figures' gesture, to the ceremonial bar displayed on Stela 29 of Tikal (fig. 12) at the beginning of the Early Classic. As with other items of regalia, the serpent has been translated into an allegorical figure, a convention that synecdochically alludes to an ancient narrative that was once illustrated by scenes of wrestling or doing battle with a serpent monster (Clancy 1994b). Through time, the monster seems to become smaller and less imposing until it is completely tamed in the imagery of the ceremonial bar.

The representation of an honored person holding *weapons* is as distinctive as it is rare in the plaza imagery of the Early Classic monuments in the lowlands. Weapon holders are commonly represented in the narrative contexts of Preclassic monuments, and this figure's translation into stational compositions occurs during the first half of the 8th baktun on Stela 11 of Kaminaljuyu, where he carries a fancy, flint axe that looks too decorative to be useful as a weapon, but, nonetheless, is recognizable as such.[9]

There is only one known lowland representation of the warrior during the 8th baktun, the important Stela 5 of Uaxactun, dated 8.17.1.4.12 (A.D. 378) and carved recto-verso with similar but reversed warrior figures (fig. 20). The weaponry regalia held are a club with sharp, obsidian(?) points, and an *atlatl* or spear thrower. Holders of weapons become only slightly more common on plaza monuments during the first two katuns of the 9th baktun and are directly related to the warriors of Stela 5 from Uaxactun by costume and by the fact that they are always represented as paired figures.

The recto-verso pair of warriors carved on the lateral sides of Stela 31 of Tikal carry atlatls and shields (fig. 33), and like the warriors on Stela 5 of Uaxactun are distinguished by the simplicity of their costuming and, therefore, by the amount of body exposed when compared with the representations of honored figures who support or display other kinds of regalia. For the warriors on Stela 31, this comparison can be made simply by walking to the front of the monument to see the main figure, Stormy Sky, resplendent in jewelry and all but hidden by his costume and regalia. Such a contrast was intentional. The warrior pair is, at this time, presented by clear and simple imagery against a fair amount of background space.

The costumes of the paired weapon holders consist of beaded and feathered helmets, feathers or tails hanging from a round medallion placed at the back of the belts, bead and shell collars, and knee ruffs. By this costume they belong to an inter-regional group of figures that have been identified as a warrior sect or sodality with religious tenets, and with the Central Mexican city of Teotihuacan (Millon 1973; 1988). At Teotihuacan this costume is associated with the offering gesture and figures that have been identified by Pasztory as "priests" (1976). Although these figures are represented as pairs or in a procession of like figures at Teotihuacan and at Monte Alban, their context is not a public one. They are found on murals in residential compounds at Teotihuacan and in burial chambers at Monte Alban (Burials 104 and 105), on ceramics such as the Calpulapan bowl (Kubler 1967), and carved on wall panels (Monte Alban, "Stela" 7 and the "Stela" Lisa).

Nonetheless, Millon's perception (1973; 1978) of a warrior sect (see also Pasztory 1976; Coggins 1975; Clancy 1980, 1992) is probably a correct one, regardless of origins or the local transformations of its iconography and context. The tenets of this sect or sodality seem to have had a strong impact on the Early Classic Maya who portrayed the warrior pair on monuments in the more public arena of the plaza.

Stelae 4 (fig. 24) and 7 from El Zapote, a possible monumental pair, display the *staff holder* for the first time in the central area, that is around 8.18.0.0.0 (A.D. 396). As rendered on these stelae, the staff is a simple rod held up vertically by the main figure. The figure portrayed on Stela 7 may also hold a *bag*, but it is not until 9.2.0.0.0 (A.D. 475), that the staff is consistently joined with the ritual bag.

Two other monuments, Stela 5 of El Zapote (fig. 35) and Stela 6 of Yaxha, also represent early staff bearers/bag holders. (Stela 6 of Yaxha, however, has no readable glyphs and stylistically could range from 9.1.0.0.0 to 9.4.0.0.0.). Stela 5 from El Zapote, carved with a recto-verso field, is fairly surely dated to within the 1st katun of the 9th baktun. Its recto face, as reconstructed in chapter 6, displays for the first time the singular tripartite staff seen at Tikal on Stela 3 (fig. 51), surely dated at 9.2.13.0.0 (A.D. 488). The tripartite staff (Bailey 1972, 122–23) consists of three flexible wands joined together at intervals along their length. Between the joints the wands are variously bent or angled to separate them from one another. Perhaps Stela 6 of Yaxha and more certainly Stela 5 of El Zapote are the first monuments to present the tripartite staff, an item of regalia important for the plaza sculpture of Tikal for the rest of its monument producing history.

Importantly, at Tikal, the appearance of the staff and bag on Stelae 9 and 13 (figs. 48 and 49) occurs simultaneously with a drastic reduction in imagery, resulting in some of the simplest representations of the honored figure known from the Classic period: they are formulaic and redundant in their simplicity, clarity, and iconography, and reduced in terms of size and iconographic display and content. The best compositional comparison for these new public images, is to the warrior as it is represented on Stela 31 of Tikal and Stela 5 of Uaxactun. The bag and staff, displayed by grasping and holding gestures, not balanced or pressed to the breast, present a more pragmatic image that seems appropriate for these major changes in the image of the honored figure (see chapter 9).

Insignia

An insigne is a badge or emblematic device that typifies or identifies particular qualities. These qualities can belong to institutions, families, or individuals, and they are represented in such a way as to be recognizable as "badges" but not necessarily to be understood for their specific meanings. They are images that mix symbol and iconic representation in order to operate (play) between meanings that can be achieved as if from a text and/or as if from an image. The imagery used for Early Classic insignia is derivative, that is, it is taken from recognizable images known from ceramic and monumental iconographies and recontextualized into an insigne. Insignia are commonly chosen for pedestal imagery, but they are a rare choice for a stela. It is intriguing, therefore, that at least four stelae were so carved in the forty or fifty years that followed the turn of the baktun.

Insignia carved as main images on stelae during the Early Classic draw their motifs from both the ceremonial bar and the shield, that is, from hand-held regalia. As restatements of hand-held things, the insignia are most likely allegorical in function, but their particular use of iconographical meaning is "thick."[10] The ceremonial bar, itself, has a history that suggests it is a transformation from narrative illustration to an allegorical synecdoche (Clancy 1994b). While the artists could, and did, draw from the motifs of the actual ceremonial bar, they could, and did, draw directly from the motifs of its older narrative. Particular insignia are difficult to understand or "translate," but there is little doubt that they functioned as emblems and allegories.

The *ceremonial-bar insigne* consists of images drawn from the figure exposed within the bar's serpentine jaws and the fancy pendants attached to the heads. The first ceremonial-bar insignia were carved on cylindrical pedestals and showed the figure from the serpent's jaws seated cross-legged within a quatrefoil frame and/or a large frame of serpentine forms.[11] The quatrefoil frame offers a possible clue for the broad meaning of the ceremonial-bar manikin restated as an insigne: that it now belongs to the chthonic realm and is associated with caves and their multiple meanings, as discussed above with the seated pose. This, however, does not exclude the possibility that these emblematic figures could also represent historical figures, perhaps ancestors.

The early ceremonial-bar insignia were carved onto pedestals that may well have functioned as actual daises or seats within the plaza (Clancy 1976). (The binding motifs of the peripheries of the Early Classic pedestals from Tikal were picked up by the Late Classic sculptors of Tikal to denote thrones as they are carved in the lintel scenes of Temples I and IV.) Of interest, then, is the fact that the actual seat (the pedestal) is carved with imagery representing someone sitting in an allegorical context.

Pedestal 12 of Tikal (fig. 47) was probably carved towards the end of the Early Classic, that is around A.D. 475 (Clancy 1976). Because of its good condition (it is only worn in its center, presumably from having been used as a seat or dais), the ceremonial-bar manikin is clearly visible as a restatement of the serpent-jaw manikin carved on the left lateral side of Stela 2 of Tikal (Bailey 1972, 169) (fig. 37).

Pedestal 4 of Caracol may be a late and reduced adaptation of this ceremonial-bar insigne. It displays an enlarged Ahau glyph carved on its circular top, framed by a quatrefoil and superfixed by two dots understood as signifying the day 2 Ahau, which may be 9.3.0.0.0. If its date has been properly reconstructed, it represents the first of many "Ahau altars" carved at Caracol (Clancy 1976; Beetz and Satterthwaite 1981). Through its quatrefoil frame it reflects the chthonic iconography of the earlier emblems and thus may signal how we are to understand the day sign, Ahau. In this emblematic context would it denote "normal" time and duration?

The main images of Stela 1 of Yaxha (fig. 45) and the stela from Corozál, near Tikal (fig. 46), display insignia drawn from the enframing serpent poles attached to the fancy ceremonial bar. The serpent-pole-as-insigne is rendered as a vertical rod, to which is tied or appended images of marginal figures, earflares, and graphemic shapes.

The serpent poles have been variously understood by scholars (Bailey 1972; Coggins 1975; Clancy 1980), and, because they are inhabited by small marginal figures, they have been likened to the sinuous serpent held in the arms of the figure depicted on the Seattle Stela (Schele 1985a). As depicted on the two monuments from Yaxha and Corozal, the emblematic serpent poles are represented as an off-center axis more appropriate to the vertical display of stelae than the circular fields of pedestals. The insigne is a construction for joining up and down, or the top and bottom of the stela panel, and the serpent poles appear to be emblematic for the more expected human figure in plaza imagery.[12]

The *shield insigne* is taken from, or is the same as, the shield held by the warrior on the right-hand side of Stela 31 of Tikal (fig. 33). This shield is rectangular and decorated with a goggle-eyed head wearing a barrel-like headdress topped with tassels and feathers. Stela 32 of Tikal (fig. 44) and Stela 11 of Yaxha (fig. 43) both represent this insigne as a full-figured, full-frontal warrior wearing a rectangular mouth mask or nose piece and a necklace that appears attached to the circular earflares. On both stelae the right hand is raised to chin level, and on Stela 32 one can just make out that it holds an atlatl, while the figure on Stela 11 holds both a spear and a shield.

Goggle eyes and a mouth mask are often attributes of the so-called Storm God of Teotihuacan (Pasztory 1977; 1988, 54) and a fertility-rain deity traditionally called Tlaloc, the Nahuatl name given to this deity by the later Aztecs. The peculiar barrel-shaped headdress, called the "tassel headdress" by Clara Millon (1973; 1988), along with the goggle eyes and the mouth mask, however, also belong to the costume iconography of the warrior sodality that appears throughout Mesoamerica during the Early Classic period (discussed above).

Illustrations of this iconographic set, which includes the warrior costume and shield imagery are also found on "Teotihuacan-style" Esquintla censers from the southern region of Guatemala. Janet Berlo (1984), in her careful iconographic study of the Esquintla censers, finds comparative, stylistic, and archaeological evidence for dating them to the late 4th and early 5th centuries, that is between 8.17.0.0.0 and 9.1.0.0.0. Although the censers exhibit various iconographic schema, many illustrated by Berlo (ibid.) and Hellmuth (1975) display heads with similar, barrel-like headdresses, mouth masks, earflares, and necklaces, even hands raised to chin level holding emblems or weapons (see Berlo, ibid., pls. 195, 132, 101, 99, 98, 96, 91, 89, and 85).

These censers compose the headdress and necklace together into an architectonic frame or stage for the face, and this compositional scheme appears to reiterate in three dimensions the "deity" figures posed frontally on the murals of Teotihuacan displaying necklaces and earflares as one piece of jewelry. (See, for example, Mural 3 from Portico 11 of the Tetitla compound [A. Miller 1973, 146].) The Teotihuacan images are composed by isotropic, bilateral symmetry; the censers and the stela emblems are not. It is as if the isotropic image (a cult image?) were vivified by the narrative use of gesture. Nonetheless, this probably explains why the necklaces worn by the goggle-eyed figures on the stelae from Yaxha and Tikal are shown as if attached to the earflares rather than draped around the shoulders.

Stela 15 of Cerro de las Mesas in Veracruz is the only other known freestanding monument to display a goggle-eyed frontal figure, but it is not clear that it belongs to the iconography of the warrior.[13] Like the Maya stelae displaying insignia, the carving on Stela 15 is "quite different in character from that on the other stelae at the site" (Stirling 1943, 44). It displays a full-frontal face and an upper torso resting on two cartouched glyphs (the Short Count date, 1 Ocelot, 4 Water [ibid.]) in the center of a designed field of repeated hands or shells. Goggle eyes and a mouth mask adorn the face, which is framed by squared earflares attached to a necklace. The figure of Stela 15 wears a crested bird helmet with jaguar ears and feathers. (It is similar to the helmet worn by the seated figure of Curl Nose on Stela 4 of Tikal [fig. 21].) The monument's date of carving, however, is not clear. Because it is anomalous, its style is difficult to reckon. For stylistic reasons, Stirling (1943, 48) suggests Stela 15 is a later monument than the stelae of Cerro de las Mesas that date between 9.1.0.0.0 and 9.4.0.0.0 (A.D. 455–514), and while these latter stelae provide important comparisons for certain Early Classic Maya monuments, the anomalous Stela 15 may be a later reflection of the Maya warrior emblem—or it may be more focussed on the fertility aspects associated with the goggle eyes at Teotihuacan.

If the goggle eyes do signal a fertility deity or spirit, then a meaningful connection between warrior and fertility deity is expressed by the images of the sides of Stela 31 and the insignia depicted on Stela 32 of Tikal and Stela 11 of Yaxha. A similar ideological juxtaposition is known to exist for the twin temples of the Templo Mayor in the Mexica capitol of Tenochtitlan dedicated to Huitzilopochtli and Tlaloc (Townsend 1982).

The Early Classic Maya used the iconographies of the ceremonial bar and the shield to create insignia clearly considered proper for display in the plaza context. The ceremonial-bar manikin was used for pedestals, the ceremonial-bar serpent poles for stelae, and the shield emblem was anthropomorphized and presented as if it were an honored figure albeit frontally. The two important items of regalia—one local and old, and one inter-regional and new—are restated as insignia for plaza display. They make up a rare set of main images whose use only lasted for the few decades before and after the turn of the baktun.

SECONDARY IMAGES

When secondary images are included in the composition there is a marked difference in their scale or size relative to the main image, and usually they are smaller. Thus, these images are not the main focus of the plaza monument, but extend or relay basic intentions for meaning in the main image. Because they are always depicted as somehow different from the main image, this difference is understood as intentional, and it suggests secondary images could have either an opposite or apposite connection to the main image.[14]

Throughout the Classic period secondary images were optional, in that they may or may not be present in the compositional field. However, for the first plaza monuments of the Early Classic period, the full panoply of secondary imagery is employed. There are four kinds of secondary images: basal (bottom), supernal (top), and supplementary images, and marginalia. Basal and supernal imagery have specific and separate locations within the compositional field, while supplementary images and marginalia can be inserted into the main figure's field. The disembodied head, discussed above as hand-held regalia, can be represented within all types of secondary imagery. The bound figure is another important secondary image used in basal imagery and as a supplementary figure within the main image, but never as a supernal image. Marginal images are tiny animate creatures inserted into any area of the image field—costume, regalia, supernal, or basal images.

Basal Images

Basal images are usually, but not always, rendered in smaller proportions than those of the main figure. Differences are also created by a contrasting compositional mode, iconography, or carving techniques, and sometimes the basal image is a glyphic text. Functioning as a context for the main image, basal images (like supernal images) can be understood as "commentaries" about the main image because they represent a "different" picture. Without disputing their representational values, the metaphoric connotations expressed by these images are plain.

The basal image literally supports and metaphorically locates the main image, and although its imagery is sometimes enclosed within an actual frame, the soles of the main figure's feet always provide a clear horizontal line for dividing the main image from the basal one (see fig. 38).

The "place" being stood upon has been interpreted variously, but always metaphorically: as an emblem or insigne for place, polity, or town; as symbols of ancestral and dynastic power; or as symbols of more personal meaning that evoke particular deeds or events upon which the main figure claims to stand. Given the actual configuring of the Early Classic basal images, it seems likely that literal denotative meaning of support, like a pedestal, as well as the several metaphoric connotations cited above were often embedded together.

The *bound figure* used as a basal image is a small figure that may or may not wear a costume but usually is given some kind of identifying headdress. The bound figure has almost always been interpreted as a captive taken in battle by the main figure (Dillon 1982, 43; Schele and Miller 1986, 210), and its different, smaller, scale is assumed to represent a hierarchical difference in status. This interpretation is syllogistic in that it equates description with interpretation by assuming a simple, denotative use of imagery, and, subsequently, it assumes that the primary function of ancient Maya plaza imagery was historical documentation. Certainly it can be assumed that the power of rule would be proclaimed on plaza monuments, but as the bound figure is presently understood there is no place for metaphor or allegory (or humor and irony) in our understanding of the image.

The non-monumental Leiden Plaque (8.14.3.1.12 [A.D. 320]) (fig. 14) represents the first known instance where a bound figure is pictured in the basal region. It is not formally separated from the main image but contrasts with the main figure by its small scale, horizontal orientation, and its narrative illustration of a relatively active and dynamic figure lying on its belly with bound forearms in front of its raised and turned head. Its knees are bent, the feet up. The pose of this little figure has been dubbed the "belly-down pose" and becomes a distinctive attribute of basal, bound figures at Tikal. In fact, this pose is one of the more convincing reasons for considering Tikal as the provenance of the Plaque.[15] The little figure wears a distinctive headdress, but no other costuming is visible.

Included within the basal panel of Stela 39 of Tikal (fig. 18) is that polity's emblem glyph. More central and indeed more striking is the small, bearded captive wearing an elaborate headdress. He is represented by an articulated profile with his shoulders and arms shown frontally. The pose is dynamic, rendered as if swimming, much like the figures depicted on the famous Diker bowl (M. Coe 1973, 26–27), the engraved vase in the Dumbarton Oaks collection (B-208-MAP), the Liverpool vase (Schele and Miller 1986, 208), the carved bones from Chiapas de Corzo (Agrinier 1960), and the "Flying Olmec," Monument 12, from Chalcatzingo (Grove 1987, 122–23). It is significant that these comparable images are ones that have consistently been identified as mythological figures, supporting, in this case, a mythological "place" or "other" signaled by the bound figure on which the main figure stands. Given the presence of the Tikal emblem glyph, one could assume a metaphoric connection being drawn between the mythic person and/or place and Tikal. Schele and Freidel (1990, 145, 147; and see Stuart and Houston 1994, 58) read the small glyphic statement as "Tikal Sky Place," and consider it a locative phrase. It is interesting, then, that a sky place is referred to in the basal portion of the stela panel and could signal the complementarity of opposites, but surely the swimming, bound figure represents more than the fact of its binding.

As on the Leiden Plaque, the little hands of the bound figure of Stela 39 are tied together at the wrists to recreate the symmetrical ceremonial-bar gesture. On the Leiden Plaque, this duplicates the gesture of the main figure, who holds a flaccid ceremonial bar, while the bound hands of the swimming figure on Stela 39 do not reiterate its main figure's gesture. The full gesture made by the main figure on Stela 39 is not known, due to breakage, but it is clearly asymmetrical as one lower arm is visible and the other is not. The meaning of the ceremonial-bar gesture is enriched and augmented in its use as a gesture created by binding. On the Leiden Plaque its duplication is an extension by apposition; on Stela 39 it is an extension created by difference, perhaps as opposition. Both examples bring to mind the linguistic convention of *diafrasmo*, or semantic parallelism, where saying the same thing in two (at least) different ways extends meaning.

As represented on 8th-baktun monuments, the most common basal image maintains a clear formal connection to the Preclassic Izapan "*signature*" (Stirling 1943, 62–67; Suzanne Miles 1965, 251; Quirarte 1973, 33; 1974) rendered as an architectonic structure with disembodied heads at either side of it (fig. 36). As with the disembodied heads used in regalia, these are sometimes appended with "hats" of emblem glyphs identified with particular cities or polities (Stuart and Houston 1994, 57ff.). The form of the signature is very close in configuration to the ceremonial bar and reiterates by its basal position certain earthly and chthonic meanings that have been associated with the bar.

The signature may be the basal image depicted for the rock carving at San Diego (about forty kilometers east of Yaxchilan), thought to be a Preclassic piece (see Schele and Freidel 1990, 88). Its next known appearance is on Stela 1 of Uolantun (fig. 28) dating from 8.18.0.0.0 or 8.19.0.0.0 (A.D. 396 or 416). Since the Uolantun stela prefigures in so many ways the compositional mode and iconography of Tikal's Stela 31, one could suppose that Stela 31 also carried the signature. The signature is used for the wraparound stelae of Tikal (Stelae 1, 2, and 28 [figs. 36, 37, and 38]) carved some time in the first two katuns of the 9th baktun. On these stelae, the main images are wraparound compositions, but the basal images are carved only on the front panels. They are spatially associated with the almost hidden frames of the front panels and express their differences in scale as well as by a carving technique that uses only an engraved line with no indication of background. Stela 28 of this group includes the bound figure atop the signature.

The *bird head*, or mask, appears as a basal image for the first time on Stelae 1 and 3 of Tres Islas (figs. 39 and 41), probably dating to 9.2.0.0.0 (A.D. 475) (see Mathews 1985, 11). It is a conventionalized bird head that combines bird features with eccentrically shaped glyphs or day signs (especially *cauac*, which also suggests hardness and stone). This broad-beaked (raptorial) head is presented in profile and is enormous relative to the human figures that stand on it. It is comparable to the "principal bird deity" identified by Bardawil (1976; see also Stone 1983, 207–17; and Cortez 1986), except that it lacks the distinctive wings. It is important to note that both stelae at Tres Islas also have conventionalized birds in their supernal region.

Monument 26 (a stela) from Quirigua (fig. 42) is fairly surely dated at 9.2.18.0.0 (Jones 1983). The basal mask is a frontal depiction of the same broad-beaked bird whose bilateral symmetry follows the isotropic mode of the main figure. Sharer (1990, 73) identifies it as an earth monster, and its basal position certainly suggests earthly, chthonic associations. The bird-as-earth-creature is another explicit paradox—much like a feathered (flying) serpent. No supernal image is carved for Monument 26, but the headdress helmet is rendered as a bird very similar in configuration to the basal mask.

The *pedestal insigne* is used on Stela 2 of Tres Islas (fig. 40), a uniquely composed monument depicting by the wraparound field a two-figure narrative scene supported by a large basal panel that covers fully one-third of the sculptured front panel. Like Stelae 1 and 3, it dates to 9.2.0.0.0 (A.D. 475). The basal image wraps around the monumental shaft in an asymmetrical design; low on the right lateral side, high in the front, and a little lower on the left. The basal imagery has scaled off in some places, but what can be seen is a complex image with scrolls, disembodied heads, and glyphic shapes rendered like the basal birds on Stelae 1 and 3. The complex design surrounds a cross shape, centered on the front panel, that may be an angular version of the quatrefoil frame. Within is a seated figure holding a ceremonial bar by the symmetrical gesture and wearing the netted bead skirt associated with the feminine. The iconography of the emblematic pedestals, displaying a seated figure in a quatrefoil frame surrounded by serpentine scrolls, was surely the inspiration for the basal imagery of Stela 2. Although it is more easily argued for the Late Classic period where there is good evidence that basal imagery on stelae represents imagery found on pedestals (see Clancy 1976), Stela 2 may be an early example of this obvious connection between pedestals that functioned as daises and basal panels that illustrate pedestals.

The frequency of basal imagery drops rather dramatically at Tikal after 9.2.0.0.0 because during the 3rd katun, contextual images that extend or relay meaning are no longer part of the plaza display. Only one monument, Stela 3 of Tikal (9.2.13.0.0 [A.D. 488]) (fig. 51), includes a basal image. It appears to be a widening of the frame as it runs beneath the main image, and is engraved with what has been likened to the bundle represented as the main sign of the Tikal emblem glyph (Bailey 1972, 134; Clancy 1980, 84). Although it is likely that Stela 3 was anciently reset (W. Coe 1990, 734–35), when it was first photographed its basal image was buried so the feet of the main figure appeared to stand on the ground (see Maler 1903, 2(2): pl. 15).

Supernal Images

During the Late Preclassic period, the supernal image was more complex and narrative in function than its later, Early Classic, counterparts in the lowlands. The great anthropomorphic birds descending from supernal "signatures" on Izapan monuments (Stela 4, for example), or the entwined and looming serpent-bird with a human head in its mouth depicted behind and above the main figure on Stela 1 of El Baúl, hardly seem to be related to the single, disembodied head of the lowland, Early Classic monuments. The downward orientation of action or gaze, however, is maintained and is part of the metaphoric connotations associated with the supernal image during the Early Classic period. Different realms are being positively illustrated, and a sort of gravity or attraction is suggested by the direction of the gaze.

Unlike basal imagery, there are no formal means by which the supernal image is separated from the main image. The transition between headdress and supernal image does not produce the distinctive division provided by the horizontal line of the profile feet of the main image as it stands on the basal image (see fig. 33). The visual impression is that the supernal image is in the same space as the main image. Its claim to contrast lies in its small scale and in the downward and vertical orientation of its gaze, or "direction."

The supernal image depicted on the Seattle Stela (fig. 16) is a human-like head blinded by its own headband ornaments that faces downward from within the open jaws of a serpent. The three-pronged, blinded eye is characteristic of some disembodied heads identified as indicators of "place" when they occur in the lower or basal regions of the stela (Schele and Freidel 1990, 146–47), and it could be supposed to mean the same here.[16] The serpent's body, long and undulant, physically connects the supernal image to the main figure, who holds the body like a ceremonial bar. The close connection between the main figure and the supernal image is graphically stated on this early stela.

A single *disembodied head* used as a supernal image has its first Early Classic appearance on Stela 29 of Tikal (fig. 12) and is rendered as a human-like head wearing a serpent-like headdress. The serpent's snout is curled upwards and it wears glyphs as its headdress. Unfortu-

nately they cannot be read. On Stela 4 of the same site (fig. 21) the supernal head is anthropomorphic, an early depiction of God K (Coggins 1975, 145). The supernal image on Uolantun's stela (fig. 28) also appears to be anthropomorphic. The connection between main image and supernal head seems to be in the gaze of the small head and the implications of gravity and attraction. Is the main figure's power to attract these entities into experiential realms being portrayed?

Stela 31 of Tikal displays a disembodied deity head gazing downward (fig. 33). The head is grotesquely human with a squared eye and a hand substituting for the lower jaw. Costumed with jewelry and a richly arrayed headdress, it looks down along the centerline of the main image, Stormy Sky. The head is in fact a partial bust with one arm in the cupped-hand gesture—the same as Stormy Sky's gesture used to hold a disembodied head. The little bust is thought to be Stormy Sky's father, Curl Snout, because its headdress is seen as an elaboration of his name glyph, a saurian or serpent-like creature with an upwardly curled nose (Coggins 1975, 186). That the identity of Curl Snout, the parent/ancestor, is being evoked seems very possible, but the similarity of Curl Snout's headdress to the headdress worn by the supernal head of Stela 29 (fig. 12) suggests that the two small heads may also have been the same entity. Certainly Stormy Sky identifies himself with the figure on Stela 29 in other ways. He wears the same helmet as the main figure on Stela 29 and carries the same disembodied JC head with the Tikal emblem glyph.

After the turn of the 9th baktun, the supernal image of a downward-gazing head is amplified by a recollection of the Preclassic anthropomorphic bird-creature with outspread wings. It is different, and perhaps significantly so, from the wingless bird head identified by its large beak represented in the basal panel. That a bird should be important to both the supernal and basal regions, however, is an interesting equivalence.

A *winged bird* occupies the supernal areas of the warrior pair represented on Stelae 1 and 3 of Tres Islas (figs. 39 and 41). On Stela 1 the anthropomorphic bird head has a sharply curving beak and is centered between outstretched wings. It is strongly reminiscent of supernal birds on the Terminal Preclassic monuments: Stelae 2 and 4 of Izapa and Stela 11 of Kaminaljuyu, which also depict warriors. On Tres Islas Stela 1 the bird's lower jaw has been substituted by an emblem with two knots. What this substitution means is unclear, but the lower jaw of the disembodied, supernal head on Stela 31 of Tikal is also substituted by a hand.

The bird iconography is continued on Stela 6 of Yaxha and Stela 3 of Uaxactun (fig. 56) with almost identical images for both monuments. The heads are smaller and seemingly less critical in terms of their visual effect than the birds of the Tres Islas monuments. Furthermore, the heads are not centered in the top, but in the upper-left-hand portion of the main sculptured panel. The heads are human-like and are framed between a wing that rises to the top of the stela and one that is suspended from the chin. On Stela 3 of Uaxactun, a bird's claw is visible next to the lower wing.[17]

Like the basal image, the supernal image extends the meaningful context of the main figure. Carved within the field of the honored figure, the supernal image provides an elaboration of the powers and attributes of the main figure. The supernal position opposes the earthly, chthonic realms alluded to in the basal area but may also indicate "place." This place, however, is not different from that of the main figure's, and its connection to the main figure is as a natural attraction, like gravity.

The common interpretation for supernal disembodied heads is that they are depictions of ancestors (Coggins 1975, 140; Marcus 1976, 35, 43; Schele and Miller 1986, 183). That these heads should represent visions or ancestors is in line with the idea that the supernal image is attracted to, and personally connected with, the main figure.

Supplementary Images

Supplementary images are secondary images inserted into the main image's field. They do not illustrate a narrative connection with the main figure because, although they may have suggested one, this connection is not explicitly illustrated. During the Early Classic period, supplementary images are bound figures and graphemic emblems.

Supplementary images of *bound figures* are found in the same field as the main figure, and while they are actively posed figures, often appearing as if supplicating or pleading, their presence does not alter or interact with the stational portrayal of the main figure (see fig. 17). They are contrasting commentaries but, by being in the same space as the main image, they do not appear to function emblematically like the bound figure in the basal image. The supplementary bound figure is depicted as crouching or kneeling, facing toward the main figure, and usually bound at the wrists. In their action, they are compelling narrative figures shown in an attitude of supplication but receiving no answering gesture on the part of the main figure composed in stational or isotropic modes.

The bound figures represented on the Uaxactun stelae do not actually touch the base line on which the main figure stands (fig. 17). They appear to float. It is unlikely this was lack of attention to detail on the part of the sculptors. Although no claims for direct influence can be put forward, floating, supplementary figures are known from the Late Terminal Preclassic period. The two supplementary, seated figures on Stela 18 of Izapa do not sit on the basal signature as does the main figure they accompany. Similarly, the supplementary figure of Monument 2 from El Mesón, Veracruz, floats just above the given ground line. (This little figure from El Mesón seems to express the same attitude of supplication as the Uaxactun figures.) That these figures, as they are used at Uaxactun, float above the ground line of the main figure emphasizes their role as functional attributes and de-emphasizes their being understood as part of a realistic scene. However, the supplementary bound figure on Xultun, Stela 12 (fig. 19) kneels directly on the ground line of the main image.

The narrative potential in the postures taken by bound figures is exemplified on Stela 20 of Uaxactun (9.3.0.0.0 [A.D. 495]) (fig. 52) where six bound figures, all in different and realistic poses, are portrayed throughout the multi-paneled composition. The figures on the lateral panels of the stela are depicted within doubled columns of glyphs. They do not have common ground lines and like the 8th-baktun bound figures of Uaxactun, they appear to float. They wear headdresses and earflares, and the figures on the right side wear back ornaments. They were probably matched in their relatively rich costuming by the two bound figures on the front panel, but these have been too worn or destroyed to be certain.

The supplementary bound figures express a quality of realism in their awkward poses, curved backs, and upraised hands, as representations of supplication or apprehension. Their metaphoric, even symbolic, functions are indicated by their narrative postures rendered within a stational context where no interaction is illustrated, and where the realisms of scale or gravity are not necessary. An explanation for these bound figures is that, like the ceremonial bar and the extroverted gesture, they represent a reduction of an old and well-known narrative into one synecdochic image that becomes part of the main figure's attributes. Thus, these little figures may have come from a complex literature of once-known references now difficult to reconstruct, but we can suggest that the narrative or story told of supplication and abasement and of a separation, detachment, perhaps even a "conquest," of these attributes on the part of the main figure.

The supplementary images called *graphemic emblems* are, for the Early Classic monuments, either glyphs or disembodied heads, which like the bound figure appear in different imagistic roles. Used as a supplementary image, it is difficult to determine whether a head should be considered as a glyph with greater symbolic value or as a disembodied head with iconic, representational value. Of course, these emblems could have been intended to be understood in both ways. For these reasons they are classed as graphemic emblems.[18]

Because both kinds of graphemic emblems—heads and glyphs— were placed at the feet of the main figure, it is likely that, while they expressed different meanings, their "commentary" about the main image was structurally similar. The heads at the feet of the main figures carved on Uaxactun stelae (5, 4, and 3) (figs. 20, 23, and 56, respectively) have been interpreted as glyphic expressions of place or polity (Schele and Freidel 1990, 145–47). This interpretation is a likely possibility, but at the same time it should be noted that while disembodied heads in other compositional contexts wear emblem glyphs as hats, the supplementary graphemic head does not appear to do so. Furthermore, at Uaxactun at least, the graphemic head appears to take the same place in the composition as the bound figure used as a supplementary image. Again, the implication is that the content is different but the structural and functional intent of the images is the same.

Marginal Images

Little figures can be found inserted into the ancient Maya plaza image, and, like disembodied heads, they can appear anywhere in the composition. Their tiny scale and active, narrative postures are the means by which they are recognized, and I call them *marginalia*. The little images include animals, anthropomorphs (deities or spirits), and sometimes human figures, and it may be that some images of plants also functioned as marginalia.[19]

The functional uses and meanings of marginalia in ancient Maya art are opaque. However, marginalia is used throughout the history of Classic Maya art and needs a greater effort than has been achieved here for the Early

Classic period. As secondary images, they certainly extend the meaning of the main image through contrast, but whether this contrast signaled oppositional or appositional meanings, or both, is impossible to determine at this time.

Tiny figures posed in an active narrative mode enter the plaza image as part of the hand-held regalia, and especially as part of the fancy ceremonial bar. They are first seen in the Seattle Stela (fig. 16) where four little figures cling to the undulant body of a serpent, and three half-bodied figures fall head-down along the seriated wing-like shape attached to the main figure's right shoulder. Linda Schele (Freidel, Schele, and Parker 1993, 101ff.) has interpreted the little figures clinging to the serpent as representing the zodiacal constellations equivalent to Capricorn, Sagittarius, Libra, and Virgo aligned on the ecliptic and crossing the Milky Way at dawn on the day she believes is the dedicatory date of the stela, March 18, A.D. 197.[20] If she is correct, then these marginal figures function in an appositive manner by positioning the honored figure in the same relative position as the Milky Way.

The Seattle Stela's marginalia are directly comparable to those carved into wraparound stelae of Tikal. On Stela 1 of Tikal (fig. 36) marginal figures inhabit the fancy ceremonial bar where it is rendered on the sides of the wraparound shaft. Below the large serpent heads, four fantastic creatures twist around the serpent poles and appear to be in conversation with tiny partial busts of more human-like beings who inhabit the feathers of the wings. Each creature and bust is rendered by different gestures and facial expressions, creating lively little scenes for any who would look closely enough.

Above these marginal conversations, little manikin figures crouch in the jaws of the ceremonial bar serpents' mouths. The crouching figure on the right side is not identifiable at this time, but the crouching figure in the left-hand serpent's mouth can be identified as God K or the "axe god" because his forehead looks like a hafted axe. Along with his unknown counterpart, who turns his head to look back towards the front of the stela, his pose and facial expression are active and lively. On Stela 2 of Tikal (fig. 37), the inhabitants of the serpents' jaws are similarly rendered, but with a different iconography. The figure on the left-hand side looks human and is comparable to the emblematic image carved on Pedestal 12 of Tikal (fig. 47).[21]

As small-scaled insertions of narrative into stational or isotropic compositions, marginalia are contrastive images. They could illustrate or allude to meanings that may not even be implied by the main image, they could be visual puns with rebus-like readings, but they surely illustrate stories as their narrative postures indicate. These "stories" were meaningful in some way, perhaps to the main figure, or perhaps as local, even idiosyncratic, ideas about the plaza image itself.[22]

Marginalia as they were used in the Early Classic plaza monuments, which was not often, may illustrate vestiges of Preclassic narratives, but such an argument is not entirely compelling because there are few actual comparisons to be made, but then, the sampling is small, and the possibility of local invention and intention is great.

Fig. 7.   Polol, Altar 1. (Photo courtesy Ian Graham.)

CHAPTER FOUR

The Beginnings

The 8th Baktun to 8.17.0.0.0 (A.D. 278–376)

Polol, Altar 1
(fig. 7)

MOST OF THE CARVINGS FOUND AT THIS SITE DATE from the Late Classic period (Morley 1937–38, 3: 407–13). There has been no argument, however, that the fragment called Altar 1 from Polol was carved at a very early date. Morley (ibid., 402–3) placed it in his Early Period, and Proskouriakoff (1950, 110) suggested that it was an 8th-baktun piece. More recently, Gary Pahl (1982), has suggested it may date from the 7th baktun. This last must remain tentative because the central glyphic column was carved in a very low relief and is now mostly obliterated.

The fragment shows a pair of figures with fancy headdresses facing one another across the column of badly worn glyphs. The figures are carved in relatively high relief accented by deeply drilled discs carved at the sides of the faces, like treble earflares. These are actually short chains of interlocked discs attached to the headdress, much like the chain attached to the headdress held up by the honored figure on Stela 31 of Tikal (fig. 33) and prefigured on Stela 1 and Altar 13 of Abaj Takalik (fig. 9).

The monuments from Abaj Takalik were probably direct influences in the making of the Polol piece. Pahl (ibid.) compares it to Stelae 2 and 5 (fig. 8) of Abaj Takalik because it follows the same compositional arrangement of a pair of figures separated by a column of

glyphs displayed by the Abaj Takalik stelae. Stela 2 appears to be from the early 8th baktun, and Stela 5 displays two Long Count dates in the central column, 8.2.2.10.5 (A.D. 83) and 8.4.5.17.11 (A.D. 126). These comparisons suggest that the Polol piece is, in all probability, a Late Preclassic monument from the 8th baktun.

The Polol fragment, however, may be that of a stela and not an altar. The figured pair is surrounded by a tightly beaded and narrow frame, like the frames carved around the oddly shaped stelae from Abaj Takalik, and may have followed the Abaj Takalik stelae in their odd but careful shaping, as well as in the compositional arrangement and certain iconography. Lundell (1934), making the first report of the Polol monument, called it Stela 6, while Morley (1937–38, 3: 402) reclassified it as an altar because its remaining, completed edge is rounded. If the arc of the top is reconstructed into a circular field, the two figures would be seated. This, of course, is a distinct possibility. However, Lundell's photographs, on file at the Peabody Museum in Cambridge, show less of a curving-in on the right side of the fragment than do the drawings of Morley (ibid., 403) and Pahl (1982, fig. 1a), suggesting that the comparison with the oddly shaped stelae of Abaj Takalik may be, in fact, a very strong one.

The comparison of compositions suggests the sculptor of the Polol piece had a good knowledge of the

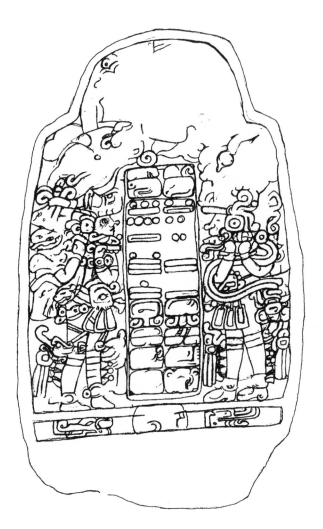

Fig. 8.   Abaj Takalik, Stela 5.
(Drawing by Flora Clancy after
John Graham, et. al. 1978, pl. 3.)

Fig. 9.   Abaj Takalik:
A) Stela 1, B) Altar 13.
(Stela 1 drawing by Flora
Clancy after
S. Miles 1965, Fig. 17C.
Altar 13 drawing by Flora
Clancy after
John Graham et. al.
1978, pl. 5.)

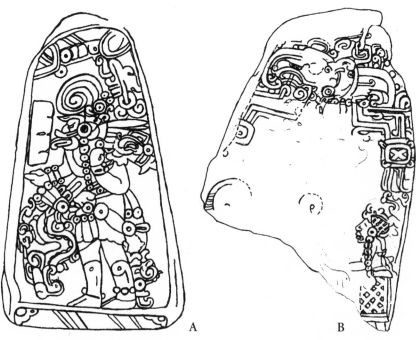

A

B

monuments carved at Abaj Takalik, but his or her style of carving the monument does not compare to any known monument from either the lowlands or the highlands: very little background space is visible, most outlining relief cuts are deep, and each shape is separately defined with little spatial reference to its neighbors. The effects of light and shadow are mysterious, expressive, and confusing, because the expected allusions to three-dimensionality made possible by a planar relief technique are not apparent. The Polol piece is ambiguous and expressive when compared with contemporary southern relief work, and demonstrates an important difference between lowland and southern carving styles of the 8th baktun.

Uaxactun, Stela 10
(fig. 10)

Anciently redressed to serve as a pedestal, perhaps for Stela 9 (fig. 15) with which it was found (Morley 1937–38, 1: 176), Stela 10 is a large fragment that not only shows close iconographic links to the southern Preclassic sites of Kaminaljuyu and Abaj Takalik, but also displays certain affinities in carving style as well. While Morley (ibid., 177, 238) considered Stela 10 to have been carved after Stelae 18 and 19 (fig. 17), that is, after A.D. 357, it is now presumed to be the first stela carved at Uaxactun (Proskouriakoff 1950, 103–4; Thompson 1970, 59). It may have been carved earlier than A.D. 278 (8.12.0.0.0), but if so not by much. Suffering from recarving and natural wear, its glyphs cannot be read and its early placement is based entirely on style.

Like the Polol monument, Stela 10 represents a pair of figures, but with the recto-verso field. The imagery is badly worn on both sides of the stela, and the paired figures can only be delineated from their waists down. They each stand off the centerline of their panel—one to the right side, the other to the left. They do not appear to wear sandals, but large knotted anklets can be seen, as well as carefully drawn feet that show the profiled line of the toe, ball, arch, and heel. The anklets are very similar to those of Stela 11 of Kaminaljuyu, and the carefully drawn feet compare with that stela as well as with Stelae 3 and 12 from Abaj Takalik.

The two figures, with thick belts worn low around their waists, stand in the typical Early Classic broad-profile pose. Each shares its panel with large scrolled forms, which on the back sides of the figures presumably belong to the watch-fob motif that hangs from the belt. How the

larger and carefully outlined scrolls to the front of the figures fit into the imagery is unclear, but they are comparable to the imagery of Stelae 1 (fig. 8) and 3 from Abaj Takalik and the miniature Stela 16 from Kaminaljuyu (Parsons 1986, 29–30). By these comparisons, we may reconstruct the figures on Stela 10 as displaying a sinuous serpent or a ceremonial bar with serpentine scrolls falling from one of its ends.[1]

Although little else can be said about the carving style and quality of line used on Stela 10, the comparisons with certain monuments from Abaj Takalik and Kaminaljuyu (especially Stela 3 of Abaj Takalik) are strong and more consistent than those found for the Polol monument.

What sets Stela 10 apart from the southern monuments is its use of the recto-verso field. Drawing heavily on highland iconography and carving styles, the sculptor, nonetheless, creates a new and complex field for the imagery. The direct similarities between the iconography of the two figures and their reversed poses indicate that the properties of the recto-verso field were carefully considered. Stela 10, then, is one of the first, if not *the* first, stelae to present this composition as a strategy of plaza display, the function of which is to engage the viewer in active participation with the imagery of the monument. What inspired the sculptor or the patron cannot be historically determined, but Stela 10 marks Uaxactun as an innovative center where plaza art was meant to inspire public interaction, not just public reaction.

Tikal, Stela 36
(fig. 11)

The surface condition of the so-called Stela 36 of Tikal is not good, and details of its image are difficult to make out in most areas of the panel. Its shape is not dissimilar from the reworked pedestal shape of the Uaxactun Stela 10 and it has been variously declared to be an altar, a miscellaneous stone, and finally a stela (Bailey 1972, 114; Jones and Satterthwaite 1982, 76). It may be coeval with Stela 10 of Uaxactun as it was probably carved before Stela 29 of Tikal (fig. 12) (C. Jones 1991, 108).[2] Although only the gross outlines of the image can be seen, Stela 36 is innovative in its representation of a seated figure supporting disembodied heads.

The image of Stela 36 is surrounded by an incomplete frame of uneven width. It is wide at the bottom of the image, clearly carved on the right side (behind the seated figure), becoming thinner as it arches across the top to disappear behind the regalia and glyphs carved on the

Fig. 10.   Uaxactun, Stela 10, Recto-verso. (Photo after Morley 1937–38 V: pl.58. Drawings courtesy Ian Graham.)

left side of the panel. Jones and Satterthwaite (1982, 76) consider the bottom part of the frame wide enough to be the butt that would support the monument as an upright stela. However, where the bottom edge is unbroken, it is nicely curved and shaped, an unusual but not unheard of finishing for the butt portion (see Stela 20 of Tikal as a Late Classic example of a rounded and finished butt). It seems proper to consider the type and therefore the function of this monument as an open question. If Stela 36 is a stela, it begins the unique Tikal 8th-baktun tradition of portraying seated figures on upright stelae by altering the more usual proportions of the stela to resemble those of a pedestal.

Stela 36 was found in an outlying group known as Santa Fe, at the far end of the airstrip, and associated with a complex of three tombs and Manik ceramics that would date from the Late Preclassic to Early Classic (ibid.). Because of looting, the exact nature of the association is unknown: Stela 36 may have been an integral part of the burial complex or associated by proximity. Given its anomalous shape and iconography, it may have been a more "private" piece of sculpture carved specifically for use in or with the burial and not intended for public display.[3]

An honored figure displaying two disembodied heads sits on a throne, probably a jaguar throne if it is this beast's head showing in front of the figure's bent knee. As discussed above in chapter 2, seated figures are more commonly found carved on pedestals. That is, seated figures are usually images with special references to caves and chthonic regions, and perhaps burial.

The supporter of disembodied heads becomes an expected plaza theme, but when Stela 36 was probably carved, somewhere between A.D. 238 and 278, freestanding plaza monuments portraying individuals in a stational mode were still new, or at least rare, events. As depicted in Stela 36, the two disembodied heads are exaggeratedly large: one is held by the cupped-hand gesture, the other by the flat-hand gesture. The head held by the cupped-hand gesture cannot be identified, but the other head is the jaguar-eared, cruller-eyed emblem associated with a jaguar deity and/or the sun god (the JC head is discussed under "Regalia" in chapter 3). On Stela 36, the JC head is qualified by the main sign from the Tikal emblem glyph added to look as if the god's hair was tied into a bun and suggesting that it was directly associated with the city of Tikal. The JC head's association at Monte Alban, in Oaxaca, with elite burials compares with Stela 36's similar context of burial.[4]

Fig. 11. Tikal, Stela 36.
(Photo courtesy University of Pennsylvania Museum, #69-43-85.
Drawing by William Coe reprinted from *Tikal Reports 33A* by Jones and Satterthwaite 1982 courtesy University of Pennsylvania Museum, Philadelphia.)

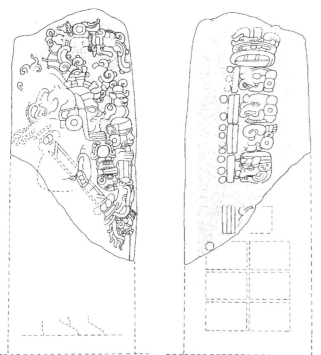

Its unusual location, so far from the known plaza centers in Tikal, its innovation in the representation of a seated figure, and its pedestal-like shape all conspire to make difficult our evaluations of Stela 36's original function and intent. It seems to have little in common with the new plaza function established by the recto-verso imagery of Uaxactun's Stela 10, and its several iconographic, formal, and contextual associations with burials are strong.

Tikal, Stela 29
(fig. 12)

Stela 29 is a large fragment with only the bottom third of the shaft missing. It was found, associated with Pedestal 13, about twelve meters east of Structure 5D-9 in a dumping ground (Jones and Satterthwaite 1982, 61) and therefore original contextual associations are uncertain. Coggins (1975, 138) assumes it was originally located in the North Acropolis, while Laporte and Fialko (1990, 41) consider it very possible that Stela 29 was originally set up on the small platform in front of Structure 5D-86-5, and that the figure portrayed on this stela was buried in the same structure (PNT-021). If this is so, the context for Stela 29 was the Commemorative Astronomical Complex with its concrete markings of the solar equinox and solstice passings.

Stela 29 displays within an unframed panel an honored figure in broad profile, supporting a disembodied head with the flat-hand gesture and pressing a ceremonial bar to his chest with the cupped-hand gesture.[5] The disembodied head is the same emblematic JC head held by the seated figure on Stela 36 (fig. 11). On top of this head rests what Peter Mathews (1985, 44) has tentatively identified as the name glyph of the honored figure, Scroll-Ahau-Jaguar, the first ruler of Tikal from the Jaguar Paw dynasty (Laporte and Fialko 1990; Schele and Freidel 1990, 140–43). The JC head is repeated just below and behind the figure's left hand, presumably as part of the belt assemblage. Here, as with Stela 36, the main sign of the Tikal emblem glyph makes up the top of the head as hair. On Stela 29 the repetition of the JC head with different "hats" suggests a semantic parallelism between the name of the honored figure and the name of his place.

Fig. 12.   Tikal, Stela 29.
(Photo courtesy Patrick Clancy.
Drawings, front and back, by William Coe reprinted
from *Tikal Reports 33A* by Jones and
Satterthwaite 1982 courtesy University of
Pennsylvania Museum, Philadelphia.)

On the back of Stela 29, the glyphic text is a Long Count date that can be clearly read as 8.12.14.8.15 (July 6, A.D. 292). The Short Count, 13 Men 3 Zip, can be calculated, but it and all other glyphs were lost with the missing bottom third of the shaft. This is the earliest known Long Count recorded in the Maya lowlands, but perhaps as significantly it is the first monument to represent the glyphic text as separate from the main image. This apparently was done by using the idea of reversed pairing first seen in the recto-verso imagery of Stela 10 at Uaxactun. Text and image are connected, but not visually.

The glyphs, as they can be seen on Stela 29, devote a large amount of space to recording the Long Count, the passage of time qualified and quantified into a history, while the image of the dynast is put (actually) on the other side of history, separated, but still connected and related. This "separation" may be a clue as to how the Early Classic Maya confronted traditional (Preclassic) philosophies about community, personal power, and individuality. That an individual, Scroll-Ahau-Jaguar(?), could claim he *was* Tikal (through the repetition of the JC heads) was likely a difficult thing to do within traditional Maya community values, where even today power is vested in groups with offices or positions of power being shared by rotation among members.[6]

What seems to have happened, distinguishing the Early Classic from the times before, is that ancient Maya religious and philosophical thinking shifted from an exclusive (Preclassic) point of view to an inclusive one. Fundamental ideas and concepts did not change but were reinterpreted to allow the inclusion of an individual and even foreign ideas (here possibly represented by the JC head) into the traditional themes of communal life. Cyclical realities were separated, but not disconnected, from the image of the individual. The different, but apparently necessary, historical themes concerning uniqueness and difference occur with a kind of intellectual objectivity for which we have little trace before its clear statement on Stela 29 of Tikal, where the individual is portrayed with as much focus and potency as the themes of time.

The formal conditions of the stone on which the glyphs and image of Scroll-Ahau-Jaguar have been carved support such speculation. No frame and very little background can be detected; the only context for the image is the stone shaft itself with most of its natural "imperfections" visibly interfacing with the relief-carved imagery. The honored figure seems to appear out of the stone, as if the sculptor were responding to its suggestive "powers," and

the fairly radical changes in portrayal demonstrated by Stela 29 were "natural" ones.

Tikal, Pedestal 13
(fig. 13)

Given that Stela 29 and Pedestal 13 were found in the same "dump," it is still not certain that they were originally paired together. However, there is little question that the pedestal was carved close in time to the production of Stela 29 (Jones and Satterthwaite 1982, 61, 80). The pedestal is a fragment and it is difficult to construe the imagery that remains on what was its circular top face: the large, open jaws of a serpent below or next to which a miniature deer rests on an emblematic head. Like Stela 29, it is carved without a background or a frame.

The periphery of Pedestal 13, however, is framed with images of binding and is structured by a quadripartite design. Four vertical lappets are carved to look as if they fall from the top of the pedestal to cover a rope that horizontally wraps around the periphery, binding shield-like shapes spaced between the lappets. The lappets are decorated with cartouched glyphs that by their outline look like day signs but are hard to identify as such.[7] Pedestal 13 initiates this quadripartite design, which is carved onto the peripheries of pedestals and images of thrones throughout the remainder of Tikal's Classic period art history.

Pedestals carved to look as if they were bound by a rope or ropes can be found during the Middle Preclassic at the Olmec sites of Laguna de los Cerros (Monument 9) and San Lorenzo (Monument 15) (Clancy 1976). It was never a common monumental theme, even for the Olmec, and it is rare elsewhere in the Classic Maya area, except for its use at Tikal and Copan.[8] It is difficult to imagine that an Early Classic patron or sculptor actually saw the Olmec examples carved a thousand years earlier, and it seems more likely that both express a similar underlying and potent idea about binding. On Pedestal 13, the theme of binding may be connected with ideas about time, given the apparent day-sign cartouches. Certainly in the Postclassic period there are abundant references to time being parceled into year-bundles.[9]

Leiden Plaque
(fig. 14)

A small jadeite celt, not quite twenty-two centimeters in height, the Leiden Plaque was a costume item, one of the celts that hung from the belt of an honored person, as it itself depicts. The plaque looks like a maquette for a stela

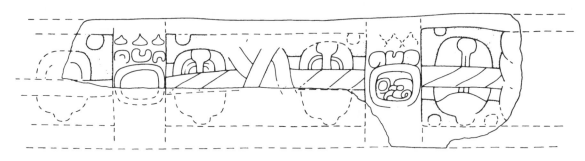

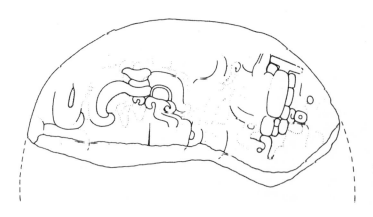

Fig. 13. Tikal, Pedestal 13.
(Photo courtesy University of Pennsylvania
Museum, #59-4-1041. Drawings, top and
periphery, by William Coe reprinted from
Tikal Reports 33A by Jones and Satterthwaite
1982 courtesy University of Pennsylvania
Museum, Philadelphia.)

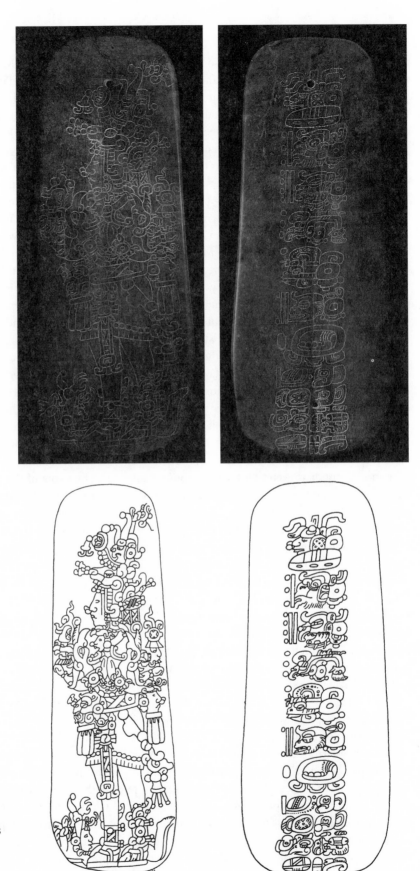

Fig. 14. Leiden Plaque,
Recto-verso. (Photos courtesy
Leiden Rijksmuseum voor
Volkenkunde, Holland. Drawings
courtesy John Montgomery.)

and is beautifully engraved with a verso text and a recto image of a wasp-waisted figure standing in articulated profile pressing a flaccid ceremonial bar to its chest with the ceremonial-bar gesture. A small, bound figure is displayed behind the main figure's feet. Because of its well-preserved iconography, it is included in most studies and discussions of 8th-baktun monuments (Proskouriakoff 1950, 105; Bailey 1972, 45–53; Coggins 1975, 123; Schele and Miller 1986, 120–21; Mathews 1985, 43–44).

The Leiden Plaque was found in 1864 near Puerto Barrios, Guatemala, close to the Caribbean coast (Leemans 1878). Ever since the definitive study by Morley and Morley (1939), however, it has been considered an 8th-baktun "monument" from Tikal. The Morleys' attribution of provenance was based on its iconographic similarities with the costumes and regalia represented on the early-9th-baktun stelae of Tikal, Stelae 1 and 2 (figs. 36 and 37). Stylistically, however, they considered the Plaque to have been carved at the time stated by its Long Count date, 8.14.3.1.12 1 Eb 0 Yaxkin (A.D. 320). Most scholars have accepted the Morleys' reconstruction of provenance and date, but Proskouriakoff (1950, 105) felt that there were not enough comparative monuments to make a firm stylistic assessment and, in a sense, this is still true. While a few monuments have been added to the corpus of Early Classic plaza sculpture since Proskouriakoff made this statement, the best comparisons for the Leiden Plaque continue to be monuments dating from the early years of the 9th baktun. Generally, dates given with the precision of the Long Count are contemporary to the dedication of the monument that bears them, but the Leiden Plaque is not a monument, and its Long Count date may not refer to the time of its making. Proskouriakoff's caution is still a proper one. In fact, celts hanging from belt heads, as depicted on the Leiden Plaque, do not appear in the monumental corpus until 8.17.0.0.0 (A.D. 376) with Stela 39 of Tikal (fig. 18) and Stela 12 of Xultun (fig. 19).

There are good reasons to question a Tikal provenance. Iconographically, the flaccid ceremonial bar is only known to be used on monuments from the southeastern and eastern areas (Copan and Tulum), but, again, the examples of flaccid bars are from 9th-baktun monuments, most of which actually date from the early Late Classic period (Clancy 1994b). A good southeastern comparison from the early 9th baktun, not known to the Morleys, is to Monument 26 of Quirigua (fig. 42), a stela dated fairly surely at 9.2.18.0.0 (A.D. 493) (C. Jones 1983) and displaying a frontal figure holding a flaccid ceremo-

nial bar. Because Monument 26 also bears such strong compositional and iconographic similarities with Stelae 1 and 2 of Tikal, it forms the basis for suggesting that Quirigua was, during the Early Classic period, a Tikal outpost (ibid., 15; Jones and Sharer 1980; Morley, Brainerd, and Sharer 1983). The presence of Stela 26 in the southeastern area, offering similar iconographic comparisons and bearing a date as close to the Leiden Plaque as we assume the comparable Tikal stelae do, weakens the arguments for a Tikal origin of the plaque.

There are, however, two strong components of the Tikal-origin argument: the glyphic text and the belly-down figure behind the feet of the honored figure. The belly-down bound figure, as it is rendered on the plaque, is only comparable to other representations from Tikal, the first comparison being found on Stela 28 (fig. 38), also unknown to the Morleys, and probably of early-9th-baktun date. If the plaque were of a later date, the unique belly-down posture would strongly suggest a Tikal origin because of its almost exclusive use at that site (Clancy 1976), but the fact is that the representation of the bound figure on the Leiden Plaque is the first known bound figure for any Classic work of imagery. It is therefore suggestive of a Tikal origin, but does not constitute conclusive evidence.

The name of the person given in the text is Moon-Zero-Bird, and Mathews (1985, 44) thinks this may be the same as the person mentioned in the Tikal text of Stela 31 (at D6) associated with the 14th katun of the 8th baktun (see fig. 33). Moon-Zero-Bird is generally referred to as the next known Tikal ruler after Scroll-Ahau-Jaguar of Stela 29 (see Schele and Freidel 1990, 143), and the Leiden Plaque would be the only known portrayal this ruler.[10] Mathews (1985, 44) considers the last glyph recorded on the Leiden Plaque to be an early form of the Tikal emblem glyph and compares it to the text (B6a) on Stela 4 of Tikal (fig. 21).[11]

The separation of the text onto the back side of the plaque, recalling the new arrangement for monumental image and text seen on Stela 29, may also be particular to Tikal at this time. However, engraved celts, as a class of objects, often separated glyphs from image in this fashion and it is difficult to know whether the composition of the celt influenced the stela or the other way around.[12] Given the above considerations of comparable compositions and iconographies, and site of finding, it is best to be cautious in our assumptions about the reconstructed provenance of Tikal and an 8th-baktun date for the Leiden Plaque.

Uaxactun, Stela 9
(fig. 15)

Stela 9's Long Count date is generally understood to be 8.14.10.13.15 8 Men 8 Kayab (A.D. 328).[13] It was found in association with Stela 10 (recarved as a pedestal) (fig. 10) in the Main Plaza of Group A at the southern end of the causeway that links Groups A and B, having no particular orientation to any structure. The context of its placement seems to be secondary (Ricketson and Ricketson 1937, 160–61). Morley (1937–38, 1: 150, 241–42) speculates that it may have originally stood where Stela 20 (fig. 52) now stands, in front of the pyramid E-VII-sub in the early Group E, the Commemorative Astronomical Complex, and when Stela 20 was erected in 9.3.0.0.0 (A.D. 495), Stela 9 was removed to Group A. Stela 9 has much in common, stylistically and iconographically, with Stelae 18 and 19 (fig. 17) of Group E, both dated at 8.16.0.0.0 (A.D. 357), and while all three stelae, like Stela 29 of Tikal, separate the main image from the text, no name glyphs or events have been deciphered for these Uaxactun stelae.

Stela 9 is an irregularly shaped shaft whose uneven and pitted planar surfaces make the details of the image and the text difficult to determine. The main figure and a supplementary bound figure are surrounded by a wide frame that is carved to follow the irregularities of the shaft. The standing figure is represented by the broad profile and cradles a disembodied head or a manikin in his right arm with the cupped-hand gesture.[14] His left arm drops naturally and seemingly holds nothing. Scrolled motifs appear to originate at the belt level and drop behind the figure, ending in a coil, which may be a snake. Ian Graham (1986, 5: 155) is noncommittal in his drawing, but Schele and Freidel (1990, 143) suggest, correctly, that it is the belt-fob motif.

Another item of costume iconography is of interest. Both the Copeland and Graham drawings show the figure wearing a long necklace made of tubular beads separated by round ones. The tubular beads make the necklace angle rather than curve around the body, and the whole thing reaches to below the figure's waist. This piece of jewelry is associated with the extroverted gesture as well as the Jaguar Paw clan of Tikal. Its appearance at this time at Uaxactun is of interest, if only because it hints at the complexities in the relationships between Tikal and Uaxactun, especially with regard to the lineal origins of the ruling dynasties in this primary region of the Early Classic Maya.[15]

In front of the figure is a small kneeling figure holding his bound wrists in front of his chest. Graham (1986, 5:

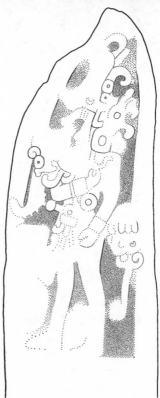

Fig. 15.   Uaxactun, Stela 9.
(Photo after Morley 1937–38 v: pl. 59.
Drawing courtesy Ian Graham.)

Fig. 16.   Seattle Stela. (Drawing by Flora Clancy after
Easby and Scott 1970 #169.)

This little figure floats above the carved ground line and takes an emotive, narrative pose for which it receives no response from the stationally composed main figure. Because of its small size and lack of gravity, it seems difficult to assume that its fundamental meaning was as an illustrative document about capture and captive. As a secondary image, the bound figure would relay information about the honored one, and given the way these two figures are depicted, it can be argued that the relationship between them was metaphorical. One could speculate about such themes as "the binding of hope" or "the conquering of death."

Seattle Stela
(also known as The Hauberg Stela)
(fig. 16)

The Seattle Stela is a small piece, measuring eighty-four centimeters in height. It lacks provenance, but its excellent condition suggests that it was buried in ancient times before it was damaged by circumstances, natural or otherwise. It is now in the collection of Mr. and Mrs. John H. Hauberg in Seattle.

The Seattle Stela shows a single figure in broad profile turned towards a panel of glyphs and set off by a clearly planed background. The little figure either wears a mask or is an anthropomorph characterized by large round and spiraled eyes, a large front tooth, and a curl from the corner of its mouth.[16] This figure is drawn with the distinctive Early Classic wasp-waist, wide buttocks, and thick thighs. It stands on a basal panel of glyphs that extend the vertical panel into an architectonic shape, suggesting a partial niche or doorway.[17]

Elegantly and simply costumed, the honored figure uses the cupped-hand and flat-hand gestures to embrace a long serpent that coils over its left shoulder and across its chest to rise upwards to the top of the stela and become the supernal image of a downward-gazing head. Schele (1985b) believes this is an early depiction of the vision serpent and the flat hand as actually depicting the scattering gesture, because "letting blood" is associated with such serpents, and this action may be referred to in the main verb of the text (at A7).

Four small figures with anthropomorphic faces that are similar to the main figure's are shown grappling along the serpent's body, and may somehow allude to the ancient (Olmec?) narrative of wrestling with a monstrous serpent. These four little figures wear headdresses, and one, the figure just to the right of the main figure's

155) is again noncommittal, but I think there can be little doubt that the bound figure is carved as if floating just above the main figure's right foot. Laporte and Fialko (1990, 41) report that a mural of similarly posed captives was painted on the interior wall of Structure 5D-86-5 at Tikal, the same building in which Stela 39 was found (fig. 18). The building belongs to the Manik II (ceramic) phase, and this could mean that the captives were painted on its wall about the same time, or shortly after, Stela 9 of Uaxactun was carved. Similar bound figures were carved on the tops of columnar altars at Río Azul (ibid.; G. Stuart 1987, 18). Both the painted figures and the Río Azul figures wear fancy back ornaments, and the little figure kneeling in front of the head holder on Stela 9 may have had such a costume.

shoulder, wears a headdress directly comparable to that of the belly-down captive figure depicted on Stela 28 of Tikal (fig. 38). Schele (1985b, 145) likens this particular headdress to that worn by the anthropomorphic head (God III) held in the left arm of Stormy Sky as he is depicted on Stela 31 of Tikal (fig. 33). With both comparisons the headdress as it is rendered at Tikal is directly associated with that site's emblem glyph. More recently, Schele (Freidel, Schele, and Parker 1993, 99ff.) understood this stela to be an iconographic display of the ruler who, by holding the undulating serpent (ceremonial bar), personifies the ecliptic along which ranges, in proper order, the constellations we call Capricorn, Sagittarius, Libra, and Virgo.

An erose, wing-like shape arches away from the main figure's right shoulder and falls to the ground. Headdown, three little truncated figures fall along its path. These marginal figures are also comparable to the truncated figures carved on the extraordinary wings worn by the figure on Stela 1 of Tikal (fig. 36). Formally, the erose form balances the arching serpent coiling over the figure's left shoulder. It is engraved with graphemic and textural markings.

The Seattle Stela is masterfully conceived as an interplay between ambiguity and structure, angle and curve, and open and closed forms. The remarkable regalia physically and metaphorically form a context for the figure by its placement, and here the graphic qualities of the serpent are telling. As it rises between the figure and the glyphs to become the supernal image, it does so with angled turnings while, as it crosses the body and descends behind the figure, it does so with sinuous curves. The angled, rising serpent body and opposing pendent, erose "wing" effectively create a barrier between the figure and the niche-like glyphs. On the other side of the figure, however, the arrangement of images is open and less structured, evoking a suggestion of unseen images at the unframed top and right sides—especially as the four marginal figures clinging to the serpent all look in this direction, opposing the directional movement of the main figure. As one's eyes move from right to left across the face of the monument, the arrangement of imagery becomes regular and more static, until the image field is ended, framed, by the straight lines of the glyphic panels on the left and bottom edges.

All heads, human and others, are lightly modeled and thus distinguished from the other images that are carved in flat, planar relief with little abrasion at the edges of the planes. The general reliance on planar relief and engraving creates an intricate and delicate web of light-catching edges contrasting with darkened, shadowed lines. In the use of these specific carving techniques, the Seattle Stela could be compared to Stelae 10 and 11 from Kaminaljuyu, but there is a quality to the carved edges and lines that signals its lowland origin. The carved lines of Kaminaljuyu monuments seem more formulated, finished, and self-consciously deployed than the line of the Seattle Stela. On this monument the lines, by contrast, seem spontaneous, expressive. Perhaps the ancient sculptor worked more directly on and with the stone, while the Kaminaljuyu artist worked from a carefully prepared cartoon.

The visual tensions within the compositional mode and the enlivening manipulation of surface mark the Seattle Stela as Early Classic in conception if not in date. Linda Schele (1985b) reconstructs the Long Count date as 8.8.0.7.0 3 Ahau 13 Xul (A.D. 199), given the composition of the stela and especially the irregularities of the calendrics that are associated with early, usually Preclassic, monuments. However, the style of costuming and the iconography of the Seattle Stela consistently relate to monuments from Tikal with late-8th-baktun, early-9th-baktun dates and suggest that a later date than the one favored by Schele is possible. Although stylistic assessment of early monuments is hampered by the lack of comparable examples, the reconstructed date of 8.15.7.5.4 3 Kan 12 Zotz' (A.D. 344), rejected by Schele (ibid., 137), is the one that matches more closely the iconographic comparisons made for the Seattle Stela.

One good argument for the 8.15.7.5.4 date is that it does not require changing and then explaining the numerical prefix of the month date as 13 rather than the given 12. Furthermore, a panel composition that includes a glyphic text next to the main figure may be as much a geographic feature as a chronological one. The eastern Maya area, modern Belize, may well have kept this arrangement well into the Classic era. Stela 11 of Uxbenka, probably of late-8th-baktun date, and Stela 2 of Pacibatun of the early-9th-baktun date both display a panel of glyphs on the front face of the monument. Clearly, the precedence for this type of arrangement is found, during the late Preclassic, in the southern sites of El Baúl and Abaj Takalik. How knowledge of such a composition came to the lowlands may well have been down the Motagua Valley and up the Belizean coast and then into the central Maya area.[18] This could argue for an eastern provenance for the Seattle Stela and, indeed, Schele (1985b, 138) tentatively considers the emblem glyph carved at A12 to be that of Kohunlich in southern Quintana Roo.

Uaxactun, Stelae 18 and 19
(fig. 17)

After Morley's (1937–38, 1: 160–67) efforts, few scholars have discussed these two stelae because they are badly worn and difficult to make out. This is especially true of Stela 18, where Ian Graham (1986, 5: 173–75) does not try to publish a drawing of its front face. Both stelae were found set up, along with a plain, third stela, in front of the central stairs of the long East Platform in the Commemorative Astronomical Complex (Group E). Stela 18 is the northern monument of the three, set just to the north of the East Platform stairs. Stela 19 (fig. 17) is the central monument placed directly in front of the stairs and on the axis that marks the equinoxes. Plain Stela E-1 was just to the south of the stairs. Both the carved stelae were set at odd angles to the north-south axis of the East Platform and Ricketson and Ricketson (1937, 130–31, 160–61) make it quite clear that this anomaly was not due

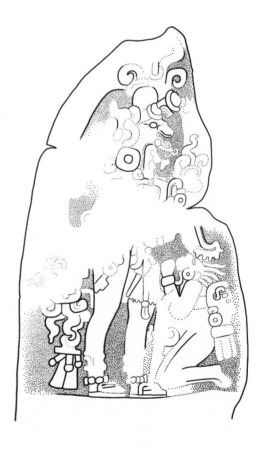

Fig. 17.   Uaxactun, Stela 19. (Photo after Morley 1937–38 V: pl.55d. Drawing courtesy Ian Graham.)

to the monuments shifting in position through time. From the archaeological evidence (ibid., 288) they believe Stelae 18 and 19 were reset in front of the East Platform at the same time Stela 20 (fig. 52) was set in its place before the western pyramid, Structure E-VII—that is, around 9.3.0.0.0 (A.D. 495). They do not speculate where their original settings might have been. Morley (1937–38, 1: 161, 165), however, considers Stelae 18 and 19 to be in their original positions. It is not clear, therefore, who commissioned the two stelae and who is portrayed on their front panels. The glyphs do not reveal any readable name.

Stelae 18 and 19 depict standing figures in broad profile holding the same gestures as the figure on Stela 9. What is supported in their cupped hands cannot be precisely identified, but these may be disembodied heads rather than ceremonial bars as suggested by Morley (1937–38, 1: 161, 165). The honored figure is most visible on Stela 19 (fig. 17), and on this panel he is elaborately dressed wearing a tall headdress and a belt-fob chain. His body type is wasp-waisted, and one can assume the same type of figure for Stela 18. Both stelae depict a kneeling figure bound at the wrists as if floating above the main figure's feet. On Stela 19, this little figure with its spiky hair wears a fancy belt with an ornamental back head. He tilts his head back to look up at the large and looming main figure but, as depicted, gets no response. What little remains of the imagery and glyphs of Stelae 18 and 19 shows that originally they were carefully composed and carved with planar and modeled relief cuts. The cuts outlining the images are expressive of what they portray: that is, the spiky hair of the bound figure on Stela 19

contrasts with the neat curving scrolls of the belt fob, which in turn contrast with the long, curved lines of the bare legs of the main figure. The expressiveness, however, seems more carefully manipulated, perhaps bespeaking greater patronage control, at least for Stela 19, than is evident for Stela 9 or the earlier Stela 10.

While Stelae 18 and 19 closely follow the imagery and composition of the earlier Stela 9, the Long Count date, 8.16.0.0.0 3 Ahau 8 Kankin (A.D. 357) recorded on their back, or verso, glyphic panels represents the first recording of an even period ending. There is no general agreement as to the significance of this "first."[19] It seems reasonable to suggest that this new kind of date may have had something to do with the astronomical function of the complex in which the stelae were placed, but this suggestion is weakened by the possibilities of resetting.

The ceremonial-astronomical context of Group E may date from the Late Preclassic; certainly the pyramid E-VII-sub is Late Preclassic. The erection of freestanding public monuments would have been an intrusive or additional act in an already established context, no matter when the stelae were set up. What changes, signaled by the addition of stelae into these plaza spaces, is the more active role played by the public in this plaza's ceremonies, and the humanity of the ruler as he is personified in human scale on the stelae in contrast to the large stucco masks of E-VII and E-VII-sub. Stelae 18 and 19 were set up in Group E in front of the equinoctial center of the East Platform. Rather than marking the solstitial extremes, the focus is at the center, the points of balance within the solar year.[20]

Fig. 18.   Tikal, Stela 39. (Photos, front and back, courtesy Karl Herbert Mayer.
Drawings, front and back, courtesy John Montgomery.)

CHAPTER FIVE

Foreign Images

8.17.0.0.0 to the End of the Baktun (A.D. 376–435)

Tikal, Stela 39 (fig. 18)

Found within the Commemorative Astronomical Complex of the Mundo Perdido area, Stela 39 is a large fragment of the lower half of a stela (Ayala Falcón 1987). It was found reset into Room 3 of Structure 5D-86-7th, the central, equinoctial, structure of the East Platform, and associated with a burial (PNT-019) thought to be that of the person portrayed on the stela (Laporte and Fialko 1990, 43–45). An honored person standing on a bound basal figure is depicted on the front panel, and the main glyphic statement is carved on the back panel. The gesture and full regalia of the figure are difficult to reconstruct, the dedicatory date is in question, and, thus, the identification of the person portrayed is also in question.

Along with the two known monuments carved previously at Tikal, Stela 29 (fig. 12) and "Stela" 36 (fig. 11), both of which are very different in composition and style, Stela 39 represents yet another carving style, as well as new iconography. Unlike the monuments carved at Uaxactun, the early monuments of Tikal are varied enough to suggest that the patrons of Tikal were quite experimental with ideas about plaza sculpture, and that they had access to various sculptors or schools with different carving styles through which to express these ideas.

The front panel of Stela 39 is bound by a small, plain frame, but the sculptor felt free to overlap the frame with imagery extending from the main image. A careful system of planar relief and abraded cuts creates an active surface that is more visually lucid than the relief work on the previous monuments of Tikal. The quality of the outlines, however, is more carefully controlled, and as a result the image is not as expressive. There is a sureness in the execution of the relief that bespeaks a well-schooled tradition of carving that may be the result of local development within the school that produced Stela 29, but the possibility remains that the patron brought in a sculptor from the highlands or from the eastern (Belizean) regions because the style of carving on Stela 39 is really quite different from the works produced earlier at Tikal and Uaxactun.

The glyphic statement on the back of the stela mentions the important name, Jaguar Paw (or Jaguar-Paw-Skull) at A2z. Because the upper part of the text is lost, it is not clear whether this Jaguar Paw is the protagonist of the stela, and thus the person portrayed, or whether this name is part of a parentage statement naming the father of the person to whom the stela is dedicated (see Schele and Freidel 1990, 145 n. 41). This problem is not resolved by the completion of a katun statement at A7z, which can be read as either "17th katun" or "19th katun." At this time, however, most scholars agree that it is the completion of the 17th katun and that the person portrayed is Jaguar Paw (Ayala Falcón 1987, 601; Laporte and Fialko 1990, 42,45; Schele and Freidel 1990, 144–45). If the 19th katun was, indeed, the intended statement, then Stela 39 would be a monument of Curl Snout, a later ruler of Tikal, whose monuments (Stelae 4 and 18 [figs. 21 and 22]) were placed in the context of the North Acropolis and were carved with entirely different styles, compositions, and iconographies. It is hard to explain why their patron would have had Stela 39 carved as well, another possible reason for considering the 17th-katun date the more likely one. Still, the succession of early rulers at Tikal remains unsettled.

For the moment, however, it is not too presumptuous to call the patron or person portrayed Jaguar Paw, whether he be the ninth successor (Schele and Freidel 1990, 144) or the third ruler of Tikal (Laporte and Fialko 1990). Jaguar Paw is shown standing in a three-quarter pose (probably the broad profile) wearing sandals and fancy anklets. A pendent belt-fob motif overlaps leg bands tied just below the figure's knees. Two complex pendants hang on either side of the main figure. The one on his right side can be seen to consist of three hanging celts (shaped like the Leiden Plaque [fig. 14]) as well as knots and other scrolling pendants. Its composition is matched by a pendant on the other side. The attachment points of the pendants are lost, but they look like the lappets that hang either from fancy ceremonial bars or from large belt heads that extend out from the belt as do the heads on the later Stela 31 of Tikal (fig. 33). It is this last reconstruction that is favored.

The one visible hand holds, actually grasps, an object not seen before. It looks like an eccentric flint or a fancy axe. Both Ayala Falcón (1987, 646) and Schele and Freidel (1990, 145) consider that the jaguar paw pendent on the honored figure's groin is actually attached to this axe as its "working end." This may be so, but it also very like jaguar-paw icons seen on Stela 1 of Uolantun (fig. 28) and Stela 11 from Uxbenka, where it as part of the front belt hanging.

While the jaguar-paw pendent is a telling motif in the identification of this figure as, indeed, a member of the Jaguar Paw clan dynasty, it is also an important part of the costume worn by several figures exhibiting the extroverted gesture. Another item in this costume is the long, angular necklace of tubular beads, first seen on Stela 9 of Uaxactun (fig. 15). Here it may be part of Jaguar Paw's outfit if the long decorated bar that hangs just below his belt (and is at the top left of the fragment) is part of this necklace. With this reconstruction, the figure was posed performing the extroverted gesture and wearing the angular necklace and jaguar-paw belt hanging. The extroverted gesture, as a pose for public display, also appears at this time at the sites of Xultun (Stela 12 [fig. 19]) and El Zapote (Stela 6), and while it could be described as bellicose, no example of its use is known to be associated with a depiction of an actual weapon.

In the basal image of Stela 39 a small, bearded figure is portrayed with his hands bound together at the wrists and raised in front of his chest so that they poignantly recreate the ceremonial-bar gesture. He wears an elaborate headdress, his profiled face is half-darkened, and, except for his shoulders and arms, his body is also shown in profile. The profile of the near leg, bent at the knee, is that of the belly-down pose first seen on the Leiden Plaque (fig. 14). The profile of the far leg, bent and drawn up towards the chest, is that of the swimmer and comparable to the poses of mythological figures carved or engraved on pottery and bones where they are identified by their iconographic contexts as creatures of primordial watery realms (Schele and Miller 1986, 208) and from other dimensions or times.

The little basal figure on Stela 39 represents, then, a powerful iconographic synthesis of the bound figure and the mythological swimmer, rendered with the added impact of the ceremonial-bar gesture, which also draws together two very different conditions, rulership and bondage. The brilliance of this image is its graphic merging of the swimmer with the image of binding and captivity. The little figure may emblematically indicate that the ruler was bound to duties that were defined, in part, by a necessary knowledge about realms beyond those experienced in everyday life.

Such an interpretation does not necessarily preclude the one more usually given for bound figures: that they represent documentary evidence for the ruler's prowess in battle and captive taking. Certainly actual captives could have been made to act the "part" of the emblematic metaphor in ceremonial or ritual dramas that took place on the steps, terraces, or the pedestals placed in the public spaces of the plaza (see Miller and Houston 1987). However, as images carved on stelae, the metaphoric and narrative content of the bound figure would have been as significant, if not more so, than its capability of recording the actual or dramatic event of captive taking. Regardless of how this basal image is interpreted, the pose and iconography clearly reveal its metaphoric complexity and the multi-leveled intentions behind it, and that Jaguar Paw uses it as his base and his support.

What may be denotative information in this basal image would be in the glyphs that make up the little headdress worn by the bound figure and in the short glyphic text on the right side next to the figure's upraised calf. The text is a locative statement that contains the main sign of Tikal's emblem glyph and is read as "Tikal Sky Place" (Schele and Freidel 1990, 145–47; Stuart and Houston 1994, 58, 60). Like the headdresses of most secondary figures, that of the bound figure incorporates in its design identifying name glyphs or emblems, in this case, looking very much like the glyphs for Moon-Zero-Bird associated with the Leiden Plaque, which may denote a person or a place. If it is a place, the seeming paradox of naming a sky place and a bird place in the basal portion of the stela will be met again when a mythological bird head becomes an important basal image (see Stelae 1 and 3 of Tres Islas [figs. 39 and 41]). If the headdress denotes a person, then Jaguar Paw is supported by his ancestor, Moon-Zero-Bird, who is depicted with the same gesture last seen in his "portrait" on the Leiden Plaque. While the glyphs particularize information, they do not lessen but enhance the metaphoric readings for the stela's imagery. Thus, on Stela 39, Jaguar Paw stands on an emblematic, bound figure who is directly associated with a place within, or somehow associated with the city of Tikal: an emblem, with the potential to fuse (confuse) mythical and historical ideas, and vivified (personified) to support the office of Jaguar Paw and his public persona at Tikal.

Xultun, Stela 12 (fig. 19)

The present location of Stela 12 is unknown, having been looted from Xultun around 1975 (von Euw 1978, 5: 39). What remains is a photograph taken in the 1920s. In a sense, the single photograph makes this another fragmentary monument. The photograph shows the monument whole and in reasonably good condition. What we cannot know is whether its sides or back were carved. Morley (1937–38, 1: 392–93) could see no trace of glyphs but surmised that this lack may be due to wear rather than to the original state of carving. Its iconography and carving techniques point to 8.17.0.0.0 (A.D. 376) as the earliest prob-

Fig. 19.   Xultun, Stela 12. (Photo courtesy Peabody Museum, Harvard University, #H-21-1-20. Drawing courtesy Ian Graham.)

able date for its dedication, while Proskouriakoff's (1950, 104–5) style date of 8.15.0.0.0 ± 2 katuns (A.D. 337 ± 40 years) places this date at the late end of its stylistic range.

The main figure is portrayed as wasp-waisted and thick-thighed in an articulated profile. There is, compared to previous lowland monuments, a fair amount of background space around the figure and an attempt seems to have been made to create something like a figure-field dichotomy. Such a perception is reinforced by the plain frame that surrounds the panel and overlaps the imagery, rather than the other way around, as seen on Stela 39 of Tikal. Morley (1937–38, 1: 392–93) calls this fact "pleasing," and, indeed, the whole figural image is beautifully organized to take up—to energetically fill—the enframed space without creating an impression of abbreviation or compaction.

The honored figure is rendered as a dynamic and graceful figure displaying a disembodied head by an extroverted gesture in the presence of a small bound figure kneeling at his feet. It is not clear what he holds in his left hand, as the motifs in the photograph are hard to read, and this is reflected in von Euw's drawing (1978, 5: 39). Perhaps it is something similar to the fancy tool held by Jaguar Paw on Stela 39 of Tikal. The Xultun figure wears the necklace made of long tubular beads associated with the extroverted gesture. Whether the jaguar paw is part of the belt hanging is open to question.[1]

The use of a defining frame and the tentative, but nonetheless observable, efforts to create a background for the figure are formal traits, which can be traced in their earliest lowland examples to Xultun with Stela 12 and to Uaxactun (Stela 5 [fig. 20]). Another affinity with Uaxactun is the kneeling bound figure posed in the same pleading manner as those carved on Stelae 9, 18, and 19 (figs. 15 and 17) of Uaxactun, except that the little Xultun figure does not float. This accords with certain conceptual changes concerning public displays that can be detected in the 17th katun, whereby greater emphasis is placed on the meanings of the imagery and less on the monument itself as the revelatory source of the image.

Cerro de las Mesas, Veracruz, Stela 9

The advent of the extroverted gesture, possibly on Stela 39 of Tikal and certainly on Stela 12 of Xultun, is connected in some way to the monument tradition of Cerro de las Mesas in Veracruz. How or why the connection existed is not clear because the archaeological record is incomplete (Arnold 1994; Stark and Curet 1994). None-

theless, from this point in time until the end of the Early Classic period, the site of Cerro de las Mesas should figure in any effort to reconstruct the history of Maya public art (M. Miller 1991, 35).

Stela 9 of Cerro de las Mesas displays a kneeling figure in broad profile brandishing a club or axe with the extroverted gesture. In his other hand he holds a small round shield. Above, in the badly worn supernal area, there may be a feathered creature whose tail continues down the right side of the panel and then turns to the lateral side as it reaches the figure's feet—a small bit of wraparound imagery.

Stela 9 has been termed "Olmecoid" in style (Bernal 1976, 146) because of the way the figure's facial features and headdress are rendered, and, in fact, there is a quality of roundness imparted to the shaping of the figure that is generally "read" as Olmec-like. However, Stela 9 is one of those monuments whose style is difficult to place and therefore was quite differently understood by Stirling (1943, 48), who "was inclined to place it with the more recent group," that is, late in the sequence of the Cerro de las Mesas monuments.[2] Proskouriakoff (1950, 174) considered Stela 9, because of its costume, to be Early Classic, belonging to the group of stelae at that site having glyphic statements: Stelae 5, 6, and 8 (figs. 25 and 26). These three stelae, by their style and stated dates, were carved between 9.1.0.0.0 and 9.5.0.0.0 (A.D. 455–534), and will be discussed more carefully below because they too have important affinities with Maya stelae of the same era.

Based on the natural, or human-like, proportions of the figure, Stela 9 may have been carved some time during the 8th baktun, perhaps during the last half. This is earlier than Proskouriakoff's (ibid.) assessment, but later than Bernal's (1976, 146). Figural proportions change at Cerro de las Mesas from natural representations to conventional figures with the squat proportions of 1:5, head to body height. The difference between the bodily proportions of the two dated stelae, 6 and 8 (fig. 26), is telling in this regard: the figure on the earlier Stela 6 is six heads tall, while the figure on Stela 8 is only five heads tall. The figure portrayed on Stela 9 would be about six and a half heads tall if it were standing. Thus, Stela 9 may be a Late Preclassic monument carved during the 8th baktun, and probably before Stela 12 of Xultun.[3]

Except for its upright orientation, the pose of the kneeling figure on Stela 9 is not unlike that of the swimmer or the bound figures on the stelae of Uaxactun and Stela 12 of Xultun. Its Olmec-like face could even be a mask, an heirloom worn to match, historically, the same narrative reference implied by his extroverted gesture; that is, the ancient narrative about a struggle with a serpent (see chapter 3).[4]

The appearance of the extroverted gesture in the Maya lowlands could well be related to its use on Stela 9, but on the Maya stelae, or at least as seen on Stela 39 of Tikal and Stela 12 of Xultun, the illustrated components of the narrative are divided between the main figure and the secondary, basal figure: the extroverted gesture is enacted by the main figure, and the kneeling/swimming pose is struck by the little bound figure. This division probably signals a reinterpretation or a retelling of the ancient story by the Early Classic Maya for the new purposes of the plaza monument. It also supports the supposition, signaled by the ceremonial-bar gesture adopted by both the bound figure and the main figure, that the meaningful "connections" between the two figures were strong and deep.

Uaxactun, Stela 5 (fig. 20)

Stela 5 was found *in situ* in front of the stairs of Structure B-VIII, a pyramidal platform supporting a small temple on its top (Ricketson and Ricketson 1937, 159) and

B

A

C

Fig. 20.   Uaxactun, Stela 5, Recto-verso.
A) Front, B) Back, C) Front, drawing
Photos courtesy Peabody Museum, Harvard
University, #H-21-2-218 and 40-10-1.
Drawing courtesy Ian Graham.)

thought to be a funerary monument because of the impressive burial (Burial 1) contained within (A. L. Smith 1950, 52; and see Schele and Freidel 1990, 447–48 n. 51). Stela 5 was set along the central axis of the structure and is associated by proximity with Stela 4, which was set in line with Stela 5 but off the axis of the structure, and with Altar 1, a carved boulder.

Stela 5 is carved recto-verso, and its famous image of the warrior is matched by a similar but reversed warrior, now badly worn, on its other broad panel. The two lateral sides are carved with glyphs, also badly worn but with a few readable details, most notably the Long Count date, 8.17.1.4.12 11 Eb 15 Mac (A.D. 378). On the well-preserved and often-published figural panel, there is a small glyphic statement in the upper-right-hand corner.

Stela 5 shows each reversed image carefully enclosed by a wide frame. Like Stela 12 from Xultun (fig. 19), this frame is matched by a fair amount of background space as evidence of an effort to create a neutral field for the figure. Also like Stela 12, this seems tentative because the background has not been carefully planed and still intrudes as a visually positive factor. On the other hand, the visual qualities produced by the way the background and the imagery are handled on Stela 5 are radically different in technique and style from those of the earlier Stelae 9, 18, and 19 (figs. 15 and 17). Using the recto-verso field of the very early Stela 10 (fig. 10), the sculptor(s) of Stela 5 produced Uaxactun's most singular plaza image for which little local precedent can be found. In terms of carving techniques, the closest comparison is with Xultun Stela 12. In terms of its iconography, Stela 5 is locally innovative, representing a pair of warriors with the regalia and costume that belong to an inter-regional group of warrior images (Clancy 1980, 51–53; Schele and Freidel 1990, 145–47).

Stela 5 is apparently the first unequivocal representation of a warrior carved in the Maya area. The squat figure is represented in a broad-profile pose with the conventional proportions of 1:5½, head to body height. He is shown grasping an atlatl in his left hand and a club tipped with nobs or blades in his right. His costuming is unusual with only the earflares, wristlets, beaded collar, and sandals represented in an expectable but simple manner. The plain wide belt has a glyph or emblem in the front, and a plain cloth panel pendent from the back. Plain thick bands or ruffs are tied around the knees and ankles. Truly unusual is the short jacket that looks like the cotton armor described by Landa (Tozzer 1941, 35, 121;

and see Hassig 1992, 126 and n. 124), worked at the hems around the waist and arms, perhaps with quilting, to be stiff and stand out. A long panache arches from the back of the jacket or from an unseen back ornament and falls to the figure's calves. The headdress is a large thick turban or helmet surmounted by a fairly realistic bird, perhaps a quetzal with long tail feathers. The helmet with feathers (the bird's tail), the atlatl, the wide belt, the long panache at the rear of the figure, and the knee ruffs are all traits of the inter-regional costume. Not included in this costume/regalia iconography on Stela 5 (but appearing shortly on Stela 18 of Tikal [fig. 22]) is the image of a goggle-eyed creature.[5]

The profiled figure of the honored warrior shares his panel with a disembodied broad-beaked bird head resting on the ground line at his feet. This head is the combined image of a bird head with an aged, bearded human-like head wearing a three-pronged "blind-fold." It is similar to the bird head in the short glyphic statement in the basal panel of Stela 39 of Tikal (fig. 18). On Stela 5, a glyph and scroll rise from the head, and three projections defining an ovoid form (glyph?) are placed in front of the face. This head has been identified as a significant but untranslated part of a place-name phrase (Stuart and Houston 1994, 11–12; and see Schele and Freidel 1990, 146–47).[6] On Stela 5, however, by its placement within the figural panel at the feet of the honored figure, this head replaces the bound figure of Uaxactun's earlier stelae and therefore also reflects in some way the meanings of the little bound figure. Furthermore, as rendered and positioned on Stela 5, the disembodied head is similar to heads depicted on the Preclassic Stelae 1, 3, 22, 23, and 67 of Izapa (Quirarte 1973; V. Smith 1984) where they are most often associated with watery signs.[7]

The bird-head-as-place-sign is described by Schele and Freidel (1990, 146–47) and Stuart and Houston (1994, 11–12) as denoting an actual place. Stela 5, however, represents the bird in an inversion of natural habitat, suggesting a metaphoric rather than denotative meaning. The disembodied head also draws together many associations: it is inspired by ancient icons from the south; it is a substitution for the kneeling bound figures; and it functions as a qualifier of a place. While the main figure is depicted with a new clarity and wears the new costume of a warrior, these things can be accounted for by direct comparisons with other, albeit foreign, monuments. The disembodied bird head, however, seems to be uniquely innovative in its syncretism.[8]

Stela 5 initiates an important iconographic theme, the warrior pair, at the same time the extroverted gesture is entered into the plaza display. The extroverted gesture is associated with the "normal" Maya iconographies of costume and regalia, but its gestural expression is unlike the usual cradling and supporting gestures of the previous plaza monuments. The new iconographies of the warrior and the extrovert may represent two different responses to an historical event or situation that was inter-regional in its scope and powerful in its effects on the lowland Maya.

What the nature of this event was, figures heavily in recent efforts to reconstruct the Early Classic histories of Tikal and Uaxactun (see Marcus 1976; Coggins 1979b; Mathews 1985; Fialko 1987; Laporte and Fialko 1990; Culbert 1988; Schele and Freidel 1990). The name of Smoking Frog of Tikal remains readable on the right side of Stela 5 at B9-C9, indicating that the fortunes of Tikal and Uaxactun are closely tied together. Furthermore, the Calendar Round 11 Eb 15 Mac of Stela 5's Long Count is mentioned on two monuments of Tikal: the Ballcourt Marker and Stela 31. In some reconstructions these facts are thought to mark a war between the two sites. While there is a general acknowledgment that the warrior in his foreign costume, as depicted on Stela 5, is an important aspect of this event, these reconstructions have never taken into account the fact that Stela 5 represents the warrior as a reversed pair, or that all Early Classic plaza representations of warriors are in fact pairs, as seen on Stela 31 from Tikal (fig. 33) and Tres Islas Stelae 1 and 3 (figs. 39 and 41). Thus, the warrior was originally understood as a pair or as twins, and this suggests some kind of allegorical or metaphoric content. The similarly attired figures at Teotihuacan and Monte Alban are also represented as pairs (Monte Alban Tomb 104) or as paired figures in processions. The Mexican examples are mainly from murals found in tombs or the interiors of buildings, that is, in private, or at least recondite, contexts. While Stela 5 uses the foreign, inter-regional iconography of the warrior and the keeps idea of procession or pairing, it changes the context of this image and theme into the more public one of the plaza.

If Smoking Frog was the patron of Stela 5, he had carved a monument at Uaxactun that recontextualized the Mexican theme of the warrior pair into a public image of power. This singular choice, by its radical difference from what had been carved on all previous plaza monuments, also points, importantly, to the fact that the plaza image of the honored person was being redefined by using foreign, though perhaps not alien, ideas and icons.

Tikal, Stela 4 (fig. 21)

Stela 4 was set in front of Structure 5D-34 of the North Acropolis. As with the location of Stela 5 in Uaxactun, this may represent a change of monument placement from the Ceremonial Astronomical Complex to another kind of ceremonial plaza space. Stela 4 is associated with a plaza structure (5D-34) thought to enclose the tomb of the figure portrayed. However, as Stela 4 was found set upside down, its original association with the North Acropolis is a matter of reconstruction.

Smoking Frog's name also appears in the glyphic text carved on the back of Stela 4, along with the name of Curl Snout (A7a and B5b, respectively). In all historical and dynastic reconstructions, Curl Snout (or Curl Nose) is considered the patron and protagonist of this stela and of Stela 18 (fig. 22) carved about a katun later at Tikal, and to be the probable occupant of Burial 10 within Structure 5D-34.[9] The Calendar Round date carved on the back of Stela 4, 5 Caban 10 Yaxkin, has been assigned to the Long Count date of 8.17.2.16.17 (A.D. 379) as marking the accession to rulership of Curl Snout. This is the usual date given for the monument, but as Mathews notes (1985, 44), the last glyphs of the statement refer to the completion of the katun, and imply that the Long Count date of 8.18.0.0.0 (A.D. 396) may be its date of dedication.

Both the monuments associated with Curl Snout and the goods in his tomb, Burial 10, bear more consistent and stronger evidence of foreign, Mexican imagery than does Stela 5 of Uaxactun. These associations have led many scholars to consider Curl Snout a crucial character in the dynastic and political histories of the Early Classic Maya: he was a foreigner who intermarried into the Tikal Jaguar Paw dynasty and usurped rulership (Coggins 1975, 142ff.); or he was related to Smoking Frog and from a local but rival Tikal lineage, now strong enough to bid for rulership (Laporte and Fialko 1990); or he was the son of the Jaguar Paw portrayed on Stela 39 and nephew of Smoking Frog, and ruled at Tikal under the protection of his uncle (Schele and Freidel 1990, 153–58, elaborating on Mathews 1985).[10]

Stela 4 depicts the honored figure seated on a throne displaying the disembodied JC head by the old flat-hand gesture, and cradling, by the cupped-hand gesture, what may be a shield, a head, or a ceramic pot with three legs—a cylindrical tripod vessel usually associated with

Mexican ceramic production at Teotihuacan and in Veracruz (see Drucker 1943). He is in the presence of (or has attracted into his field) a downward-gazing supernal head of God K. The seated pose is functionally related to the pedestal-like proportions of the monument because of its requirements for space. Like Stela 5 from Uaxactun, the body of the figure is conventionalized into squat proportions, but on Stela 4 there is an added emphasis on the head and shoulders in terms of size and by the extraordinary use of a frontal face rather than a profile one. He sits on a throne of unclear design: mouth scrolls emerge from its edge.[11] Falling behind the throne is Curl Snout's back ornament of pendent feathers or tails like those worn by Smoking Frog on Stela 5 of Uaxactun.

No frame is carved around the image, and there is no effort to make a clear visual distinction between the figural shapes and the background. In terms of carving techniques, Stela 4 is decidedly conservative in its evocation of the "revealed image" in a natural field. It is difficult not to see this as an *apologia* for the iconographic anomalies of the frontal face and the odd costuming, which are new and foreign. Facing similar problems for

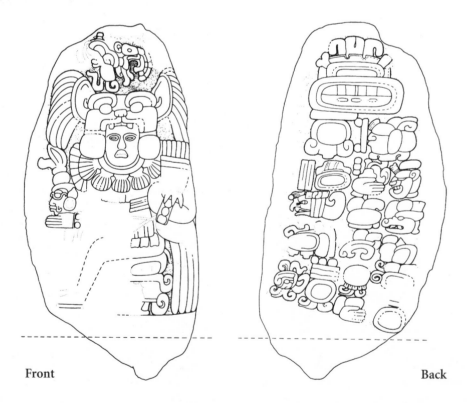

Front   Back

Fig. 21.   Tikal, Stela 4. (Photo courtesy Patrick Clancy. Drawings, front and back, by William Coe reprinted from *Tikal Reports 33A* by Jones and Satterthwaite 1982 courtesy University of Pennsylvania Museum, Philadelphia.)

the combination and synthesis of old and new ideas about plaza imagery, the sculptors of Tikal used strategies similar to those deployed by the sculptor(s) on Stela 5 at Uaxactun. They revised the old frameless panels of Stela 29 that separated image and text by means similar to the recto-verso field, and associated the new regalia and costuming with at least one old image of a disembodied head: the jaguar-eared, cruller-eyed head, held in the flat right hand of Curl Snout, perhaps with the Tikal emblem glyph as first seen on Stela 36. The supernal head, identified as God K or God II of the Palenque Triad, may also hold evocative associations with ancient imagery, but its formal history is obscure (however, see Coggins 1975, 145).

Everything else is extraordinary on Stela 4. If one were to look from Stela 39 (fig. 18) to Stela 4, it would be hard to guess that they were from the same site and were carved within two to eighteen years of one another. However, it must be remembered that Tikal had not yet developed a consistent set of imagery for its plaza monuments. The patrons and sculptors of Tikal were apparently open to, and willing to engage in, the kind of iconographic and formal experimentation seen on Stela 4, and on Stela 18, Curl Snout's other plaza stela. With Stela 4, the sculptor was able to integrate the unusual desires of the patron into a convincing and intriguing image centered in, and dominated by, the striking frontal face, which is modeled rather than receiving the planar treatment given to the rest of the image.

The fully frontal face rendered in relief is rare in general, and Stela 4 represents its first known use on plaza monuments. The idea was very likely influenced by the large stucco heads common to public architecture (see A. Miller 1986), which in turn fit the general perception that frontal faces represent a deity image (Klein 1976). Reifying the frontality of the face is the animal-head helmet with wonderfully large ears from which arching feathers fall. Along with the plain earflares, the helmet maintains the bilateral symmetry of the face, and completing this focus is a necklace of large pecten shells curving from earflare to earflare under the chin. Such an isotropic arrangement could be a reflection of a knowledge of the Esquintla censers being produced in the south, or even the frontal "deities" painted on the walls of Portico 11 of Tetitla, Teotihuacan (see chapter 2). It is difficult, however, to find a precedent, local or foreign, for the use of a frontal face to represent a human, and the few that can be cited are from the Olmec sculptural traditions of the

Middle and Late Preclassic periods—assuming that the colossal Olmec heads represent humans because they look human. Another possible inspiration may have been Olmec jadeite masks and heads that were kept as heirlooms by the later Maya (E. W. Andrews V., 1986; Schele and Miller 1986, 119–20; Freidel 1990). Both the stucco heads and the heirlooms, by their evocation of ancient imagery, would be useful for a strategy of validation. Furthermore, the frontal face would cast an aura of timeless, god-like qualities around Curl Snout.

Around the chest and waist of the figure, the symmetry and proportions of the head and headdress are dropped, and unfortunately it is at this point that the stela has suffered the most damage. Probably originally obscured by costuming, and now obscured by damage, Curl Snout's body is shown unnaturally articulated, turning from frontal to profile, so, as reconstructed, he sits in profile, feet to the viewer's left.

Curl Snout's gestures are traditional and asymmetrical. The flat hand and the cupped hand are used to display the JC head and an unidentified, possibly foreign, item of regalia. For an iconographic strategy, he may have emulated Scroll-Ahau-Jaguar's Stela 29 (fig. 12) presentation of old and new emblems. It is significant, however, that what had been a new and perhaps foreign emblem (the jaguar-eared, cruller-eyed head) a hundred years ago, on Stela 29, is now reused as the old emblem.

The seated portrait and the representation of a throne have been iconographically associated with ideas of cave and burial. The formal requirements of this active posture are not really suited to the usual panel field of the stela, and apparently the evocative, iconographic associations to cave and burial were more important than monumental shape. With the old and traditional carving style, the use of the supernal head, and the traditional gestures, Curl Snout's plaza monument represented a definite, if not extreme, change in traditional plaza imagery, and this in turn may signal a different conception for plaza ceremony. With the use of anachronisms and foreign imagery, Curl Snout shows himself to be almost god-like as well as disproportionate in terms of human measure. If the supernal head is an ancestral statement, he does not claim a human ancestor, but a deity. His vision of rulership apparently required a *disconnection* from public expectations and the traditional plaza image of the ruler (see Andrea Stone 1989).[12]

One thing he did *not* do was proclaim himself a warrior. Historically, however, we know he was very closely tied, perhaps even related, to the warrior Smoking Frog, supposedly portrayed on Stela 5 of Uaxactun. However we eventually understand the political histories of the 17th katun, it must be acknowledged that Curl Snout's personal philosophies and agendas, as expressed publicly, were at odds with those of Smoking Frog.

Tikal, Stela 18 (fig. 22)

The Long Count date on Stela 18 has been reconstructed as 8.18.0.0.0 (Jones and Satterthwaite 1982, 42–43), suggesting that it and Stela 4 were both carved for Curl Snout and erected at the same time (ibid.). The glyphic statement carved on the back panel of Stela 18, however, has been badly damaged and eroded: Curl Snout's name glyph does not seem to appear, but Smoking Frog's does at B11. Stela 18 is now part of the stela row in front of the North Acropolis, but Jones and Satterthwaite (ibid.) suggest it was originally set up in front of Structure 5D-34-1st.

Stela 18 repeats and extends the programmatic intentions of Stela 4. The head of the figure portrayed on Stela 18 has been lost, and what remains suggests that the seated pose is identical to that of Stela 4: a frontal face

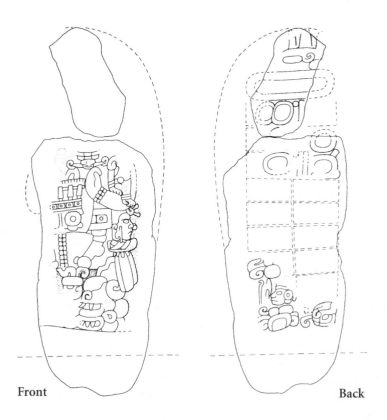

Front

Back

Fig. 22. Tikal, Stela 18. (Photo courtesy Patrick Clancy. Drawings, front and back, by William Coe reprinted from *Tikal Reports 33A* by Jones and Satterthwaite 1982 courtesy University of Pennsylvania Museum, Philadelphia.)

and shoulders with profiled hips and legs. As with Stela 4, the stone shaft was left in a fairly natural and rough state, the image panel is unframed, and the planar relief cuts were masterfully executed. The only differences between the two monuments are in the iconographies of costume and regalia.

On Stela 18, Curl Snout (if this is the correct attribution) showed himself wearing a more traditional costume—at least this is true for the belt and its pendent features, the back belt head with celts, and the hanging belt fob. Again using the old cupped-hand gesture, he holds a small but unidentifiable manikin. The main figure's right arm is lost; it may have held the foreign-looking shield or pot that rests in his lap. This new emblem, goggle eyes under a tiered and barrel-shaped headdress, becomes specifically associated as a shield emblem with the warrior pair on Stela 31 of Tikal (fig. 33). It will also be used as a main image for the rare monuments displaying insignia rather than portraits. (See Stela 32 of Tikal [fig. 44] and Stela 11 of Yaxha [fig. 43], below.)

On Stela 18, the honored figure sits on a throne that is the same disembodied locative head with a trilobed eye seen on Stela 5 of Uaxactun (fig. 20) but here made large and associated with a mountain or hill (Stuart and Houston 1994, 83–84) and perhaps with water and rain by what looks like a *cauac* sign placed on top of the head. If Stela 18 portrays Curl Snout, then he is shown seated on a place that had been specifically associated with Smoking Frog at Uaxactun.

Uaxactun, Stela 4 (fig. 23)

Stela 4 is a fragment with only a small amount of imagery left, while on the back panel the glyphic text is in better condition (Graham 1986, 5: 141). Its Initial Series date, 8.18.0.0.0 (A.D. 396) is fairly certain. Like Stela 5 of Uaxactun (fig. 20), with which it is associated, it was found *in situ* in front of Structure B-VIII, and it may also mention Smoking Frog in its text on the back panel at B5. Stela 4, then, could have been carved under Smoking Frog's aegis as Schele and Freidel (1990, 153) believe. Laporte and Fialko (1990), however, consider Stela 4 to have been the monument of the man in Burial A-29 at Uaxactun, who they identify as a fraternal nephew of Smoking Frog. Despite the fragmentation, it can be seen that an effort was made to foreground the figure by establishing a level, and visually neutral, background, which is reinforced by the straight edges of a plain wide

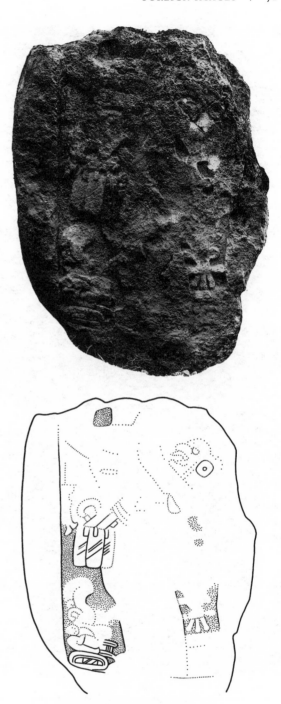

Fig. 23. Uaxactun, Stela 4. (Photo courtesy Peabody Museum, Harvard University, #H-21-2-20. Drawing courtesy Ian Graham.)

Fig. 24. El Zapote, Stela 4.
(Photo courtesy Ian Graham.)

frame. Thus, Stela 4 extends the suggestion of figure on field seen on Stela 5, but its contrasting composition and iconography are intriguing.

The main figure on Stela 4 displays the extroverted gesture along with the cupped-hand gesture to cradle a disembodied head. The figure may wear the long, tubular necklace, but this is not clear. One can see celts pendent from a belt head and the traditional belt fob hanging at the back of the figure's legs. In front of the figure's feet rests an emblematic head similar to the one seen on Stela 5. On the ground line, behind his feet is an unidentifiable object, possibly another disembodied head (see Copeland's drawing), in that it is also portrayed with three projecting bars from its beak. This is the only recognizable icon shared between Stelae 4 and 5. On Stela 4 the costume and regalia are traditional, while the use of the extroverted gesture is new.

In the discussion of this gesture as it is portrayed on Stela 12 of Xultun (fig. 19), it was postulated that the warrior and the extrovert were conceptually connected, perhaps as a kind of iconographic polemic. This seems to be the case for the two monuments associated with Smoking Frog at Uaxactun. The conceptual relationships between Stelae 4 and 5 may not be readily perceived as those of pairing, but there must be some significance to the linking of the foreign costume iconography of a warrior pair to the traditional costume iconography of the extrovert because this describes—and predicts in broad terms—the iconographic program of Stela 31 of Tikal (fig. 33), a stela whose well-preserved text mentions the momentous events that took place in the times Stelae 5 and 4 were erected at Uaxactun. If the disembodied heads at the feet of the main figures functioned as place-names, then the iconographic events depicted on the two stelae may be linked to the same location, just as they are, in fact, linked by proximity to Structure B-VIII. Thus, it would be logical, although not necessarily correct, to suggest that the shared disembodied head referred to the building.[13] If Stela 4 displayed two locative, disembodied heads, then the event signaled by the extroverted gesture may have been performed twice in two different locations.

El Zapote, Stelae 4 (fig. 24) and 7

Stela 4 is in better condition than Stela 7 and has been dated at 8.18.0.0.0 (A.D. 396) (Marcus 1976, 31). If this is the correct dedicatory date, then Stela 4 introduces into Maya plaza imagery, among other things, the iconographic theme of the staff holder. While its date is uncertain, Stela 7 also represents a staff holder and may have been conceived as the pair of Stela 4. They are both remarkable because of their aberrant carving styles, their representation of staff holders, and because of their costume and gestural iconography. Furthermore, Stela 4 may be a portrait of a woman.[14] Very little archaeological information is available to assess their context.

If Stela 4 and 7 are a monumental pair, and if they represent, respectively, a woman and a man, then they predict Stela 5 of the same site depicting a man and a woman paired by the recto-verso field (fig. 35). It is a pairing of opposites, male and female, and while it could be conceptually linked with the ideas behind the paired iconographies associated with the current rulers at Uaxactun and Tikal, it suggests a different kind of opposition, and perhaps a less subtle one.

If the monuments were set up next to each other, they would face one another, with the woman looking to the viewer's right, and the man to the left. They each hold plain, rod-like staffs and are dressed in simple costumes consisting of large—almost enlarged—motifs. The female wears several neck pieces: a chin strap with a medallion precisely like the one worn by Scroll-Ahau-Jaguar on Stela 29 of Tikal (fig. 12), two differently beaded collars, and a long necklace that may be the tubular kind associated with the extroverted gesture. Below this necklace is a braided mat motif that may be attached to it, or may be part of the belt. The mat motif has direct analogies in the later Stelae 9 and 13 of Tikal (figs. 48 and 49), both dating to the 2nd katun of the 9th baktun (A.D. 475). Most of her headdress is lost, except for a pendant hanging with beads spaced along its edge. The male on Stela 7 is dressed similarly but with a shorter skirt. He lacks the many necklaces, especially the tubular beaded one, and the mat motif, and his headdress is a round helmet with a long flap hanging over his left ear and shoulder. It can be directly compared with the headdress worn by the figure of Stela 7 of Tikal (fig. 53), dated to 9.3.0.0.0 (A.D. 495). With his right hand he holds the plain staff, and while it is not clear what he does with his left hand, he may hold a bag or repeat the gesture of the woman.

The woman grasps her staff with her left hand and with her right hand performs the offering gesture also known as the "scattering gesture." If correctly identified, it is another innovation associated with these two stelae.

Here the offering gesture is similar to the flat-hand gesture, but the hand is more realistically rendered with curved fingers and does not support or hold anything. Other than on these two stelae, its next appearance in Maya plaza sculpture is on Stela 27 of Yaxchilan, dating to 9.4.0.0.0 (A.D. 514), and it becomes a major gestural theme during the Late Classic (see Schele and Miller 1986; Love 1987). Outside the Maya area, as discussed in chapter 2, the offering gesture is linked to the costume and regalia worn by the warrior pairs. The gesture also occurs on monuments at Cerro de las Mesas during the Early Classic, where its contextual associations, that is the costuming of the main figure, are closer to those known for the Maya (see below). Thus, the gesture can be associated with the warriors of Stela 5 of Uaxactun, by tracing iconographies outside of the Maya area. When the gesture appears on Stela 4 of El Zapote, it does so in the thematic context of a pair, which may also allude to the warrior but does not in any way visualize the connection.[15]

The carving style, exemplified by Stela 4, is severe with a clear and simple use of planes. The relief cuts outlining the body and costume parts are squared, giving the image a crisp look. Within the outlines, the defined shapes are flat with little interior working. On Stela 4, an exception to this technique is the mat motif, which is modeled in order to make explicit the design of its plaiting. This difference creates a visual focus that suggests a certain importance given to this icon. Although the figure takes up most of the panel space outlined by the frame, the background is a level and distinct plane. The carving style of Stela 7 is difficult to assess because its surface shows greater wear. The relief-cut outlines appear to have been abraded and not square-cut.

On Stela 4 there is an intriguing difference between the styles of carving and outlining used for the glyphs and for the images. The glyphs, carved on the lateral sides of the monument are modeled shapes with abraded edges and intricate interior detailing. Their style is much more the expected one for this period than is the severe planar style of the images.

The disparity in the styles of carving used for image and text emphasizes the already existing differences between image and text and suggests that here they were conceived as a complementary comparison to elicit the same sort of juxtaposition between the new and foreign, and the traditional and ancient seen for the monuments of Curl Snout of Tikal and Smoking Frog of Uaxactun. On Stela 4, the new and foreign iconography and carving style, however, can be fairly certainly aligned to contemporary monuments at Cerro de las Mesas in Veracruz.[16]

Cerro de las Mesas, Veracruz,
Stelae 3, 5, 6, and 8 (figs. 25 and 26)

It may be that the framed and glyphless Stela 3 is the earliest of this group, but such a judgment is tentative until more archaeological work is done at Cerros de las Mesas (see Stirling's 1943 chronological reconstruction).[17] I am assuming, however, that since Stela 9 of Cerro de las Mesas, discussed above with Xultun, Stela 12, is stylistically an 8th-baktun monument, the site was erecting monuments at the time when Stelae 4 and 7 of El Zapote were carved. I do not wish to argue for which direction influence traveled (surely it went both ways), but I do want to suggest that the connections are strong enough to have been the result of direct, historical contact between Cerros de las Mesas and El Zapote.

These four stelae represent an honored figure making a offering gesture. All are panel compositions, and Stelae 5, 6, and 8 include a glyphic text within the main image towards which the figure faces, like the Seattle Stela (fig. 16). Stelae 6 and 8 have Long Count dates, 9.1.12.14.10 (A.D. 468) and 9.4.18.16.8 (A.D. 533), respectively. Nothing can be read on the glyphic panel of Stela 5, and Stela 3 never had one. Stela 3 is the only monument that is framed, and it bears the closest affinity to Stelae 4 (fig. 24) and 7 of El Zapote in terms of carving techniques. However, all these stelae show the enlarged costume and regalia motifs of Stela 4 of El Zapote.

Shared features consist of the carving style, which is aberrant at El Zapote, and the offering gesture new to Maya plaza imagery. The ancient Maya chin-strap medallion and the unusual headdress pendant seen on Stela 4 of El Zapote (and Stelae 29 and 31 of Tikal [figs. 12 and 33], and Stela 1 of Uolantun [fig. 28]) are also shared iconographic features, but they are used differently at Cerro de las Mesas. The medallion is the central motif of the belt assemblage turned upside down from its Maya counterpart. It is clearly rendered on Stelae 6 and 8, and I think it is present on Stela 3, but so enlarged as to make the attribution questionable. Mary Miller (1991, 31) calls this particular motif an "eye." The headdress pendant with beads spaced along its edge can be seen on Stela 6 of Cerro de las Mesas used as a belt pendant ending with a leaf-like point. Here, the beads may have been intended to look as if they fall from the offering hand, even as they are attached to the pendant.

Less specific comparisons should also be mentioned. The figure in Stela 5 of Cerro de las Mesas displays the extroverted gesture seen on the earlier Stela 9 and points downwards with his right hand. This may or may not have been intended as the offering gesture. The figures of Stelae 3 and 8 of Cerro de las Mesas stand on a basal panel carved as a frontal mask. The mask looks like the frontal version of the eyeless profile faces found on Izapan stelae. The basal disembodied heads on Stela 3 of Izapa were compared, above, to the disembodied heads used as locative emblems at Uaxactun, and perhaps a similar function may be assigned to this basal motif at Cerro de las Mesas. The frontal mask as a basal image, however, does not appear in the Maya area until 9.2.18.0.0 (A.D. 493) on Monument 26 of Quirigua (fig. 42).

The severe carving style and the simplified costuming will be taken up by the group of stelae depicting staff holders carved at Tikal after 9.2.0.0.0 (A.D. 475). Coming as they do after the production of Stelae 31, 1, 2, and 28, they represent another major stylistic break in the history of plaza art at Tikal, and one that owes much to Stelae 4 and 7 from El Zapote: the severe carving style, reduced imagery, and the iconography of headdress, staff, and mat motif. Whether the later Tikal patrons were also concerned with Cerro de las Mesas in Veracruz cannot be determined, but the hypothetical link between El Zapote and Cerro de las Mesas, based on carving style and iconography, is a strong one.

El Zapote, Stela 3 (fig. 27)

At this time there is no way to date Stela 3 other than to say that it bears a strong resemblance in its carving style to both Stelae 4 (fig. 24) and 7. It is broken in two pieces near its middle and has suffered from the efforts of looters to saw off its image. The upper part, above the break, looks like the "severe" style of Stela 4, while the lower section has weathered to look like the softer, more abraded, carving of Stela 7. The panel of Stela 3 is surrounded by a strict frame and no imagery overlaps it.

The honored figure is depicted by a broad-profile pose and makes the extroverted gesture. He wears the expected tubular and long necklace. At chest level a jaguar head extends out from under the upraised arm as if from

Fig. 25. Cerro de las Mesas, Veracruz:
A) Stela 3, B)Stela 5.
(Photos courtesy Patrick Clancy.
Drawings by Flora Clancy.)

A

B

A

a belt. It appears to be on top of three pendent celts. If it is a belt head, the belt is worn very high, and there is another belt depicted at waist level. This strangely positioned jaguar head could be a "translation" of the jaguar-paw motif associated with the extroverted gesture, but usually worn pendent from a belt so as to cover the groin of the main figure.

Two disembodied heads rest on the ground line on either side of the figure's feet. The left head is now missing, having been sawn off and looted after the original photograph was taken (Ian Graham, personal communication 1991). Looking at the photograph it is hard to identify the head at the back of the figure's legs, but it certainly wears a glyphic "hat." The head on the right appears to wear as its headdress the Tikal emblem glyph topped with scrolls. There are two locative heads, then, with one almost certainly claiming a location in Tikal.

The extroverted gesture of Stela 3, along with its stylistic similarities to Stelae 4 and 7, could represent a program similar to that of the two monuments associated with Smoking Frog of Uaxactun. First a pair of foreign images is displayed: the recto-verso warrior pair of Stela

B

Fig. 26.   Cerro de las Mesas, Veracruz: A) Stela 6, B) Stela 8.
(Photos courtesy Patrick Clancy. Drawing by Flora Clancy.)

A

B

Fig. 27.   El Zapote, Stela 3,
Front Face A) Top, B) Bottom.
(Photos courtesy Ian Graham.)

5 at Uaxactun (fig. 20) and the paired set of staff holders, Stelae 4 and 7, at El Zapote. This is followed by images of an extrovert who wears traditional costuming: Stela 4 of Uaxactun (fig. 23) and Stela 3 of El Zapote. Iconographically, then, the two stelae of Uaxactun provide precedents for the later Stela 31 of Tikal, while the pair of foreign-looking figures at El Zapote provides the precedent for the stelae of Tikal carved after 9.2.0.0.0 (A.D. 475).

Uolantun, Stela 1 (fig. 28)

Uolantun is a small site, so close to Tikal it could be considered an outlier or "suburb." Stela 1, the only monument found at Uolantun, was erected in front of a pyramidal mound; its top, the supernal image, was anciently recarved to serve as its pedestal. The likelihood of resetting and reuse suggested to Jones and Satterthwaite (1982, 108) that Stela 1 may have been carved elsewhere (Tikal?) and moved to its position at Uolantun. Stela 1 of Uolantun was severely fractured and damaged by looters in the late 1970s, and its pieces are now stored at Tikal (ibid., 106–7).

The Initial Series date as read by Morley (1937–38, 1: 262–66) is the one most commonly accepted, 8.18.13.5.11 (A.D. 409), while Stela 1's dedicatory date is thought to be either 8.19.0.0.0 (A.D. 416) or 9.1.10.0.0 (A.D. 465) by Jones and Satterthwaite (1982, 107–8). Both dates are at the late end of Proskouriakoff's (1950, 104) style range, 8.17.0.0.0 ± 2 katuns.

Stela 1 represents the extrovert in an unframed panel with both the supernal and basal areas defined by motifs: a downward-gazing head at the top, and the lowland version of the "Izapan signature" at the bottom. Given the experimentation and innovation in iconography and carving styles that have been described for the monuments of Tikal, Uaxactun, and El Zapote, Uolantun's Stela 1 is a decidedly conservative monument, specifically drawing on the early iconographies of Stelae 29 and 39 of Tikal (figs. 12 and 18). This may explain why its style graph produced an early date, and also suggests that style cannot be used without question in choosing which dedicatory date, 8.19.0.0.0 or 9.1.10.0.0, is the correct one.

This is an important question because most reconstructions of Tikal's history (following Coggins [1975, 146–47]) consider the figure portrayed on Stela 1 to be a person of the Jaguar Paw dynasty deposed from Tikal at the time when Smoking Frog and Curl Snout were active. If so, the earlier dedicatory date must be correct. The strong iconographic affinities between Stela 1 and Stela

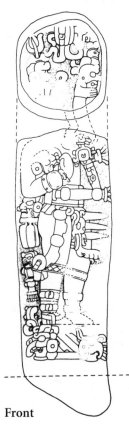

Front   **Back**

31 of Tikal (fig. 33) present another question. If the earlier dedicatory date is accepted, then much of the imagery on the front of Stela 31 was prefigured on Stela 1 of Uolantun. The later dedicatory date would suggest that Stela 1 was not only conservative, but derivative.[18]

Regardless of which date actually reflects the time when the monument was carved, it was carved by a master very much in control of technique and artistry. The outlining cuts and planar distinctions were handled with grace and confidence. The twisting perspective of the articulated costume motifs rendered as frontal and others as profile is done with a conviction that precludes the perception of awkwardness. (This is best seen by looking at the monument itself, or, as must be now, the photographs, because the drawing cannot show how this twisting was actually handled in its dimensional relief.) Whoever the patron of Stela 1 was, he had access to skilled artists.

The figure on Stela 1 lifts high a disembodied head with the extroverted gesture, and cradles another in his right arm with the cupped-hand gesture. His costume includes the distinctive helmet with a bone roach and the chin-strap medallion worn by Scroll-Ahau-Jaguar of Stela 29 (fig. 12). (This is the same chin-strap medallion that was depicted on Stela 4 of El Zapote, and on several stelae from Cerro de las Mesas, there used as a belt medallion.) The head held aloft by the figure on Stela 1 resembles that held by Scroll-Ahau-Jaguar on Stela 29, where it is thought to express his name. From Stela 39 of Tikal (fig. 18) come the long tubular necklace and the jaguar paw pendent from the belt, here looking decidedly phallic. The knee bands seen on Stela 39 are also worn, along with a belt fob and a head with celts on the back of the belt.

If Stela 1 were dedicated at the 8.19.0.0.0 date, this would be the first time the "signature" is used as a basal image for a lowland monument. It is a synthesis and/or a restatement of the old Izapan basal image and the secondary images of the two disembodied heads found at

Fig. 28. Uolantun, Stela 1.
(Photo after Morley 1937–38 V: pl. 66b.
Drawings, front and back, by William Coe
reprinted from *Tikal Reports 33A* by
Jones and Satterthwaite 1982 courtesy
University of Pennsylvania Museum, Philadelphia.)

the feet of Smoking Frog on Stela 4 from Uaxactun (fig. 23). Uolantun's monument depicts the two locative heads as actually joined by an architectonic arrangement of motifs. The head on the (viewer's) right is the locative bird head with the three bars projecting from its beak. The left head wears a twisted and scrolled headdress and may also be the broad-beaked bird.

The supernal head wears the Tikal emblem glyph as a hat. This head is badly worn, but in the drawing published in Jones and Satterthwaite (1982, fig. 76) it does not look like a human head and may represent God K (as did Curl Snout's supernal head on Stela 4 of Tikal) (fig. 21), but here specifically attached to Tikal's polity emblem.

It is not hard to argue that the two heads in the basal panel functioned as locatives for two places conceptually or actually linked by the main figure who stands on them. The three heads in the supernal region, however, are intriguing. The head held aloft to touch the chin of the downward-gazing head may be an ancestor if its "hat" has been properly interpreted as the name, Scroll-Ahau-Jaguar (Stela 29 at Tikal), and more speculatively, the glyph on the matching head to the left could be the main figure's name, if it is part of his headdress. The downward-gazing head with a Tikal place sign as its hat is problematic. It is similar to the Tikal locative at the feet of the main figure on Stela 3 of El Zapote (fig. 27) and, yet, by its position in the panel, it supposedly should refer to an ancestor. Of the known Early Classic stelae, none exhibits in its supernal imagery signs identifiable with an actual site.[19] Much in the carving style, composition, and iconography of Stela 1, found at Uolantun, refers back to earlier monumental works at Tikal—ones that precede the new and foreign images that entered into the plaza around 8.17.0.0.0 (A.D. 376). Iconographic items from the earliest monuments of Tikal and from the southern highlands, such as the basal panel (and, perhaps, the God K head), may represent the same sort of effort to maintain traditional iconographies that was suggested for the extroverts carved on Stela 4 of Uaxactun and Stela 3 of El Zapote. Because of the greater preservation of details on Stela 1 of Uolantun, traditional icons can be identified and specifically traced to Stelae 29 and 39 of Tikal.

The turn of the baktun was just about to happen (or had just happened), and this historical event was not likely to be taken lightly; millenial perturbations (for good or for ill) would have been prevalent. While the very idea of the freestanding Early Classic plaza monument is predicated on a philosophy that engaged the individual and allowed for foreign icons, the return to traditional iconographies suggests, if not a back-lash effect, at least a reaction of some sort to the iconographic extremes represented on Stelae 4 and 18 of Tikal, Stela 5 of Uaxactun, and Stelae 4 and 7 of El Zapote.

Fig. 29.   El Zapote, Stela 1. (Photo courtesy Ian Graham.)

CHAPTER SIX

The Turning of the Baktun

9.0.0.0 to 9.1.0.0 (A.D. 435–55)

El Zapote, Stela 1 (fig. 29)

THE APPEARANCE OF STELA 1 IS UNEXPECTED IN TERMS of the history of Maya plaza monuments up to this point and in terms of what is known about monument production at El Zapote. It displays, within a framed panel, not an honored person, but the anthropomorphic baktun-other, and, for the first time, a main figure is rendered by the profile pose that, up till now, had been reserved for the depiction of bound secondary figures. Everything else suggests a normal public image: the headdress, costume, flat-hand gesture, and basal panel (mostly destroyed) are rendered as if the image were an honored one. With these expected traits there is as well the sense of conservatism displayed on Stela 1 from Uolantun. Even the carving style displays no hint of the "foreign" method seen on the earlier Stelae 3, 4, and 7, except that the background is a well-defined plane. There is a nervous wiry quality to the outlines, to the rendering of the scrolls emanating from the anthropomorph's mouth, and in the detailing of the headdress, but the quality of the line and the rendering of interior details are traditionally Maya in style and akin, in fact, to the manner in which the glyphs are carved on the sides of Stela 4.

The glyphs carved on the back panel give the Initial Series date of 8.19.10.8[?].9 9 Muluc 7 Tzec (A.D. 426). Other dates given in the text could bring the dedicatory date of the stela within a few uinals, or Maya months,

before or after the turning of the baktun. If the glyph supported by the anthropomorph's flat-hand gesture expresses 8 Ahau, then this may refer to the turning of the baktun at 9.0.0.0.0 8 Ahau 13 Ceh (December 8, A.D. 435), but this is not the likely dedicatory date. Coggins' (1990) perception that there was a prohibition against dedicating public monuments to the actual turning of the baktun is probably correct because only a few mention this date in their texts and none is known with certainty to have been dedicated to this millenial date. This is in direct contrast to the practice of dedicating monuments to katun endings, started with Stelae 18 and 19 of Uaxactun eighty years previously.

Despite the supposed dedicatory prohibition, or really because of it, Stela 1 was carved to mark the turning of the baktun by portraying not a human but an anthropomorph wearing the costume of rulership. The image must be metaphoric, showing the baktun-other as "ruler" of the millenial change, but it is not clear why the powers of history (cyclical history) at this particularly potent point in time required the image of an anthropomorph in the guise (costume and context) of the honored human (see Stuart 1996).

Xultun, Stela 20 (fig. 30)

Xultun is another site that was erecting plaza monuments in the Early Classic period, and like El Zapote it

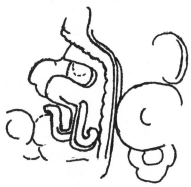

Fig. 30.   Xultun, Stela 20, with Drawing of
Face by Flora Clancy. (Photo and drawing
courtesy Ian Graham.)

lacks archaeological definition. Both sites are at present
understood to be provincial to Tikal and Uaxactun (see
Marcus 1976, 33–35).

Stela 20 of Xultun was carved from a poor-quality
limestone (von Euw and Graham 1984, 5: 70) and has
suffered badly through time. Nonetheless, the published
drawing (ibid., 5: 69) is conservative, and the area around
the head of the figure is left more-or-less featureless but
at the same time suggests a very small and poorly pro-
portioned head within the jaws of a large animal-like
headdress. In the photograph one can see that a curved,
underslung animal jaw matches the animal head, and,
indeed, a line of small beads in front of the earflare
marks the edge of the real headdress. The large round
earflare is in correct proportion only if this reconstruc-

tion of the baktun-other is accepted. Otherwise, it is aberrant and inexplicably large.

Like those of Stela 1 of El Zapote (fig. 29), the imagery and carving techniques are conservative, and the head-dress, costume, regalia, and basal panel are all rendered as if an actual ruler were being portrayed. For Stela 20, however, no frame can be detected for the image. The basal panel is like that of Uolantun, Stela 1 (fig. 28) with two disembodied heads framing a signature structure.

Two things stand out: the panel of glyphs at the lower-left edge of the main image panel, and the extroverted gesture associated with an undulating serpent supported by the baktun- other's left arm, probably in the cupped-hand gesture. A glyph panel within the main image and the undulating serpent are traits associated with monuments from the eastern Maya area, such as the Seattle Stela (fig. 16), Stela 11 from Uxbenka (not discussed in this text), and Stela 35 of Copan (fig. 31). It is necessary to remark, therefore, that while the undulating serpent appears at Xultun well outside its expected realm to the east and the south, there is a strong possibility that it was perceived as regalia proper to the turning of the baktun. Given certain similarities to the Uolantun stela—the gesture, the basal panel, and the conservative style—the undulating serpent/ceremonial bar might be another "millenial" reminder of the more traditional alignments (historical, cultural, and probably economic ones as well) to the south and east held by the Jaguar Paw dynasty. Because of its antiquity, the undulating serpent may also have been used to evoke a sense of the inherent originating powers in the turn of the baktun.

The first glyph of the main panel text of Stela 20 is prefixed by the number 6. This could be 6 Ahau, perhaps marking the first katun after the turn, 9.1.0.0.0 6 Ahau 13 Yaxkin.[1] Stephen Houston (1986, 8) reconstructs the Initial Series date on the left side of Stela 20 as 9.0.0.0.0 8 Ahau 13 Ceh. While these glyphs are very worn, at Cp11 a reference to the completion of the 9th baktun is fairly clearly expressed. Like Stela 1 from El Zapote (fig. 29), however, it is unlikely the Xultun stela was actually dedicated to 9.0.0.0.0, but it is not surprising that this date is important to its text.

Copan, Stela 35 (fig. 31)

Stela 35 is a stela fragment that only shows the figural image from chest to ankles. The top and bottom parts are missing as well as the edges, which have been battered, chipped, and broken. The piece was found within Struc-

ture 4 of the Main Plaza and may have been involved in the dedicatory rituals performed in its construction, because the stela, by style, is earlier than the construction of the building. No glyphs remain on the fragment, so, based on stylistic assessment, Baudez (1983, 186–87, 190) considers this monument to be of late-8th-baktun date and no later than 9.0.0.0.0 (A.D. 435).

The image represents a recto-verso pair shown in the same, but reversed, articulated-profile pose. Both figures hold an undulating serpent by the ceremonial-bar gesture and wear similar, but not identical, costumes. The carving and outlining of the relief are a mixture of planar levels and modeling with engraved lines providing rich textural details. An ornate and complex image results from the complete delineation of costume motif and detail. Despite the attention to detail, however, the sculptor(s) worked to create visual contrasts (or tensions). The intense detail of the skirt contrasts with the clear sweep of the legs, and the arched bow of the serpent, made prominent by its planar level, is contrasted to the easier curves of the belt and its pendent attachments. The quality and feeling of the piece are exuberant and expressive. While Stela 35 represents the recto-verso pair in traditional costume, it is not a derivative work, and it occurs at the beginning of a corpus of plaza images at Copan that are distinctive for their iconography and carving style.

Baudez (ibid.) sees as much influence from the southern Preclassic traditions of iconography as he does for iconographic affinities with contemporary lowland monuments.[2] Compositionally, however, the piece is closer to the lowland development of the recto-verso field in that the paired images are identical in regalia and pose and similar in costume, but pictured as the reverse of one another.

The undulating serpent held by the ceremonial-bar gesture is rendered more like the serpents of Stela 20 of Xultun (fig. 30) and Stela 11 of Uxbenka. Later bars at Copan will be rendered as "flaccid," like the curved bar represented on the Leiden Plaque (fig. 14). While the flaccid body is characteristic of Late Classic monuments from the eastern and southeastern Maya areas, the coiling serpent may be related to the turn of the baktun and the baktun-other. With the heads of the figures from Stela 35 missing, it is possible to speculate that one might be the grotesque head of the baktun-other, and the other, rendered as human, because such a recto-verso pair is so depicted on the later Stela 5 of Copan (ca. 9.13.15.0.0 [A.D.

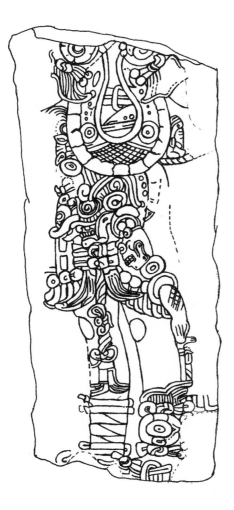

Fig. 31.   Copan, Stela 35, Recto-verso. (Drawings by Flora Clancy after photos in Baudez 1983: 188-89.)

706]). If so, Yax-K'uk-Mo', or his son, was represented in this recto-verso portrait as paired to, or as a twin of, the baktun-other, and if this reconstruction is correct, the use of the recto-verso composition clarifies the implied relationship between human ruler and baktun-other seen in the other monuments discussed above.[3]

The way the knees are indicated as modeled circles on Stela 35 is intriguing. This odd trait continues at Copan well into the Late Classic period.[4] Because of their continued use, knee circles, at least originally, may have been more than a stylistic mannerism, and when they were carved in Stela 35, carried a particular iconographic meaning. As Baudez (ibid.) would have predicted, contemporary comparisons for this feature come from the southern highland site of Kaminaljuyu whose Stelae 4

and 19 depict a very active figure wrestling with a coiling serpent. The figure is not human; it has a grotesque face, claws for feet, and knobby knees. Because they are repeated on two monuments from Kaminaljuyu, the knobby knees appear to be important iconic traits for the narrative theme of the struggle, and provide another reason for suggesting that the original imagery of Stela 35 depicted the baktun-other.

Uaxactun, Stela 26 (fig. 32)

Only outlines remain to allow for the reconstruction the image carved on Stela 26 as isotropic in composition— a depiction of a fully frontal figure holding a ceremonial bar by the symmetrical gesture. Although the front is badly worn and damaged, perhaps intentionally effaced

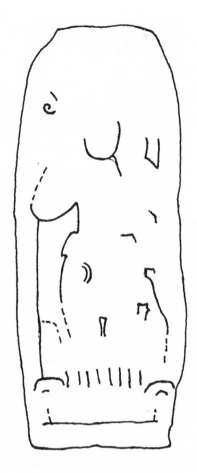

Fig. 32.   Uaxactun, Stela 26.
(Drawing after Sharer 1994, fig. 14.1.)

(Morley 1937–38, 1: 182; A. L. Smith 1950, 23), the back panel clearly shows an Initial Series Long Count date, 9.0.10.0.0 7 Ahau 3 Yax (A.D. 445), that is also considered the dedicatory date. Despite the poor condition of its imagery, the date of Stela 26, where it was found, and its isotropic composition deserve discussion. Stela 31 of Tikal (fig. 33) bears the same Initial Series date and was disposed of in a manner similar to that used for Stela 26 of Uaxactun. At Uaxactun, there is some evidence to suggest when the stela was buried.

Stela 26 was found buried within the early construction phases of Structure A-V when it consisted of three structures facing into a court, signaling its ritual functions. Stela 26 was axially centered in front of a flight of stairs giving entrance to the court (A. L. Smith 1950, 23).

Shortly after its erection, Stela 26, with its front, back, and sides painted red, was buried beneath a fourth temple added to the original three that defined the court (Morley 1937–38, 1: 179–81). Stela 22, dated 9.3.10.0.0 (A.D. 505), was directly associated with this later construction phase.[5] This means that the public life of Stela 26 would have been no longer than seventy years or so. If this reconstruction of events is correct, then the ruinous condition of Stela 26 has to be the result of intentional defacement because the early burial of monuments usually preserves them, as was the case for Stela 31 of Tikal. We are not sure who erected Stela 26, but Laporte and Fialko (1990, 57) suggest that the person in Burial A-31, placed directly in front of Stela 26, ruled at Uaxactun while Stormy Sky (Stela 31) ruled at Tikal.

The use of an isotropic composition on Stela 26 represents its first known monumental use in about six hundred years, but it is hard to imagine that the sculptors of Uaxactun were somehow familiar with La Venta's monuments (Stelae 1 and 2) to call them up as prototypes. One can more reasonably suggest that the ruler was emulating the stucco works composed isotropically that so beautifully defined the surfaces of the older public buildings of Uaxactun (Valdés 1986, 1987). Curl Snout of Tikal tried something like this with his Stelae 4 and 18 (figs. 21 and 22) but not with the same apparent conviction. Again, the possibility of Olmec-styled heirlooms may also have suggested such a composition, but the fact remains that, as with the much earlier Stela 10, the sculptors and patrons of Uaxactun resurrect or, more likely, originate a new compositional strategy for plaza art in the Early Classic, and they do so at the turn of the baktun. The connotations of this new composition and its iconographic contexts are intriguing and, as described below, may allow us to speculate that the visage of Stela 26 was that of the baktun-other.

During the 8th baktun, the symmetrical ceremonial-bar gesture had limited use, appearing on the non-monumental Leiden Plaque (fig. 14) where it is enacted by both the main figure and the bound secondary figure, and on Tikal's Stela 39 (fig. 18) where it is adopted by only the bound figure in the basal image. It is likely that this gesture appears on Stela 35 of Copan (fig. 31), which may have been carved earlier than Stela 26, but by no more than ten years. During the 8th baktun, then, this gesture is associated with bound figures and with non-monumental contexts. It is not until the turn of the baktun that it is appropriated for the plaza monument's display of the honored figure.[6]

The implications of the isotropic compositional mode and symmetrical gesture are that the ruler of Uaxactun had himself portrayed as outside of the "normal" events and actions of royal plaza display; nonetheless, his image can engage the viewer with a direct and frontal gaze (Schapiro 1973). While we have seen imaging strategies such as the representation of foreign regalia and costuming, and even carving styles that proclaimed a difference and perhaps effected a disconnection between the realm of the viewer and that of the image (see Andrea Stone 1989), Stela 26, in establishing an isotropic other-worldly difference, can do so by maintaining a connection with the viewer through frontal confrontation. Given the conflicts between old and new that had been, and were, occurring at the time Stela 26 was carved, the employment (deployment?) of the isotropic image is a brilliant solution that supports *both* the portrayal of difference as other-worldliness or, perhaps, even as the baktun-other, and the connection with the viewer necessary for a plaza monument.[7]

Uaxactun, Pedestal 3

Found within the fill that buried Stela 26 was the fragment of a cylindrical pedestal displaying a quatrefoil frame and the remains of a profile figure seated cross-legged. This fragment used to be called the Altar of Stela 26 (Proskouriakoff 1950, 106) because of its proximity to the stela. Whether it was originally paired with Stela 26 cannot be determined, and may explain why Ian Graham (1986, 5: 126) gave it its own number.

Within the quatrefoil frame, the figure is shown seated on a cushion-throne engraved with braided matting. The figure's arm extends forward and seemingly disappears into serpent forms within which can be seen a small hand emerging from the forehead of a grotesque head to touch a *kin* (day or sun) glyph. The seated figure is likewise surrounded by scrolling forms, small heads, and what may be a cartouche or shield-like frame just before its face. Not much more sense can be made of this imagery.

Pedestal 3 represents the seated figure emblematically, referring to the figures in the serpent jaws of the ceremonial bar, but this does not exclude the possibility that it *also* represents a historical figure or ancestor, but now in a context evocative of the earth or underworld. The quatrefoil frame, the seated pose, the throne, and the orientation of the monument itself all intimate that the image belongs to the chthonic realm.

There is an effort to create a smooth surface and an evenly shaped monument evident on Pedestal 3 that is not evident on the previous monuments of Uaxactun. Of course, we have no idea what Stela 26 looked like originally, and it too may have been as "finished" as the little fragment of Pedestal 3.

Tikal, Stela 31 (fig. 33)

Broken at its base, Stela 31 was found reset in a shallow pit in the rear room of Structure 5D-33-2nd, a building fronting the North Acropolis on its north-south axis. It was buried by construction fill when the building was enlarged to become Structure 5D-33-1st (W. Coe 1990, 508–9). Traces of red paint were found in the surface depressions on the back side of the stela (Jones and Satterthwaite 1982, 64). The cylindrical Pedestal 19 (fig. 34), in a somewhat more fragmented condition, was also found in this fill and is thought to have been originally paired with Stela 31 (ibid.; W. Coe 1990, 523). The circumstances of Stela 31's deposition are similar to those of Stela 26 from Uaxactun except that it was not effaced, and since Structure 5D-33-1st was constructed much later in time than the structure that covered the Uaxactun stela, we cannot know as precisely when Stela 31 was removed from the public domain of the plaza and put into the temple of Structure 5D-33-2nd. William Coe (ibid.) suggests that Stela 31 either stood with Pedestal 19 in front of Structure 5D-33-2nd or that Stela 31 was originally centered in front of the stair leading to Structure 5D-33-3rd (ibid., 503, 509).

In any case, because of the burial of Stela 31, its image and long glyphic text are in excellent condition, with only the bottom parts missing. Since its discovery in 1960, its images and text have formed a basic document for all reconstructions of Tikal's Early Classic history, and, by extension, Maya Early Classic history in general. On the back panel of the stela the text begins with an Initial Series date, 9.0.10.0.0 7 Ahau 3 Yax (A.D. 445), marking a period-ending event celebrated by Stormy Sky of Tikal, the assumed patron of the monument. The textual narrative then goes back in time to the period around 8.14.0.0.0 (A.D. 317) in order to recount certain early events and rulers of Tikal. The latest date that can be read in the narrative is 9.0.3.9.18 (A.D. 439), which is followed by a distance number that is now incomplete because of the loss of the bottom of the stela. Jones and Satterthwaite (1982, 66, 73) suggest a final date of 9.0.14.15.15 or 9.0.11.5.17. These dates are later by a few years than the Initial Series date of 9.0.10.0.0 that is nonetheless taken to be the dedicatory date (ibid.).

The stela is carved on all of its four faces. The front face shows Stormy Sky, identified by his name glyph in his headdress (Coggins 1975, 184–85), standing in a broad-profile pose holding aloft a headdress with the extroverted gesture. With his other arm in the cupped-hand gesture he holds the JC head with the Tikal emblem glyph as its headdress. Above him in the supernal realm is a downward-gazing head. Stormy Sky may have stood upon a basal panel, but this part of the stela is missing.

Stormy Sky's pose and costume are traditional and carry specific references to the plaza monuments of earlier rulers at Tikal, rulers *before* his supposed father, Curl Snout (Jones and Satterthwaite 1982, 68). The bone-roach helmet with the small scrolled head at its front, the rope descending in front of the ear to hold the chin-strap medallion, and the disembodied JC head with the Tikal emblem glyph are each specific quotations from Stela 29 and the costume of Scroll-Ahau-Jaguar (fig. 12). Stormy Sky's pose, his belt with the extended heads and pendent celts, and his long tubular necklace may have been inspired by Stela 39, Jaguar Paw (fig. 18).

The headdress held up by the extroverted gesture is very similar in design to that worn by the figure depicted on the Leiden Plaque. The fancy chain that hangs from its earflare assemblage, however, shows a marked affinity with the headdresses worn by the figures on "Altar" 1 from Polol (fig. 7) and with the small female(?) on Altar 13 from Abaj Takalik (fig. 9): both late Preclassic monuments. The headdress held in the upraised hand of Stormy Sky may have been the one worn by Jaguar Paw on Stela 39, but of course this is speculative.[8] What does seem clear, however, is that like Uolantun Stela 1 (fig. 28), the front face of Stela 31 is dedicated to recalling early plaza "portraits" and traditional affiliations with peoples to the south and east. Much of the surviving text on the back of the stela tells of the two early rulers whose costume and pose Stormy Sky emulated: Scroll-Ahau-Jaguar of Stela 29 and Jaguar Paw of Stela 39.

Curl Snout, Stormy Sky's father, and Smoking Frog of Uaxactun are also mentioned in the narrative, specifically connected with the events and date of 8.17.1.4.12, which is the Long Count date given on Stela 5 of Uaxactun (fig. 20). While nothing of Curl Snout's iconographic choices for public imagery appears on the front of Stela 31, he is generally identified with the supernal head because his name glyph supposedly gives form to the headdress: a saurian creature with crossed bands in his eyes and a long, curled snout (Coggins 1975, 186; 1979b, 265).

The little supernal creature is shown with the sun god's square eye, three dots on its cheek, and a human hand substituting for its lower jaw. Its little arm, drawn with the cupped-hand gesture, holds a sinuous serpent with a glyph in its open mouth. If this is Curl Snout, now dead, he has been apotheosized *and* "traditionalized" by his son. In the two public monuments thought to be commissioned by Curl Snout, Stelae 4 and 18 (figs. 21 and 22), he never showed himself in traditional costumes or poses, but here he holds the ancient, sinuous serpent and is accoutered and costumed appropriately for his status as ancestor. For these reasons alone, it would be fair to question the supernal figure's identification with Curl Snout, especially because the identifying headdress looks similar in its outlines to the one worn by the supernal head on Stela 29 (fig. 12).

More reasonably, Curl Snout has also been identified with the warrior pair carved on the sides of Stela 31 (Schele and Freidel 1990, 159), and, indeed, the texts above these two figures' heads mention him in long, undated, phrases. The two sides are designed to complement the traditional imagery of the front by representing the new and foreign imagery of the warrior.

The warrior pair carved on the sides of the stela is directly related to the recto-verso warriors carved on Stela 5 of Uaxactun (fig. 20) in that they are reversed views of the same pose, gesture, and regalia. The lateral figures on Stela 31 are shorter than Stormy Sky by about a head and are simply and elegantly dressed in similar, but not identical, costumes of the inter-regional warrior. They wear beaded and feathered helmets, bead and pecten shell necklaces, and fringed knee bands. Thick cloth belts are tied with a large knot in the front, and at the back support a round medallion and pendent furry tails. Each holds an atlatl in the right hand and a square decorated shield in the left. Since they are reversed images, the figure carved on the (viewer's) right side displays the shield decoration, while the other figure carries the shield on his far arm so that only the back of the shield is seen while the atlatl is in the foreground. The shield is decorated with the emblematic goggle-eyed head wearing a "tassel" headdress that evocative of Mexican imagery, especially that of Teotihuacan (Millon 1973; 1988), and is one of the major reasons for historical reconstructions that posit emissaries or mercenaries from Teotihuacan present in Tikal at this time (W. Coe 1965; Coggins 1979a, 1979b).

The murals painted in family or clan compounds at Teotihuacan reveal that this tassel headdress is worn by

A

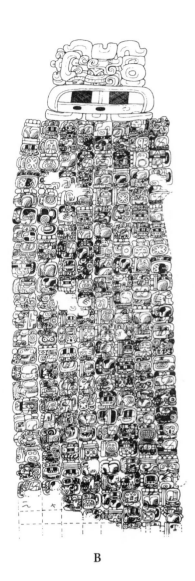

B

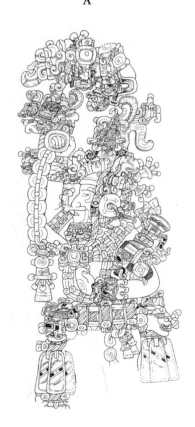

Fig. 33.   Tikal, Stela 31: A) Front, B) Back,
C) Left Side, and D) Right Side.
(Photos courtesy Patrick Clancy.
Drawings of all four sides by William Coe
reprinted from *Tikal Reports 33A* by Jones and
Satterthwaite 1982 courtesy University of
Pennsylvania Museum, Philadelphia.)

C

D

the Storm God and human-like warriors, and is also associated with the Great Goddess (Millon 1988, 122–24). The Storm God's attributes are goggle eyes, while the Great Goddess is associated with the offering gesture and bountiful hands. In the Maya area, the shield emblem consisting of the goggle eyes and the tassel headdress becomes the main image for two stelae, one at Tikal (Stela 32 [fig. 44]) and one at Yaxha (Stela 11 [fig. 43]), both probably carved shortly after Stela 31.[9]

Clara Millon (1973, 1988) suggests that the shield insigne carved on the right side of Stela 31 was that of a military sect or sodality existing throughout Mesoamerica during the Early Classic period, and because of its iconography there is little question that it is of Mexican origin. It is notable, however, that its use on monuments in a public plaza is a Maya trait, not a Mexican one, where most images of the warrior, the Storm God, or the Great Goddess—all part of this iconographic complex—are found in private contexts, such as interiors of compounds or tombs, or as private ceramic goods.

Two things make the reversed and similarly dressed figures carved on the sides of Stela 31 different from one another: their headdresses and their height. The figure displaying the shield decoration is at least half a head shorter than his reversed mate, and his headdress is a beaded or shell-spangled helmet with a floret medallion in the front and a beaded ear and chin guard that extends in front of his face to cover his mouth. The taller figure's headdress is beaded but lacks the chin guard and is configured like an animal's head with large ears and a long and fanged upper jaw that extends beyond his forehead. Clara Millon (1988, 127) identifies this animal as a coyote, but it looks like a feline head with a bird's eye and wing or tail feathers. This is the same headdress worn by Curl Snout on Stela 4 (fig. 21), along with the same pecten shell necklace. It is also comparable to depictions of the inter-regional warrior on the murals of Zacuala, Teotihuacan, and to the Feathered Feline mural in the de Young collection in San Francisco (see Millon 1988, pl. 32). The helmet-like headdress of the shorter figure can be directly compared to the beaded helmets worn by the inter-regional warriors as they are depicted at Monte Alban on the Plain Stela and Stela 7, and in the murals of Burial 105. The helmet is also worn by the paired warriors from Tres Islas (Stelae 1 and 3 [figs. 39 and 41]) in the Pasion area of Guatemala, to be discussed below. If the top part of Curl Snout's second public monument, Stela 18, were ever found, it would not be surprising if he were depicted wearing the beaded helmet.

The helmet-like headdress is not really common at Teotihuacan. Although it is described as a "Teotihuacan-style" helmet with a chin guard by Clara Millon (1988, 127), only one published example is evident in the murals of Teotihuacan, the murals from Zone 11 (see A. Miller 1973, figs. 149 and 150) and these headdresses lack the chin guard. Otherwise, the beaded or spangled helmet is known from pottery, and this, too, rarely, such as the mold-impressed bowl from Calpulapan (Kubler 1967, fig. 41; Millon 1988, 125, fig. V.14).

On the Calpulapan Bowl, the spangled helmet with a chin guard is worn by three figures in procession, led by a figure wearing the tassel headdress. A very similar procession is carved on the Plain Stela of Monte Alban where two figures wear the helmet with chin guard, one figure wears the tassel headdress, and, interestingly, one figure wears the spangled or beaded feline (or coyote) head with bird eye. Both headdresses, then, worn by the recto-verso pair on Stela 31, belong to the iconography of the inter-regional warrior sect or sodality, as do their costumes and the weapons they hold. Creating differences in the height of paired figures, whether they portray the warrior or not, however, is a distinction made at Monte Alban and in the Maya area, and, as far as I know, not at Teotihuacan.[10] At Monte Alban in Tomb 104, and on the Lápida de Bazan, the pairs of figures are distinguished by differences in height, and in the tomb, by age as well: the larger figure displays traits of old-age. The pairs may exhibit similarities in gesture, costume, or pose, but at the same time complement one another with their differences. It is a visual dichotomy, a visual parallelism, where two images at first glance look alike but after more careful scrutiny are discovered to be different in significant ways.

The sides of Stela 31 differ from the front image in iconography and in compositional field, but all three sides are carved in the same graphic style, utilizing a complex combination of carving techniques: planar relief between costume elements and overlapping body parts, abrasion of edges and cushioning of planes where the relief is too shallow to allow planar distinction, modeling of all heads and faces, and delicate incision for interior details and texture. Besides this, the major outlines of the three figures are cut directly back to the smoothed background plane and create a silhouetted image. This technique is more obvious, of course, on the sides because the compositional field presents simpler and clearer relationships within the imagery and between the image and its background.

The juxtaposition of two different compositional fields for Stela 31 is so striking that, along with the very different costume and regalia iconography, it is easy to understand how the sides have been called Mexican in style, even though they are clearly carved by the same hand or hands that carved the front. It is equally clear that this striking contrast between compositional mode and iconography was intentional on the part of the patron and sculptor(s). At the simplest level of interpretation, it places the traditional image of Stormy Sky in the middle and up front, while aligning his image with the new warrior pair and with, perhaps, new ideas about plaza portraiture.

Part of what makes Stela 31 so provocative is its complexity of conception. Its composition combines the wraparound field with the recto-verso field and by doing so opens up the possibilities for multiple interpretations. The two warriors paired by the recto-verso field have a clear precedent in Stela 5 of Uaxactun (fig. 20), and the text on the back of Stela 31 specifically refers to the date and event celebrated by the Uaxactun monument. This connection between the two monuments was certainly not an obscure one at the time Stela 31 was carved and may well have been easily appreciated as common knowledge, but why create the ambiguity inherent in the recto-verso field—are they two images as one, or one image as two—and why further complicate meaning by implicating the recto-verso pair in a wraparound scene?

The wraparound compositional field used on Stela 31 may be an innovation for Early Classic public monuments.[11] Whether it is or is not, the combining of the two fields is unique and unprecedented. What should be emphasized is that the wraparound field was ancient and could have been understood by the patron and the sculptor as evocative of long ago, half-forgotten, times. Equally possible, however, is that they had no knowledge of this ancient field and reinvented it. Given the overall brilliance exhibited in Stela 31, this also seems quite feasible.

The wraparound composition is used to convey the sense of a scene. No frames separate the three figures in the scene; only the angles around which the scene is "wrapped" make such a suggestion. Still, the outer edges of Stormy Sky's costume bend around the angles, and the implication is strong that this is a scene of a figure flanked by two attendants. Such a scene in itself is not without precedent, but comparisons take us again to Monte Alban (the mural in Tomb 104 [see Clancy 1983]) and Teotihuacan, where three-figure scenes are portrayed in the murals (Kubler 1967, 7, 10, fig. 45), and where the attendant figures are costumed as the warriors

described above or closely related personages holding ritual bags, which could be atlatls held by their wrist straps, and displaying the offering gesture (see especially the mural from Techinantla, Teotihuacan discussed by Millon [1988, 114–21, pls. 39–41]).

Stela 31 is extraordinary, certainly in its evidence of carving skills, but perhaps even more so in its conception. Ostensibly, its conception was based on an effort to bring together the old, traditional image of rulership with the newer image of the warrior pair and its associations to things foreign and, indeed, Coggins (1979b, 265) has characterized Stela 31 as Stormy Sky's objective synthesis of the two cultures, Maya and Mexican. However, synthesis cannot be said to occur at the iconographical level. Maya and Mexican icons are juxtaposed, brought together on one monument, but they are clearly separated between the front (Maya) and sides (Mexican) of the monument so that their differences are, in fact, highlighted. It is only through the more formal strategies of interweaving the compositional schema of recto-verso and wraparound fields that any kind of synthesis can be said to take place: a synthesis whose purpose might have been to clarify (or subvert) the meaningful relationships between old and new, foreign and local, father and son.

The theme of juxtaposing old and new, Maya and foreign, has been noted for the monuments of Curl Snout of Tikal and those of Smoking Frog from Uaxactun where differing gestures and costume iconographies signaled the juxtaposition of old and new. The carvers of Stelae 4 and 7 of El Zapote created stylistic and graphic differences to emphasize the iconographic ones. None of the earlier instances has the complexity or confidence of Stela 31, but their existence shows that there was a fairly general perception that the coming together of the Maya with other, foreign peoples (the Mexican) and the ideas and economies this engendered had somehow to be understood and promoted within the plaza.[12]

Tikal, Pedestal 19 (fig. 34)

Pedestal 19, if not originally paired with Stela 31, is thought to have been carved during the reign of Stormy Sky because his name glyph appears in the lower-left of the fragmented surface (Jones and Satterthwaite 1982, 81). The carving styles of the two monuments are similar, but the techniques of creating the relief are not the same. A greater amount of abrading, modeling, and cushioning, with fewer planar distinctions, was used for carving Pedestal 19, and there is no evidence that the outside edges of the images were silhouetted against the

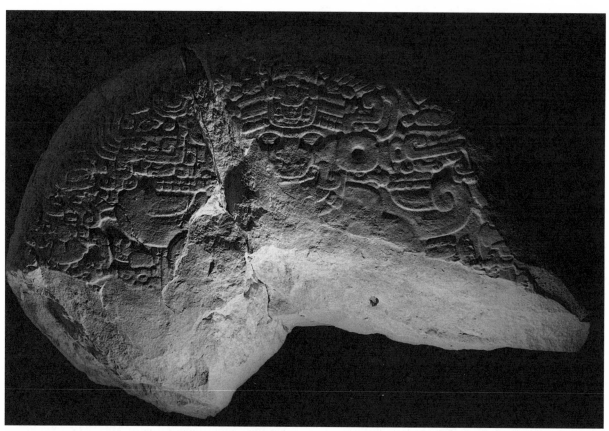

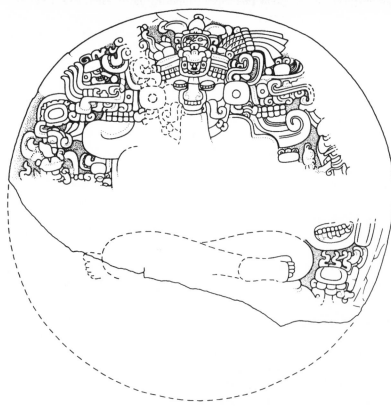

Fig. 34.   Tikal, Pedestal 19, Top.
(Photo courtesy University of
Pennsylvania Museum,
Philadelphia, #63-4-1445.
Drawing by William Coe reprinted
from *Tikal Reports 33A* by
Jones and Satterthwaite 1982
courtesy University of
Pennsylvania Museum,
Philadelphia.)

background. In fact, there is almost no background visible on the top surface.

Originally a finely shaped cylinder, Pedestal 19 is now four fragments, and a little less than half of the cylinder is lost. A fully frontal figure seated with crossed legs is represented on the circular top surface. Judging by the head and arms of the figure, it looks like the baktun-other with large bulging eyes in round sockets, high cheek bones, a broad flat nose, and curls coming from the corners of its mouth. Two saurian-like arms are bent at the elbows and uplifted to either side of the frontal face. They end with upturned "hands" as stylized serpent heads with boneless, wavy fingers protruding like tongues. Each "hand" supports an emblem with a single bead, or the sign for the number one: on the viewer's left, a disembodied head, and on the right, a glyph shape with a double-scrolled superfix. Many more glyphic emblems surround the seated figure, including the name glyph of Stormy Sky.

The full-frontal presentation is not, as might be expected, bilaterally symmetrical. There are too many asymmetries in the headdress, the different angles of the upturned "hands," and the various surrounding emblems to achieve an isotropic composition. Perhaps an allusion to the isotropic theme of timelessness and godliness was intended, along with the tension created between such an allusion and the actuality of the compositional mode.

The periphery of Pedestal 19 is lenticular and carved with images of binding: a circumferential rope and four braided knots hold in place eight ovular emblems (fruit-like, seed-like, heart-like?). Four lappets, carved to look as if they hang from the top of the pedestal to lie over the rope and emblems of the periphery, are decorated with glyphs that look like day-sign cartouches. On the periphery, then, like the earlier Pedestal 13 (fig. 13), there is a four-part, repetitional symmetry in the context of binding: four braided knots, four lappets with day signs, and eight repeated emblems.

The question remains whether the seated figure on the top of Pedestal 19 was intended to represent the baktun-other. The few representations known are usually depicted as active, asymmetrical figures (including the Late Classic dancers on Stelae A and C from Quirigua), which might explain the need for asymmetry. The allusion to the isotropic mode, however, may have been aligned to the traditional and sacred context of binding and four-part divisions supplied by the periphery. If Pedestal 19 were a mate for Stela 31, then the stela's themes of juxtaposing and composing the old and new, Maya and foreign, were shown to be empowered by the turning of the baktun and millenial change. In a sense, what could have

been disturbingly new is shown to be a different, but expectable, manifestation of events occurring because of and within the turning of the baktun.

El Zapote, Stela 5 (fig. 35)

Several stelae from the site of El Zapote have been described as having intriguing similarities with stelae from Cerro de las Mesas in terms of composition, carving style, and iconography. Only traces of this connection can be seen on Stela 5, but efforts to integrate disparate images and ideas are obvious strategies behind the composition and iconography of the stela.

Carved recto-verso, Stela 5 breaks with the expected representation of reversed but similar figures. It presents two figures in similar and reversed poses but here as male and female, each portrayed by a very different costume and regalia. The carving style is consistent, but the differences from one face to the other in the use of background space, framing strategies, and detailing of costume are of the same kind seen between the sides and front of Stela 31 of Tikal.

On what I presume to have been the front, or recto, face is portrayed a simply dressed male wearing a large grotesque mask as a headdress. A plain background allows a projection and clear locus for the figure, which is also surrounded by a neatly cut, plain frame. In the simple clarity of the male figure, it is possible to see traces of the earlier angular and severe images of El Zapote, especially Stela 7, that were comparable to the monuments of Cerro de las Mesas.

Because of damage done to the stela, by breakage and modern sawing, we cannot be sure what kind of regalia the male holds. We might suppose that the now-lost right hand, the one closest to the viewer, held a bag. Small bags held by straps are not yet common hand-held regalia for Classic Maya public imagery, but after 9.2.0.0.0 (A.D. 475) the Early Classic staff holder is usually portrayed holding a bag (see Stela 7 from Tikal [fig. 53]). The male on Stela 5 almost certainly holds a staff in his left (far) hand. In front of the figure's chest is a grotesque head wearing a glyphic "hat" topped by an arching form. This head compares directly with the heads that bind the tripartite staff held by Jaguar-Paw-Skull on Stela 3 of Tikal (fig. 51), dated 9.2.13.0.0 (A.D. 488), and it seems a likely reconstruction for the type of staff held by the male figure. If so, its appearance on Stela 5 of El Zapote is the first visible record of the tripartite staff, an item of regalia with a subsequent and long history in the plaza art of Tikal, lasting into the 10th baktun (Stela 11).

On the verso side, a richly dressed figure in a female costume stands in the same but reversed broad-profile pose as her male counterpart. The netted female costume constructed from long beads and round beads is made into a capelet and a skirt that falls to mid-calf. The rendering of the beads in low relief creates a closely patterned background for other beaded costume elements, such as the collar with a central head medallion, and the belt with front and back heads each with pendants that hang to the bottom edge of the netted skirt. The figure's headdress consists of several images: an anthropomorphic, long-lipped head with its own beaded headband to which is attached several graphemic components. One of these is a quadripartite emblem (see Kubler 1967, 33ff.; Greene Robertson 1974) that is closely comparable to the one found in the headdress of Stela 2 of Tikal (fig. 37). The plain frame that surrounds the faceted, patterned, and detailed image of the female is narrow and as visibly obscured by the overlapping images as is most of the background space.

The female's near arm and hand supports by the flat-hand gesture a square cartouch within which lies a little figure on its back, and on which rests the "Mexican year sign" (trapeze and ray sign) qualified by the number 12. Below the hand, but likely part of this piece of regalia, is a pendant shaped as a geometricized serpent head tipped by a large round bead. This item of regalia is remarkable and rare, and here it is held by the flat hand with its suggestion that it "supports" an idea rather than actual objects.

Marcus (1976, 39–41, 117, 120, 159) discusses the little reclining figure and identifies it as a lineage emblem, the "scroll baby," by noting its rather restricted occurrences on Stela 5, and on Stelae 1, 31, and 26 of Tikal, and in the hieroglyphic text of the now-lost Early Classic mural of Uaxactun.[13] The squared cartouch is held to be a sign of Mexican influence during the much later Epiclassic period beginning in the 9th century; within the Early Classic there are no other examples known. A comparison can be made with the cartouched glyphs with pendants carved on the stone cylinders known as Altars 9 and 10 of Kaminaljuyu (see Parsons 1988), and another could be made with Stelae 4 and 15 from Cerro de las Mesas. These last two monuments, however, are difficult to date. The best connection seems to be to Late Preclassic monu-

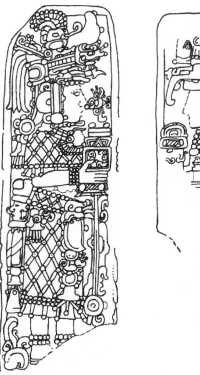

Fig. 35.   El Zapote, Stela 5, Recto-verso.
(Photo of back courtesy Ian Graham. Drawings by
Flora Clancy after Easby and Scott 1970, #170.)

ments from Abaj Takalik. Altar 13 (fig. 9) of that site displays two squared cartouches surrounding crossed bands, each with pendant forms similar to those of Altars 9 and 10 of Kaminaljuyu and with the item of regalia held by the woman of Stela 5 at El Zapote. On the Abaj Takalik pedestal, the two cartouches emanate from the mouth of a supernal head of the large beaked bird and enframe a now-missing image. Just below one cartouche and pendant is a female wearing a netted skirt.

That the squared cartouche carries connotations of foreignness (Mexican) is emphasized by the appended Mexican year sign. On Late Classic monuments this sign is most often used as an insigne in headdress assemblages. Like the square cartouch, there are no other known plaza occurrences of the year sign during the Early Classic, although it figures in the iconography of the painted ceramics found in Burial 10 (for Curl Snout) at Tikal, dated a few years earlier (Coggins 1975, 146ff.). Coggins (1983) discusses the appearances of this sign as evidence of Teotihuacan expansion. Her argument, following Adrian Digby (1974), is that the Mexican year sign represents an astronomical instrument for measuring solar movements that the Teotihuacanos acquired from the Zapotecs of Monte Alban—given its clear resemblance to the early Zapotec year sign (see Caso 1965). At Teotihuacan the trapeze and ray, as this sign is more commonly called for its use at that site, can first be seen as an emblem resembling an architectural form (see A. Miller 1973, figs. 63, 64, and 291) during the early Xolalpan period, and more-or-less contemporary with Stela 5.[14]

The regalia held by the woman on Stela 5 of El Zapote is made up of unusual, and, for the Early Classic Maya, unprecedented, insignia. When all the supposed iconographic meanings of this emblematic object—the year sign, the pendant, the square cartouche, and the scroll baby—are brought together, we might understand it as an emblem for lineage and/or rulership with ties to the south (Abaj Takalik?) and to a Mexican icon suggestive of cyclic history. That it is held by the flat-hand gesture, however, argues that it was more a conceptual amalgam of ideas represented as insignia rather like its appearances in speech scrolls at Teotihuacan, than an actual instrument or item of regalia.

The recto-verso pair of Stela 5 contrasts the costumes and sex of the honored figures through a compelling and visual contrast: a delectation for complex and dense imagery on the female side, and a clarity and simplicity of images on the male side. The male side depicts the new iconography of the tripartite staff (and bag?) with an equally "modern" use of modest and uncomplicated shapes, while the female side displays unprecedented, hand-held regalia within the context of a traditional complexity and ambiguity of image characteristic of the 8th baktun. There seems little doubt that the female regalia and the male regalia were somehow conceptually connected. Given the contrasts between the recto-verso sides, it is likely that the connection was one of polarity, or a duality in meaning and intention.

While Stela 31 of Tikal depicts two different visions of rulership side by side in an effort visually to juxtapose, to bring together, old and new orders, the sculptor(s) of Stela 5 of El Zapote synthesize(s) the old and new within a context of differences that show how the old and new forms are actually part of a much deeper reality than politics or style and, in fact, refer to basic, existential themes of duality and complementarity such as male/female, simple/complex, and front/back.

Stela 5 was carved within the aura of the millenial turn of the baktun. Its Initial Series date is 9.0.0.0.0, and while other dates were given in its now partially destroyed text carved on the narrow sides (due to modern sawing), the Initial Series date is the one usually understood as its dedicatory date (Coggins 1983; Mathews 1985, 8). This can be questioned (Clancy 1988, 197), and with the more recent perceptions of Coggins (1990) showing how rare it is to find monuments dedicated to the turn of the baktun, I consider 9.1.0.0.0 a more accurate date for the dedication of the stela, especially since the style date (following Proskouriakoff's [1950] method) indicates 9.4.0.0.0 ± 3 katuns. Specifically, the late traits are the headdresses worn by both the male and female, belt heads with profiled ear plugs, and the staff held by the male. The female's regalia is unique at this time.

Since 8.17.0.0.0 (that is, for the previous eighty years) the patrons and sculptors of public monuments had been concerned with how to illustrate the current religious and political issues raised by the inter-regional warrior sodality. For the ruling elite of Tikal, Uaxactun, and El Zapote, there was a desire and need to integrate the warriors into the regimes of the traditional dynasts and to do so within the public spaces of the plaza, most likely in an effort to achieve public support for certain changes in public and religious life such an integration would require. It seems to me that Stela 5 of El Zapote represents the most politically successful monument for these efforts. It uses an ancient compositional field; it mimics the juxtapositioning of old and new imagery in use since 8.17.0.0.0 but does so to synthesize rather than just to bring together or to juxtapose; and it solicits comparisons for this "marriage" with primal and deeply held knowledge about dualities.

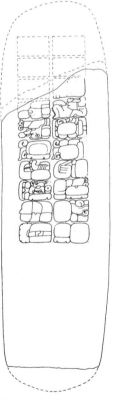

Fig. 36.   Tikal, Stela 1, Wraparound.
(Photo after Maler 1911, pl. 19,
reprinted courtesy Peabody Museum,
Harvard University. Drawings by
William Coe reprinted from *Tikal
Reports 33A* by Jones and
Satterthwaite 1982 courtesy University
of Pennsylvania Museum,
Philadelphia.)

CHAPTER SEVEN
The Wraparound Fields
9.1.0.0.0 to 9.2.0.0.0 (A.D. 455–75)

Tikal, Stelae 1, 2, and 28 (figs. 36, 37, and 38)

THESE STELAE ARE ICONOGRAPHICALLY AND COMPO-sitionally similar and have long been referred to as "wraparound stelae" (Bailey 1972, 62; Clancy 1980, 54; Jones and Satterthwaite 1982, 60). Their original settings are unknown and all three are fragmentary. Stela 1 is the best preserved and Stela 28, the worst. While the extreme elaborations of motif and icon are most striking, it is also notable that these stelae exhibit no visible reference to the foreign imagery associated with the warrior pairs.

Stelae 1, 2, and 28 are (were) beautifully shaped, rect-angular shafts of compact limestone carved with the wraparound field to exhibit an articulated-profile figure portrayed with the wasp-waisted body. All three figures stand on a basal image, but breakage at the tops of these monuments does not allow us to know whether all or any had supernal images. Each figure is shown with the remarkable regalia of wings, and each presses to his chest, by the symmetrical ceremonial-bar gesture, a uniquely complex and fancy bar. (It is possible that the ceremonial-bar gesture still carried the implications of its earlier associations with the bound figure.)

Stelae 1 and 2 were found set up as a pair within the North Acropolis in front of Structure 5D-26-1st. The carved figures faced one another in that the figure on Stela 1 faces to his left, while the figure on Stela 2 faces to his

right. Jones and Satterthwaite (1982, 9–11; and see W. Coe 1990, 786) say that the archaeological evidence strongly suggests that they were reset into this position, and al-though they discuss the clear iconographic similarities between the two monuments, they do not suggest that they were conceived as a pair. They think Stela 1 may have been first erected in the Great Plaza and/or North Ter-race, that is, in a more public space than within the North Acropolis where it was found. The lower half of Stela 2 was broken or cut off at some time in its history and reset as a pedestal (15) for Plain Stela 21 located in the Great Plaza. Jones and Satterthwaite (ibid.) do not spec-ulate on its original position. Stela 28 was found, appar-ently dumped, in an undeveloped area west of the West Plaza (ibid., 60).

The dating of the wraparound monuments is not cer-tain because their glyphic texts are worn and largely lost through breakage. Stylistically they range between 8.19.0.0.0 and 9.3.0.0.0 (A.D. 416–95), and Jones and Satterthwaite (ibid., 10) think it is likely they were carved some time between 9.0.10.0.0, the date of Stela 31, and 9.2.0.0.0, a time of considerable stylistic change at Tikal (that is, between A.D. 446 and 475).[1] However, there seems little doubt that they were carved to honor Stormy Sky. His name is recognizable in what remains of the glyphic text carved on the back of Stela 1.[2]

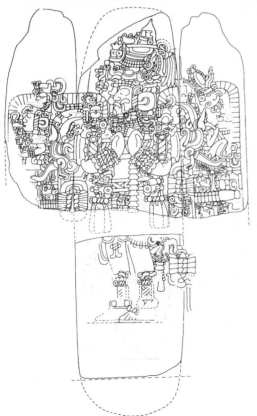
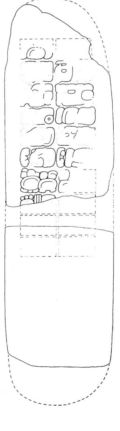

Fig. 37. Tikal, Stela 2, Wraparound.
(Photo, Flora Clancy; Drawings by
William Coe reprinted from
Tikal Reports 33A by Jones and
Satterthwaite 1982 courtesy
University of Pennsylvania
Museum, Philadelphia.)

Fig. 38.   Tikal, Stela 28, Wraparound.
(Photos courtesy University of Pennsylvania Museum,
front #59-4-501, and side #59-4-87.
Drawing by William Coe reprinted from *Tikal Reports
33A* by Jones and Satterthwaite 1982 courtesy
University of Pennsylvania Museum, Philadelphia.)

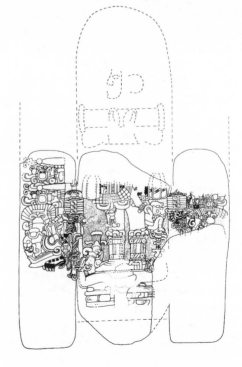

On Stela 1, the best preserved of the three monuments, the two serpent heads of the ceremonial bar expose fully figured manikins within their open mouths, and additional serpents, referred to as "serpent poles" by Bailey (1972, 56), hang pendent from their chins at the corners of the front panel. Feathered wings rise behind the main figure's shoulders, as seen on the front, and cascade down the lateral sides to frame the complex imagery. Marginal figures cling and coil around the serpent poles; miniature serpents and feline-like creatures face equally small and active busts of humans embedded in the feathers of the wings. In a less narrative fashion, Stelae 2 and 28 replace the animated busts with stacked heads arranged horizontally within the feathers of the wings.

Within the front face of the monument, the figure stands on a basal image that still reflects the Izapan signature. On Stela 1 a grotesque head with the Tikal emblem as its bound hair is paired with a cartouched *kin* sign that is itself framed by a quatrefoil shield with small serpent snouts projecting from its corners. These two emblems are connected by an undulant form and a segmented line (vertebrae?). The basal image may be glyphically restated at Bz7-Az8 on the back of the stela (Stuart and Houston 1994, 58), and certainly it carried locative meanings. Most of the basal imagery is lost on the recut fragment of Stela 2, but enough remains to show that it, too, was a signature type. For Stela 28, the right-hand head is a grotesque with the Tikal emblem for hair, while the other emblem is affixed with the number 7. A small belly-down figure with bound hands has been inserted between the soles of the main figure's feet and the two emblematic glyphs of the signature. The bound figure wears a fancy headdress and a circular nose plug, and given the way his hands are tied and held in front of his face, they continue, in profile, to mimic the ceremonial-bar gesture.

Between the three wraparound stelae, the carving techniques are similar enough to consider that one particular "school" of sculptors produced them, but not close enough to suggest one hand or master. Stelae 1 and 28 are closest in carving style to Stela 31 (fig. 33) in that they display a similar sense of plasticity and dimension in their imagery achieved by abrasion, modeling, and cushioning. In their intricate planar treatment Stelae 1 and 28 are also quite close to Stela 35 of Copan (fig. 31), especially in a similar use of relatively deep relief for the creation of vivid depths of shadow.

The relief-carved imagery of Stela 2 is realized on the surface of the stone. Modeling for the heads and head-dresses is minimal and does not conflict with the unequivocal foregrounding of the image. Cushioning is used where costuming overlaps the body, but the costume itself is rendered by square, barely abraded cuts. Everything maintains the surface of the stone, and the imagery of Stela 2 looks like a delicately filigreed cut-out laid over the monument shaft.

Background space is minimal, but where it is visible it is smooth and well defined. The basal panels, however, have no real backgrounds. On Stela 1, the basal imagery is engraved and occupies the same foreground plane as the frames that surround the front panels. This is probably the case for Stelae 2 and 28, but their basal images are too worn to say more. The complex imagery carved on the sides of the shafts was subtly achieved through gentle abrasion at the edges of shapes and delicate modeling and cushioning, but the wings, serpent heads, serpent poles, and marginalia present a field of overlapped images so densely packed that background space is practically invisible, and spatial relationships are ambiguous.

As mentioned above, plain frames actually do surround the front panels, but they are not just overlapped, they are overwhelmed by the regalia that wraps around the angles of the shaft. The only parts of the frame that are visible are near the faces of the main figures (on Stela 2) and the belly-down figure (Stela 28). The extraordinary images on the sides are not framed at their far edges away from the front.

One of the functions of a plain frame is to objectify the image (Clancy 1990). On the wraparound monuments, the honored figure is framed, but the fabulous regalia is not. Facing the stela straight on, one might see it as the more expected image of an honored person standing on a basal panel. By taking an oblique or side view, it becomes evident that the regalia exceed the objectifying frame to merge with the stony shaft on the sides. A dialectic, or perhaps more precisely, a separation, has been visually realized between the objective portrait and the resplendent regalia. (This separation is easiest to apprehend by looking at the stelae themselves; the next best way is looking at photographs. The drawings of these monuments would never provoke such an observation.) The visual separation of regalia from the figure it qualifies is subtle and masterful. On the wraparound stelae, the regalia is literally foregrounded because it alone is represented as beyond the frame.

The main figure's costume, as exemplified on Stelae 1 and 2, is fancy and traditional. The headdress (seen on Stela 2) is the early helmet type (Proskouriakoff 1950, 50) displaying the quadripartite emblem mentioned in the discussion of Stela 5 of El Zapote (fig. 35). A long segmented chain, perhaps of vertebrae, hangs from the ear plug assembly of the headdress. This is not the same as the interlocked discs attached to the headdress held by Stormy Sky on Stela 31, but surely it is a related motif. On Stela 28 this item may have been replaced by the long necklace of cylindrical beads associated with the extroverted gesture. On Stela 1, and perhaps on 2, the figure wears the beaded, net skirt associated with things feminine, while the kilt of the figure on Stela 28 is made from the skin of a jaguar. Completing the costume is a watch fob, very fancy anklets, and a thick belt with projected, disembodied heads or manikins with pendent celts.

Stelae 1, 28, and 2 were probably conceived as a triadic display. More speculatively, they may originally have been set up and arranged so that the figure in the jaguar kilt standing over the belly-down figure on Stela 28 represented the actual (present) portrait of Stormy Sky flanked by a pair of more mythical or ethereal figures represented on Stelae 1 and 2 wearing the feminine netted kilts. Freidel, Schele, and Parker (1993, 61, 92, 276ff.) understand the netted costume as that worn by the Creator Couple or their impersonators, and such an interpretation fits nicely with this speculative arrangement of Stelae 1, 28, and 2. Furthermore, this triad is very like the basic compositional schemata of the later triad of panels from the Cross Group of Palenque, where the iconography and texts suggest themes of transformation through a sequential reading of the panels, and, simultaneously, themes of equivalence illustrated through the obvious similarities of composition and iconographies in the panels (Clancy 1986).

The repetitive, redundant image, by creating a specific context for the triad as one passes by and around all three monuments, was important for the intentional meanings of the wraparound stelae. On a general level they can be understood as a series of equivalent images, but when their differences are noted, these take on greater significance because of the established context of equivalence. Interplaying similarities and differences, however, need not be unexpected conditions through which to describe a reality if the basic sense of time was a cyclical one.[3]

Tres Islas, Stelae 1, 2, and 3
(figs. 39, 40, and 41)

At the same time the wraparound stelae were being produced at Tikal, three stelae were carved at a small site on the Pasion River called Tres Islas (Mathews 1985, 11). Stelae 1 and 3 were surely conceived as a pair, each displaying one of a warrior pair costumed and accoutered very like the recto-verso pairs on Stela 31 at Tikal (fig. 33) and Stela 5 at Uaxactun (fig. 20). Peter Mathews (1985, 53, n. 2) reports that Stelae 1, 2, 3 were found *in situ* by Ian Graham in 1965 and one might suppose that they were found set in a row, their order suggested by their numbers; the warrior pair flanking Stela 2. Stela 2 (fig. 40) is now in the Museo Nacional in Guatemala City. All three have compositions and framing devices that are unusual for the imagery they represent, but, nonetheless, have intriguing programmatic similarities with Stela 31 and the wraparound stelae of Tikal.

Stela 1 (fig. 39) depicts a warrior in broad profile standing on the left side of a paneled field facing a glyphic text on the right. Stela 3 (fig. 41) displays the same warrior but in a true profile and reverses the positions of the figure and text. Because this latter monument is more irregularly shaped, the glyphic text that can be seen on the front face wraps around the angle of the shaft to the left lateral side.

Fig. 39.   Tres Islas, Stela 1.
(Photo courtesy Ian Graham.)

Fig. 40. Tres Islas,
Stela 2, Wraparound.
(Photo courtesy
Ian Graham.)

Fig. 41. Tres Islas,
Stela 3.
(Photo courtesy
Ian Graham.)

The warriors are dressed almost identically in feathered, beaded helmets with chin straps, belts with pendent tails at their backs, and knee ruffs. The figure on Stela 1 carries his atlatl by its strap so it looks like a bag. In his other hand he holds three darts or short spears. The figure on Stela 3 carries darts and gestures towards the glyphic text with his right hand. Each warrior wears a short cape with embroidered(?) panels that hang from a beaded collar.[4] Although there are small iconographic differences in costume and regalia, the Tres Islas warriors clearly conform to the iconography of the warrior pair shown recto-verso at Tikal and Uaxactun.

The warriors both stand on large basal images of the broad-beaked bird head whose headdress and earflares are composed of interlocked scrolls infixed with *cauac* (a day name) and shell signs. The outline of the bird's headdress is stepped and, except for its squared and open eye, looks like the throne depicted on Stela 18 of Tikal (fig. 22). The bird head is in profile, facing in the same direction as the warrior. All the parts of the basal bird image are outlined with narrow frames that make it look like a structure of some sort. In the supernal region, above each warrior, is another broad-beaked bird with wings spread. While the supernal bird has a long history in the southern Maya area and especially at the coastal site of Izapa (Bardawil 1976), a basal image of a bird does not.[5] The sculptors of the Tres Islas warrior pair bring the lowland's paradoxical image of a basal bird together with the Preclassic supernal bird to form an apparent opposition or apposition of signs having, one might assume, locative functions.

Stela 2 (fig. 40) is uniquely composed, depicting a two-figure scene or narrative supported by an enlarged basal panel that fully takes up one-third of the sculptured image. Both the scene and the basal panel wrap around the shaft to the right side, but only a small portion of the basal image wraps around to the left, where a glyphic statement occupies most of that side. On the front of the stela, the scene is contained by a narrow frame that separates it from another glyphic text. By their architectonic construction, the frame and glyphs create a niche or doorway-like space for the main figure: a compositional strategy used during the Late Classic by sculptors at sites downriver along the Usumacinta, and one noted above for the glyphic arrangement on the Seattle Stela (fig. 16).

The main figure of the scene appears on the front face of the monument, while a much shorter companion figure is carved on the lateral side (not shown). Wearing a long, possibly netted, skirt, the attendant may be female.

Both figures are posed in articulated profiles and carry ceremonial bars. The main figure also carries a bag. It is clear that the headdresses of the two figures are different, and the main figure's headdress may have once displayed the "Mexican year sign" described for the verso face of Stela 5 from El Zapote (fig. 35). Spalling of the stone makes further description difficult.

Despite its unique composition, Stela 2 may represent an early, if not the earliest, "niched-accession" scene of a ruler, so well known at Late Classic Piedras Negras (Proskouriakoff 1960). The niche, the female attendant, and the extraordinary basal imagery discussed below are all suggestive of this theme. Furthermore, although the text on the front panel has also suffered spalling, a verb for accession can be seen at C3. If Stela 2 were carved to be a central image flanked by two warriors, then like Stormy Sky's great monument (Stela 31 of Tikal) Stela 2 employs the wraparound composition and joins its traditional regalia to that of the warrior.

Key areas of the basal panel have been lost to the spalling of the stone; however, enough imagery remains to describe it as unusual. Centrally placed within the front panel is a framed field shaped like a Saint Andrew's cross. Surrounding the cross and wrapping around, asymmetrically, to the left and right sides are scrolled forms suggestive of the deity heads and serpents that frame the lost scene on Altar 13 of Abaj Takalik (fig. 9), which in turn was compared to the regalia held by the woman on Stela 5 of El Zapote (fig. 35). The comparison with Altar 13 continues because the seated figure within the cross wears a netted and beaded skirt like that worn by the little figure on the altar. The stela figure is seated on a pedestal and holds, horizontally, a ceremonial bar whose end heads are neatly fitted into the horizontal arms of the cross.

The enframing cross of the basal image may be an angular version of the quatrefoil frame and, thus, may be a reference to a cave. The quatrefoil used as a frame for displaying an enlarged glyph, usually the day *Ahau*, will become a hallmark for pedestals of Caracol, the first of which is thought to be carved in 9.3.0.0.0 (Altar 4 [see Beetz and Satterthwaite 1981, 41, fig. 20d]). Others continue to be carved well into the Late Classic Period. Stelae from Machaquila, a Late Classic site close by Early Classic Tres Islas, employ the quatrefoil and the enlarged glyph as a basal image on stelae (I. Graham 1967) where it is considered to function as a place sign (Clancy 1976; Stuart and Houston 1994, 33).

If it is correct to think of Stelae 1, 2, and 3 of Tres Islas as a triadic group, then, while unusually composed, they represent the now-familiar "theme" of juxtaposing old and new regalia iconographies. However, like Tikal's wraparound "triad" the Tres Islas stelae expand or "open up" the programmatic message so that additional associations can be represented. The emblematic, basal image of a figure seated in a quatrefoil/cave is flanked by the basal images of Stelae 1 and 3, the two mythical birds that signal a place or location and may be identified with the so-called Principal Bird Deity (Bardawil 1976; Cortez 1986). Since the seated figure of Stela 2 holds a ceremonial bar, it appears to restate the main image's theme, but on a different scale and in a different context. Likewise, then, the impossibly large bird heads may have been understood as somehow equivalent to the warriors who stand on them. It is of interest that in her study of the Principal Bird Deity, Cortez (1986, 84–89) finds associations between it and the mythical Hero Twins of the *Popol Vuh* (see Tedlock 1985). With the Tres Islas stelae, we can posit that the warrior pair was conceptually linked to the Hero Twins and their seminal role in the creation of this world.[6]

If this descriptive analysis for the Tres Islas stelae is at all correct, their programmatic message about equivalencies is similar to the equivalencies represented by the contemporaneous triad of wraparound stelae erected at Tikal. Looking between the two sets of monuments, broader iconographic meanings can be very tentatively sketched for both. Stela 2 of Tres Islas is flanked by the warrior pair standing on the broad-beaked bird heads that may declare their mythic identity as the Hero Twins. Stela 28 of Tikal is flanked by a different pair, the Creator Couple. Both flanking pairs, the warriors and the Creator Couple, are evocations of characters and events at the beginnings of the current world as we know them from the stories in the *Popol Vuh*, and it is they who provide the context for equivalence with the human figures—rulers—who hold ceremonial bars and are portrayed on the central monuments. While much of the above is speculation, the core of the argument is that plaza monuments now show the honored figure explicitly associated with profound, mythical histories. Where this may have been implicit all along, it is now illustrated.

Quirigua, Monument (Stela) 26 (fig. 42)

Monument 26 was found about a kilometer northwest of the site core of Quirigua in an Early Classic context (Ash-

A

B

C

Fig. 42. Quirigua, Monument 26, Wraparound:
A) Front/Top, B) Front/Bottom, and C) Side.
(Photos and drawing courtesy University of
Pennsylvania Museum, Philadelphia:
front/top #Q 79-7-260; front/bottom #Q79-7-276;
side #Q79-7-255.)

more 1980; Jones 1983; Sharer 1990), and its dedicatory date has been read as 9.2.18.0.0 (A.D. 493) by Christopher Jones (1983, 119–20). Monument 26 consists of two fragments, the upper half and lower basal portion. The middle part is lost. It is a tall, columnar shaft of blue-gray schist carved to represent the honored figure in a wraparound field. The compositional mode is isotropic and the symmetrical figure presses a ceremonial bar to his body by the expected symmetrical gesture. As with the wraparound stelae of Tikal, the main figure is completely represented on the front, while the exotic parts of the regalia take up the lateral sides. Unlike the Tikal stelae, no frames were carved to be overlapped, and, thus, no separation between figure and regalia can be detected.

The wraparound field is, in fact, a sympathetic field for the isotropic mode because it works to "project" the face and body of the figure on the front panel. When the paneled field is used to present a full-frontal figure, there is often a tension created between the shallow relief used for the image and the spatial reality of the head on the shoulders to which it refers. Stela 4 of Tikal (fig. 21) is a good example of this tension, where the face appears sunken into the stone, while the headdress and costume are presented as in the foreground.[7] On Monument 26, the frontal face and cupped hands are "foregrounded" by the fact that the lateral projections of the headdress, regalia, and costume parts actually retreat around to the lateral sides of the stela.

On the front panel of Monument 26 there is no visible background plane, although it may have been visually effective around the legs. In what survives, however, the frontal human image and the stone are completely integrated, recalling the earlier 8th-baktun efforts to integrate stone and image. For Monument 26 the sculptor(s) mostly used planar distinctions to define the overlapping parts of costume and gesture, and used modeling only for the human face and the eyes of the headdress mask. The lateral sides do have a visibly defined background, especially at the edges of the image, and thus the projections of costume and regalia are seen on the sides as separated from the stone and perhaps, by implication, from the figure.

The many comparisons between Monument 26 and the wraparound stelae of Tikal have suggested to Jones and Sharer (1980; and see Sharer 1991, 190) that Quirigua may have been colonized by peoples from the Peten or central Maya region, and specifically from Tikal, in order to control the important trade route along the Motagua River. Without denying these similarities, the differences between the Tikal stelae and Monument 26 are not negligible. The isotropic mode is perhaps the first clear difference, where the frontal confrontation of Monument 26 engages viewers by including them in a reciprocal "gaze," while the Tikal stelae imply direction and movement by their use of the profiled face and feet. The use of the frame on the Tikal stelae also creates a very different effect for the wrapped imagery that overlaps the frame to continue to the sides. Without any framing, the Quirigua image better integrates its compositional field and mode. Finally, the imagery of Monument 26 is much more simply represented than the intricacies and fulsomeness of the imagery carved on the Tikal wraparound stelae.

There seems little reason, however, to doubt Jones and Sharer's (1980) basic ideas about close ties between Tikal and Quirigua or that the sculptors of Monument 26 knew of the Tikal monuments. However, it must be admitted that they were equally aware of the monuments being carved at Uaxactun. Monument 26 is no copy. It is a fine synthesis of the new wraparound field from Tikal and the new isotropic mode from Uaxactun. With this synthesis, the sculptors and patrons created a different plaza theme at Quirigua, one where viewer interaction required by the wraparound field is positively enhanced by the reciprocal gaze of the frontal face. This basic scheme for stela composition will be followed at Quirigua and at Copan throughout the Classic period.[8]

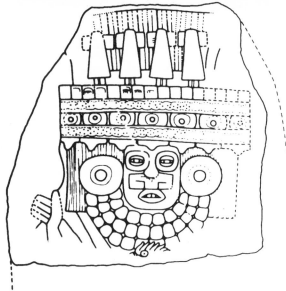

Fig. 43. Yaxha, Stela 11. (Photo after Morley 1937–38, pl. 161b. Drawing by Flora Clancy after Hellmuth 1975.)

Fig. 44. Tikal, Stela 32. (Photo courtesy University of Pennsylvania Museum, Philadelphia, #61-4-716. Drawing by William Coe reprinted from *Tikal Reports 33A* by Jones and Satterthwaite 1982 courtesy University of Pennsylvania Museum, Philadelphia.)

CHAPTER EIGHT

The Insignia

Ca. 9.2.0.0.0 to ca. 9.3.0.0.0 (A.D. 475–495)

Yaxha, Stela 11, and Tikal, Stela 32
(figs. 43 and 44)

THE DISTINCTIVE SHIELD HELD IN THE HAND OF THE warrior on the right side of Stela 31 at Tikal is rectangular and decorated with a goggle-eyed head wearing a barrel-like headdress topped with tassels and feathers. Both Stela 11 from Yaxha and Stela 32 of Tikal represent this shield as anthropomorphized and restated emblematically as a full-frontal warrior. Neither piece is strictly isotropic, however, because the gestures are asymmetrical: on both stelae the right hand is raised to chin level. These figures wear the singular headdress just described, circular "goggles," a mouth mask, and a necklace that appears to be attached to the large, circular earflares that are visually significant features for these stelae. The obvious foreignness of the shield, when translated into a figure, insured that Stela 32 of Tikal and Stela 11 of Yaxha would appear as different and aberrant, and yet they are not without precedent, given Curl Snout's choice of imagery on his monuments carved at Tikal eighty years earlier.

Stela 11 (fig. 43) is the more complete monument. It is a frameless stela displaying the warrior with conventional, squat proportions of 1:4, head to body height. The round and deeply indented earflares are modeled, as is

the beaded necklace, but otherwise, planar levels distinguish overlapping shapes. The bottom third of the stela shows a clear and leveled background plane, while the top two-thirds is filled with the regalia of shield and spear, and the great shield insigne headdress surrounded by a spray of feathers. Morley (1937–38, 3: 470–71) found Stela 11 accompanied by a pedestal in front of the East Acropolis of Plaza B and suggested that the stela may have faced the acropolis rather than the plaza. However, the bottom portion of the stela was found, much later, centered on the steps to the East Acropolis (Hellmuth 1969, 35).

Stela 32 of Tikal (fig. 44) is only a fragment that has preserved the face, parts of the shield insigne headdress, and a trace of the right hand of the figure, which may hold an atlatl. On this piece the face is modeled and all disc shapes are deeply indented. The carving is delicate and precise and not concerned with creating a sense of spatial realism. What is left in the fragment shows an enigmatic relationship between image and background. The modeling of the face cuts to a deeper level than the "background" surrounding the image, which looks like it has been purposefully pecked and roughened, perhaps in emulation of the earliest monuments with visually active fields surrounding image. Joyce Bailey (1972, 115–16) suggests that it was unfinished.

Fig. 45.   Yaxha, Stela 1. (Photo after Maler 1908,
pl. 15:1, reprinted courtesy Peabody Museum,
Harvard University.)

Stela 32 was found as part of what is called a Problematic Deposit #22, which suggests a cache-like function but also a secondary use for the goods found together in the deposit. Problematic Deposit 22 was found in front of Structure 5D-26 (the structure fronted by the wrap-around Stelae 1 and 2) (W. Coe 1990, 784).

As with Stela 15 of Cerro de las Mesas, to which these stelae compare, it is not sure when they were carved. Jones and Satterthwaite (1982, 118) place Stela 32 at the end of the 8th baktun between the 18th and 19th katuns, primarily because the frontal face compares with that of Stela 4. Coggins (1975, 182) stylistically dates Problematic Deposit 22 between 8.19.0.0.0 and 9.1.10.0.0 (A.D. 416–65), while Jones and Satterthwaite (1982, 117, table 2) give the range of its possible deposition from the end of the

Ik ceramic complex to the beginning of the Imix complex (that is, around the beginning of the Late Classic, A.D. 593–693). This of course only makes clear the latest date Stela 32 may have been carved. Equally, there is no good evidence for the dating of Stela 11 of Yaxha.

These stelae do not take the honored human as their main image, but rather an anthropomorphized insigne, or, as it is usually described, a cult image, and in this they are aberrant in terms of stelae imagery. Insignia were more normally represented on pedestals. Although the anthropomorphized shield may have appeared earlier than the ceremonial-bar insigne (discussed below), these rare events are structurally similar, in that they recontextualized icons drawn from the significant hand-held regalia of the warrior pair and the ceremonial-bar holder, and it is likely, therefore, that they were considered as conceptually related to each other. Insignia displayed on stelae enter the plaza along with, or soon after, the appearance of the baktun-other, and some kind of meaningful connection between the insignia and the baktun-other is also possible.

Yaxha, Stela 1 (fig. 45)

Stela 1 and the Corozál Stela (below) represent insignia drawn from the ceremonial bar as the main image. Stylistically they relate to monuments carved at Tikal between 9.2.0.0.0 and 9.3.0.0.0 (A.D. 475–95) and could be contemporaneous with the shield insigne stelae discussed above, or with Pedestal 12 of Tikal, to be discussed below.

Maler (1908, 4(2): 63–64) supposed that Stela 1 of Yaxha was the top part of a broken stela, reset into Plaza C. It is the westmost stela in a roughly aligned row of monuments in front of Structure XIII (Stelae 1, 2, 3, 4, and 5). Morley (1937–38, 2: 467–68) agreed with this reconstruction, but remarks that, given the existing height of the fragment, one and a third meters, Stela 1 as a whole monument would have been close to four meters high, an extraordinary height for an Early Classic monument. Both Maler and Morley identify the head of the main figure as the small profile bust seen in the lower right of the panel wearing a helmet-like headdress and facing a short panel of three glyphs. All the rest of the imagery is interpreted as an extraordinary and large headdress. If this small bust is, in fact, what remains of the "main figure," the difference between the size of the tiny head and its gigantic headdress would also be unique within the Classic Maya aesthetics for representing the human figure. This image is better construed as illustrating insignia, with its imagery drawn from the complexly designed ceremonial bars of the wraparound Stelae 1, 2, and 28 of Tikal (figs. 36, 37, and 38).

A vertical bar or pole carved just to the left of center in the framed panel supports the stela imagery that can be seen as a restatement of the lateral sides of the Tikal wraparound stelae: the serpent head of the ceremonial bar, the serpent pole, and the inhabited wings. Tied to the pole and displayed on the left-hand side are two forms, the lower one looking like an earflare, and the upper, like an enlarged "ahau bone" (a trilobed shape like the joint end of a long bone with two "eyes" and an ovular "mouth"). To the right of the vertical pole, and level with the ahau bone, is a large animal skull with a snake protruding from its mouth. Just below the skull is the little helmeted human comparable to the miniature active manikins in the mouths of serpents or the marginal figures cavorting along the serpent poles. Above the large animal skull graphemic imagery can be seen, but it is badly worn.[1]

Corozál, Stela (fig. 46)

A stela from the small site called Corozál, close by Tikal, displays as its main image insignia of a similar kind: the off-center vertical bar or pole that supports four large concentric-circle earflares attached to the left side and a vertical series of anthropomorphic heads attached to the right side. The imagery is comparable, again, to the sides of the wraparound stelae of Tikal, especially Stelae 2 and 28, where small disembodied heads overlie the wings and butt against the vertical serpent poles. The supernal region displays scrolling and intertwined shapes like serpents or vining plants, and while the condition of the stela is not conducive to a clear reading, it is worth noting that this part compares with the headdress worn by the figure on Yaxha Stela 6, and to the supernal imagery of the later Stelae 3, 5, and 6 of Caracol, dating between 9.6.0.0.0 and 9.9.0.0.0 (A.D. 554–613) (see Beetz and Satterthwaite 1981, figs. 3, 6, 7, and 8).

The glyphic text carved onto the back of the Corozál monument is largely spalled off, but the remaining glyphs are rendered in a style similar to that used for the stelae of Kan Boar and Jaguar-Paw-Skull of Tikal (Jones and Orrego 1987, 131; and discussed below). Given the comparisons drawn for both Stela 1 of Yaxha and the Corozál stela, it is a good estimation that they date between 9.2.0.0.0 and 9.3.0.0.0 (A.D. 475–95).

Fig. 46. Corozál, Stela 1.
(Photo courtesy University of Pennsylvania Museum, Philadelphia.)

Fig. 47.   Tikal, Pedestal 12.
(Photo courtesy Patrick Clancy.
Drawings, top and periphery, by
William Coe reprinted from *Tikal Reports
33A* by Jones and Satterthwaite 1982
courtesy University of Pennsylvania
Museum, Philadelphia.)

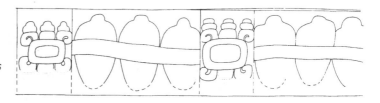

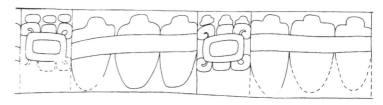

Tikal, Pedestal 12 (fig. 47)

Pedestal 12 of Tikal emblematically represents a small figure wearing beaded jewelry sitting cross-legged in the open jaws of an enlarged serpent head. As noted by Bailey (1972, 169) the image on Pedestal 12 replicates the imagery on the side of Stela 2 of Tikal (fig. 37), where a similar little figure with beaded jewelry sits in the jaws of the serpent head attached to the ceremonial bar. Like this figure, the seated figure on Pedestal 12 holds glyphs in his hands.

The pedestal serpent is beautifully positioned with its circular field. Its great jaws open a little to the left of center, thus placing the seated figure in the upper-left-hand portion of the circular panel. The serpent's body forms a frame around the circular field, twisting into a simple plait at the base of the image. It may be a two-headed serpent with a small rear head balanced at the end of the twisted plait, just in front of the seated figure. Repeated scrolls, rhythmically varying in size, arch away from the serpent's upper jaw and cartouched headdress.

The periphery of Pedestal 12 is similar to those of Pedestals 13 and 19 of Tikal. Four lappets with day-sign cartouches are carved to look like they hang over the sides from the top plane. Behind the lappets a circumferential binding holds sets of three shield- or heart-shaped forms. There are no fancy knotted plaits.

Pedestal 12 was found in proximity to Stela 6 on the North Terrace of the North Acropolis in front of 5D-32-1st (Jones and Satterthwaite 1982, 79). Stela 6, badly fragmented, displays the main figure with the new regalia and costume described below in the next chapter, but it very likely included a supernal image, traces of which can be seen on the upper fragment of the stela, and, thus, predicts the more iconographically rich plaza images of Tikal's Middle Classic period. It is dated at 9.4.0.0.0 (A.D. 514) by a Long Count date and is therefore not part of this survey.[2] Jones and Satterthwaite (ibid.) can only tentatively suggest that Pedestal 12 and Stela 6 were originally paired. If Pedestal 12 is affiliated with the group of monuments displaying insignia as main images, as I think it is, it was probably carved before the 4th katun.[3]

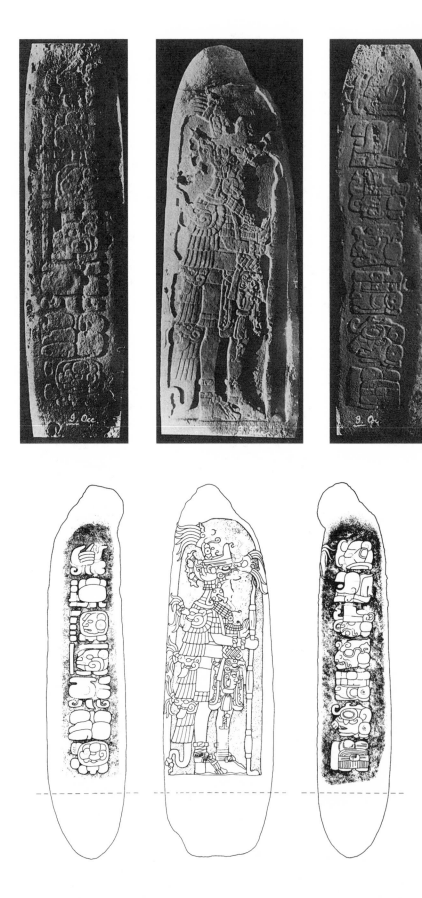

Fig. 48.   Tikal, Stela 9,
front and sides.
(Photos after Maler 1911,
pl. 20, reprinted courtesy
Peabody Museum,
Harvard University.
Drawings courtesy
William Coe.)

CHAPTER NINE

The New Image

9.2.0.0.0 to 9.3.13.0.0 (A.D. 475–507)

Tikal, Stelae 9, 13, and 8
(figs. 48, 49, and 50)

Stela 9 was placed in the Great Plaza just left or west of the central axis of the North Acropolis. It may be in its original setting (Jones and Satterthwaite 1982, 23; W. Coe 1990, 687–88). It is now part of a long row of stelae that range in date from Stela 9 to the latest known stela erected at Tikal, exactly one baktun later, Stela 11 of 10.2.0.0.0 (A.D. 869). Stela 9 represents the honored figure standing in a profile pose, while the belt and apron motifs are in an odd combination of frontal and profiled imagery. The main figure grasps a spear/staff with his near hand and gestures with his far hand turned up at the wrist.

The carving within the costumed body was done by a neat system of cushioning and planar relief, while the main outlines were silhouetted. This has resulted in the staff/spear being carved in a (relatively) dramatic relief, since it is held by the near hand away from and in the front of the body and is directly outlined by the background. The costume details have been simplified and slightly enlarged. The usual projecting belt heads with pendent celts have been reduced to just one in the front, wristlets and anklets are simple knotted bindings, no watch fob is depicted, and only one piece of hand-held regalia is included. A long necklace ending in a plaited rectangle is visible at the waist of the figure. This, and the hand-held spear/staff specifically recalls the stark image on Stela 4 of El Zapote (fig. 24) carved eighty years earlier. Interestingly enough, the figure on Stela 9, thought to be the ruler Kan Boar (Coggins 1975, 220; Jones and Satterthwaite 1982, 25), maintains the feathered wings of the wraparound stela. This piece of costuming or regalia is shown here in profile and looks like a long cape inset with feline heads sporting feathered nose beads.

Except for this rather fine piece of vanity, Stela 9, and the seven stelae that follow it at Tikal, look as if some kind of sumptuary law had been enacted. There are no contextual images and no supernal, basal, or supplementary figures. The figure stands alone within the framed panel nicely projected against its ample background plane. The monument size is reduced, imagery is revised for a simpler depiction (the less dramatic profile view of the wing/cape on Stela 9), and the cutting techniques for outlining and spacing shapes are clearer and more descriptive than evocative, and certainly less expressive than those of the wraparound stelae, or indeed, any stela erected previously at Tikal.

The glyphic text of Stela 9 is split and placed on the sides of the monument. This is the first time this arrangement is used at Tikal and may allude to the wrap-

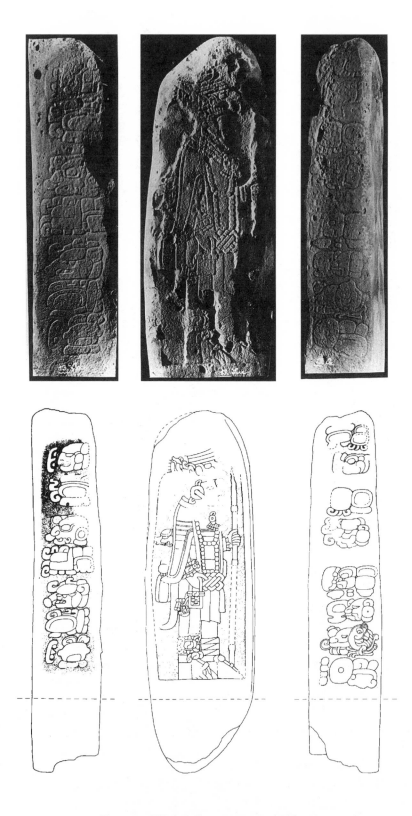

Fig. 49.   Tikal, Stela 13, Front and Sides.
(Photos after Maler 1911, pl. 25, reprinted courtesy Peabody Museum,
Harvard University. Drawings courtesy John Coe.)

114

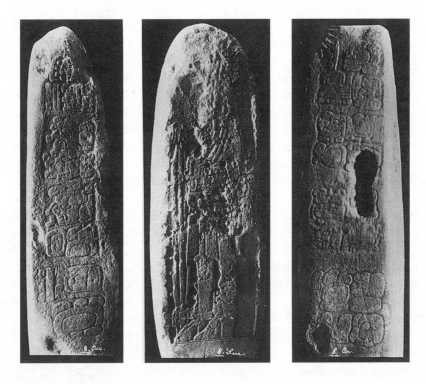

Fig. 50.   Tikal, Stela 8, Front and Sides.
(Photos after Maler 1911, pl. 19, reprinted courtesy
Peabody Museum, Harvard University.)

around compositions that had just been carved at Tikal. The glyphic columns are not framed and some feathers from the figure's headdress and the nose beads of the cape/wing felines overlap their frame to wraparound to the sides.[1] If this is a correct perception, then Stela 9 (and those that follow) places its text where the esoterica of regalia had been. Unlike the earlier Stela 29 of Tikal that used the recto-verso field to create a complementary relationship for figure and text, Stela 9 uses the wraparound field to create a continuity for figure and text.

The text of Stela 9 begins on the left side by declaring the ending of the 2nd katun (9.2.0.0.0 [A.D. 475]) with its day, 4 Ahau, but does not give the month position. Another day, 1 Men, is given at A7, also without a month position, and then on the other side, following glyphs not yet understood, Kan Boar's name and the Tikal emblem glyph end the spare text. Jones and Satterthwaite (1982, 25) consider the 9.2.0.0.0 date to be the dedicatory date.[2] Essentially, the text is as abbreviated as the imagery. Month positions are not given, nor the Long Count, and the viewer/reader would have had to have some knowledge of the events discussed in the text in order to transform what is apparently an epitomized mnemonic "text" into a coherent narrative.

Kan Boar is also named on Stela 13 (fig. 49), and this monument is even more radically reduced in size and imagery than Stela 9. Stela 13 was placed towards the eastern end of the Great Plaza stela row and may also be in its original location (Jones and Satterthwaite 1982, 33). William Coe's (1990, 731, 733) assessment, however, is equivocal on this point. Stela 13 represents a standing figure in the broad-profile pose holding the same spear/staff as the figure on Stela 9, but by the far hand. The near hand grasps a bag by its strap. Hanging to his waist is the same plaited mat seen on Stela 9. Although the headdress feathers may overlap the panel's frame (the imagery is worn here), no other motif does. The figure is carved well within the panel's borders surrounded by a clear background. Description seems to be the main function for the relief cuts outlining shapes, and denotation rather than expression is the main thrust.

Like those of Stela 9, the glyphic messages carved on the sides of the stela are not framed and are equally ambiguous about time. Kan Boar is named at B5, and here his parents are also named. The mother is designated by the glyphic sign of a clawed bird (Lady-Bird-Claw) at A7, while the glyphs at A1 name the father, who may be Stormy Sky as speculated by Jones and Satterthwaite (1982, 34). Jones and Satterthwaite (ibid., 33) do not detect any calendrical glyphs on Stela 13, but glyph B4 may refer to the ending of the 2nd katun and the last glyph on the right side, A8, may be 4 Ahau, thus repeating the terse time statements of Stela 9.

If Kan Boar's declared father is Stormy Sky, then the son now has little interest in any of his father's efforts at juxtaposing and interweaving the old imagery of the 8th-baktun dynasts with the new plaza imagery that can be traced to the iconography of the warrior pair. Kan Boar established new ideals for public imagery. He rejected the old regalia of ceremonial bars and disembodied heads, and the fancy elaborations of composition, costume, and supplementary figures. Importantly, he also rejected the outright depiction of a warrior's regalia: the spear is held like a staff on Stelae 9 and 13. As argued below, Stela 8 (fig. 50), another monument of questionable date, was part of Kan Boar's public display, and here he finally transforms the spear/staff into the tripartite staff so important to the succeeding rulers of Tikal. Because the tripartite staff occurs earlier at El Zapote (Stela 5, recto [fig. 35]), Kan Boar may be honoring this site by his use of regalia, or, more speculatively, he may have had close familial ties with El Zapote. Carving techniques that simplified the definition of imagery, the staff, and the plaited medallion certainly suggest that some sort of connection existed between the Tikal of Kan Boar and El Zapote.

Stela 8 (fig. 50) is erected near the western end of the Great Plaza stela row. It may or may not have been reset

(Jones and Satterthwaite 1982, 21; W. Coe 1990, 681). The monument displays within its framed panel a standing figure facing to the (viewer's) left in broad profile, but with the front belt assemblage shown frontally and the back belt head depicted in profile and emphasized by its large size. The figure holds the tripartite staff in his far hand and a bag in the near hand. The relief-carved outlines on Stela 8 draw some attention to the curving forms of the human body, and the stela is, in this small way, unlike Stela 13 with its more pragmatic emphasis on description. The imagery of Stela 8, while looking awkward and stiff, is, nonetheless, more realistically rendered.

Because a month position is given, the glyphic text carved on the lateral sides is only slightly less ambiguous than that of the two preceding stelae. In its arrangement of the glyphs, however, Stela 8 is closest to Stela 13, where the first column to be read has single glyphs, and the second column follows with glyphs paired in a double column that is also divided into blocks by wider horizontal spaces. The glyphic texts are not framed.

Jones and Satterthwaite (1982, 21–23) consider the best reading of the Short Count is 7 Ahau 8 Muan, with its Long Count position reconstructed as 9.3.2.0.0 (A.D. 497). Since Kan Boar's son, Jaguar-Paw-Skull, was in power by 9.2.13.0.0 (A.D. 488) as stated in the glyphs of Stela 3 (fig. 51), this would mean Stela 8 either belonged to him or to a later but unknown ruler (see also Schele and Freidel 1990, 165; and Jones 1991, 113). However, problems exist in the identification of the month glyph and, of course, the proper Long Count signaled by the Short Count date, and there are no compelling reasons that would prohibit including Stela 8 in the corpus of Kan Boar's monuments. In a parentage statement on the right side (B5-B8), the mother is identified as the same Bird Claw woman who was mother to Kan Boar; the father's name is not recognized at this time. Stela 8, then, could represent Kan Boar, a brother, or a half-brother.[3]

Stelae 9, 13, and 8 are all part of the Great Plaza stelae row, and in their laconic glyphic statements refer to Kan Boar, his father and mother and, perhaps, a brother. It is possible to speculate that these three monuments were carved in association with Kan Boar's reign during the 2nd katun, and that they were originally conceived as a triad: the short Stela 13 in the center, flanked by the caped or winged figure of Stela 9 who faces across Stela 13 to the figure on Stela 8 who looks back at both Stelae 13 and 9 and holds the tripartite staff for the first time. The triadic theme of transformation and equivalence postulated for the wraparound stelae may have been important, but it is certainly not as obvious.

In Kan Boar's radical revision of the plaza monument and its imagery there is an apparent change of focus from the horizontal, up-down hierarchies of the earlier stelae displaying supernal and basal imagery, to a vertical one that makes distinctions between front and back or left and right. This is better argued for the monuments of Jaguar-Paw-Skull that follow Kan Boar (see Stela 3 below), but this change, nonetheless, must be attributed to the patronage of Kan Boar. Of the possible sources for this new conception and, thus, new presentation, of the honored figure, the one "closest to home" is the warrior pair carved on the sides of Stela 31 with ample background space defining the figural outlines and with no contextual imagery except for supernal glyphs. These images in turn can be traced to the recto-verso pair on Stela 5 of Uaxactun (fig. 20) and to Stelae 4 (fig. 24) and 7 of El Zapote with their connections to Cerro de las Mesas. Regardless of such a proposed genealogy, however, the images of Kan Boar and Jaguar-Paw-Skull make an important comparison, by formal means, to the warrior pair of Stela 31. The new plaza image is that of the attendant, not the thing or person attended.

Tikal, Stela 3
(fig. 51)

Stela 3 was found on the terrace of the North Acropolis, just west of the stairs of Structure 5D-34. It was probably reset there some time during the Classic period (Jones and Satterthwaite 1982, 12; W. Coe 1990, 734–35). A new ruler of Tikal is represented on Stela 3 along with a complete Long Count date, 9.2.13.0.0 (A.D. 488). His reconstructed name, based on the imagery of his name glyph, is Jaguar-Paw-Skull (D1 on Stela 3). Questions remain about this figure's actual identity and his dynastic affiliations. Stela 39 (fig. 18) was the last known monument erected at Tikal by a member of the Jaguar Paw dynasty. The events following 8.17.0.0.0 (A.D. 376), possibly war between Tikal and Uaxactun, involved a new clan or dynasty called the Ma'Cuch lineage with which both Smoking Frog and Curl Snout were associated (Laporte and Fialko 1990, 45ff.). Although Schele and Freidel (1990, 153ff.) and Laporte and Fialko (1990, 45ff.) differ in their reconstructions of these events and the relationship of the characters involved, it is clear that the succession of Tikal rulers was challenged, if not overturned, at this

time. Thus, the protagonist of Stela 3 may signal the return of the Jaguar Paw dynasty to ruling power at Tikal. However, this new Jaguar Paw claims Kan Boar as his father (D6-D8), and according to Laporte and Fialko (1990, 52, 58), Kan Boar was of the Ma'Cuch lineage, so how we reconstruct the affiliation of Jaguar-Paw-Skull is still an open question. Jaguar-Paw-Skull continues the new sort of plaza image initiated by Kan Boar—with certain changes, of course, but these are not as striking as the similarities. Jaguar-Paw-Skull adds four, perhaps six, public monuments to the three erected by his "father," thus marking the forty years between 9.2.0.0.0 and 9.4.0.0.0 (A.D. 475–514) with a series of nine homogeneous, formulaic, and repetitive public images.[4]

As the first monument belonging to Jaguar-Paw-Skull, Stela 3 is the most complex in terms of imagery. It even has an incised basal image, but this is reduced to the point of obscurity, at least for present-day iconographers. Joyce Bailey (1972, 134) likens it to the bound, striated form of the Tikal emblem glyph. When Maler (1903, 2(2): pl. 15) first photographed Stela 3, it had been (re)set with the basal image buried, so that the figure "stood" on the ground; in the photograph, grass can be seen next to the feet.[5] The main figure is represented in profile and this is maintained by the costuming and regalia: there are no odd turnings from frontal to profile, or three-quarter projections, and this consistency of point of view is a feature of Jaguar-Paw-Skull's monuments. The frame of the panel is thin and is overlapped by the headdress feathers, the projecting bindings of the tripartite staff, and by the newly redefined and embellished back belt head, now properly termed the back shield. The overlapping seems to highlight and bring to the foreground these items of regalia and costume. This technique was used on Kan Boar's stelae but not with the same visual conviction that is achieved through the consistent profiling of imagery.

With the addition of the fancy back shield, the image is presented as three major verticals, the tripartite staff, the figure and its costume, and the back shield. This creates a density of imagery in the middle of the monument where the vertical divisions within the image describe differences between left and right, east and west, or front and back, rather than the hierarchies between up and down expressed through basal and supernal images framing the main figure. While the human figure remains centered in the composition, the change in the spatial hierarchy is significant. The stelae of Kan Boar and Jaguar-Paw-Skull represent the main

Fig. 51. Tikal, Stela 3, Front and Sides. (Photos after Maler 1911, pl. 15, reprinted courtesy Peabody Museum, Harvard University. Drawings by William Coe reprinted from *Tikal Reports 33A* by Jones and Satterthwaite 1982 courtesy University of Pennsylvania Museum, Philadelphia.)

figure and his reduced context of gesture and regalia within one unified panel. No obvious allusions to the unseen realms of chthonic or celestial influences are depicted, only the honored figure who appears to stand on the same ground as the viewer. The direction of the profile figure is unequivocal, his staff is in front, and the head within the back shield faces in the opposite direction. The plaza image now displays its meanings carried within the mundane forms of dress and hand-held objects. On the other hand, these seemingly more accessible images require very little of the viewer. There is no need to walk around the monument and, ultimately, little need to exercise imagination.

Uaxactun, Stela 20
(fig. 52)

Stela 20 is composed within a multi-paneled field, and all four sides of the stela are carved. No Long Count date can be discerned in its texts, but the dedicatory date Morley (1937–38, 1: 189) assigns, 9.3.0.0.0 (A.D. 495), is generally accepted as the correct reading. The stela was erected in front of the stairs of the Eastern Platform, Structure E-VII, in the Ceremonial Astronomical Complex of Group E, and aligned with the central equinoctial axis. Stela 20 represents Uaxactun's apparent conservatism, relative to its neighbor Tikal, by its very placement in the (possibly) earliest plaza context for the plaza monument. Following the earlier Stela 26 (fig. 32), Stela 20 represents the main image by the isotropic mode on the front panel, a full-frontal figure pressing the ceremonial bar to its chest by the symmetrical ceremonial-bar gesture. The headdress is large, complex, and almost architectonic in its structured symmetry. Earflares are attached to the headdress and are as big as the face they frame. Unfortunately, a fair amount of the imagery and glyphs of Stela 20 have been spalled off through time, but enough remains to realize that the sculptors of Uaxactun were representing the plaza image through patently traditional iconography. There is little or nothing about Stela 20, other than its dedicatory date expressed as a Short Count, that can be related to what was happening in Tikal's Main Plaza.

The symmetry of the main figure's pose, costume, and regalia is contrasted by supplementary bound figures presented in profiled poses: two kneel on either side of his legs, and four more are interspersed within the glyphs on the framed sides of the shaft. All wear headdresses and some also wear back ornaments. Each little figure, with hands in front of it as if in supplication, is bound at the wrists by knots of cloth that end in graceful, pendent scrolls. Through their gesture, by the curves of their shoulders and buttocks, and in the tilting of their heads, these figures are expressive and vivid in their adjuration. Like the old 8th-baktun figures on Stelae 18 and 19 (fig. 17), across the plaza from Stela 20, all the bound figures appear to float in their panels.

The front, back, and side panels of Stela 20 are each framed so that they are clearly presented as separate, paneled entities around the shaft. On the sides, the bound figures are confined within glyphic texts, and while they are rendered as gesturing towards the front panel, they do not participate with it as in a composed scene. It seems likely that they are to be literally "read within" the text and its stated or implied sequences of events. The glyphs, like the bound figures, also face towards the front panel. Thus, the glyphs on the left panel are reversed, and their prefixes, such as numerical qualifiers, are placed to the right of the main sign.

Tikal, Stelae 7, 15, and 27
(figs. 53, 54, and 55)

These stelae all name Jaguar-Paw-Skull and announce the same date, 9.3.0.0.0 (A.D. 495) in their texts. It has long been assumed that this was their dedicatory dates, and the three stelae were erected at the same time. Both Stelae 15 and 27, like Stela 3, express the date with Long Count statements. Stela 7, by noting the same date with only the Short Count, 2 Ahau 18 Muan, is closer in the structure of its text to the earlier monuments of Kan Boar. All may have been anciently reset: Stela 7 was found on the terrace of the North Acropolis in front of Structure 5D-29 (Jones and Satterthwaite 1982, 20; W. Coe 1990, 777). Thus, as Stela 3 was reset on the western end of the terrace, Stela 7 was reset on the eastern side. Stela 15 was also found reset in the West Plaza, and Stela 27 was found well away from the Great Plaza in Square F of the site map of Tikal (Jones and Satterthwaite 1982, 58–59). Its new setting was accompanied by a sub-stela cache (Cache 51), but there was no associated pedestal or, more importantly, architecture (ibid.). Cache 51, by its contents, puts the late limits for the resetting about 9.14.0.0.0 (A.D. 711) (ibid., citing W. Coe 1990).

These three stelae are closely related by their carving style, methods of framing, postures, gestures, and use of iconography. It is only in the particulars of costume and the iconographic detailings of the tripartite staffs and back shields that differences occur. They, too, may have been conceived as a triad, as was postulated for the three

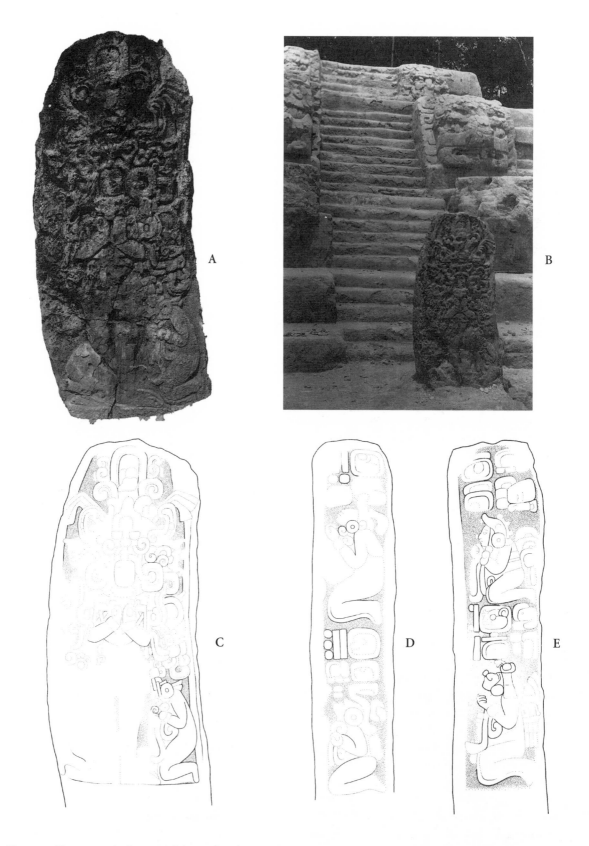

Fig. 52.   Uaxactun, Stela 20, Multi-panels: A) Front Face, B) *In-situ* in Front of Structure E-VII-sub, C) Drawing of front, and D) and E) Drawings of Sides. (Photos courtesy Peabody Museum, Harvard University #H22-4-61, and #U72-111-28, respectively. Drawings courtesy Ian Graham.)

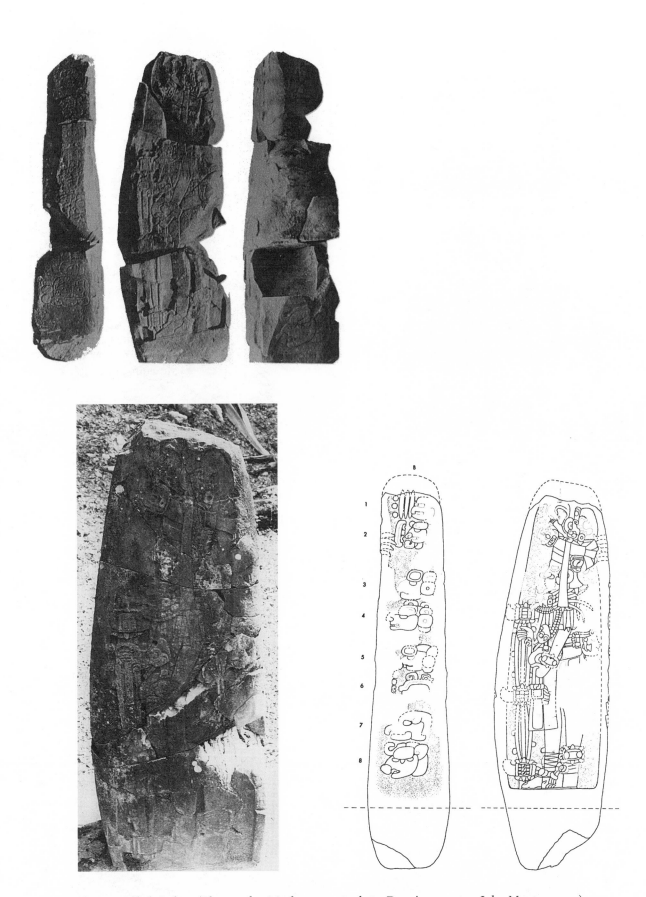

Fig. 53.   Tikal, Stela 7. (Photos after Morley 1937-38, pl. 69. Drawing courtesy John Montgomery.)

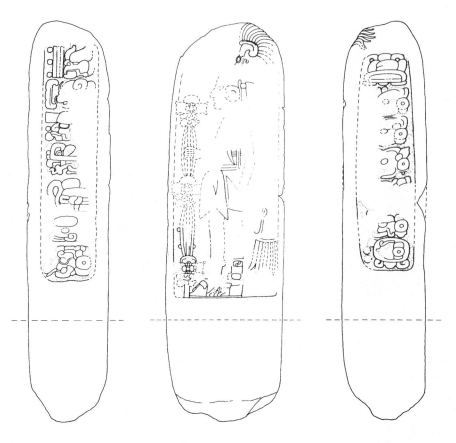

Fig. 54.   Tikal, Stela 15,
Front and Sides. (Drawings by
William Coe reprinted from
Tikal Reports 33A by Jones and
Satterthwaite 1982 courtesy
University of Pennsylvania
Museum, Philadelphia.)

Fig. 55.   Tikal, Stela 27.
(Drawing by William Coe reprinted from
Tikal Reports 33A by Jones and Satterthwaite 1982
courtesy University of Pennsylvania
Museum, Philadelphia.)

Fig. 56. Uaxactun, Stela 3: A) Front and Sides, B) Drawing of Front. (Photo after Morley 1937-38, pl. 60. Drawing courtesy Ian Graham.)

stelae associated with Kan Boar, where again, the most reduced and simple image, in this case Stela 7, was the central one.[6]

If Jaguar-Paw-Skull were a member of the 8th-baktun Jaguar Paw dynasty returned to power at Tikal, he achieved this by fully accepting the new ways in which power was imaged on plaza monuments and, thus, one suspects, the new ways in which power was exercised. He, too, represents himself as an attendant and does not claim a place within a horizontal hierarchy but in the lateral scheme of worldly things. His "support and location" is an actual plaza of Tikal without any apparent metaphoric meanings or allusions to other realms. It is of interest that all the stelae associated with Jaguar-Paw-Skull were clearly reset into their present positions. Where or how they were originally set up is unknown, but this pattern may contrast with his "father's" monuments (Stelae 9, 13, and 8) set in the Great Plaza stela row. The possibility of resetting certainly remains for these earlier stelae (W. Coe 1990, 731), but the archaeological evidence also allows us to suggest that they were found in their primary settings.

Uaxactun, Stela 3 (fig. 56)

Stela 3 was found broken in front of a low mound adjacent to Structure B-VIII. It has been determined by Ian

Graham (1986, 5: 138) that nearby Pedestal 2 had been anciently recut from what had once been the lower part, mainly the basal image, of Stela 3. Stela 3 is carved on the front with a paneled image and on the sides with double columns of glyphs. On the left side, the Long Count 9.3.13.0.0 (A.D. 507) can be read. The basal image may have originally wrapped around from the front to the sides because non-glyphic shapes can be made out below the glyphs on the right side.

The honored figure is wasp-waisted and stands in an articulated-profile pose with the face and headdress in profile, shoulders represented frontally, the waist and legs in three-quarter projection, and the feet and back shield in profile. He presses to his chest a fancy ceremonial bar designed with lappets falling from the chins of the serpent heads. On the viewer's left, the lappet is similar in design to the lappets last seen on Stela 39 of Tikal (fig. 18). On the right, this feature is either missing or concealed by a rendition of the new back shield first seen on the stelae of Jaguar-Paw-Skull at Tikal.[7] The apparent need to provide the same sort of three-part vertical division seen in the Tikal stelae of Kan Boar and Jaguar-Paw-Skull has been achieved by the asymmetricality of the fancy ceremonial bar's pendent forms: the lappet on the left and the back shield to the right frame the honored figure. Next to his legs are a pair of disembodied heads with glyphs on their heads. The one on the right is clearly the JC head.

Above the honored figure's profile face, against the frame in the upper left side of the panel, a winged head shares the supernal region with the rising and arching forms of the headdress. A little bird claw emerges from this icon that compares closely, not only in form, but by placement, with Yaxha Stela 6 (see Maler 1908, 4(2): pl. 17). Supporting the main figure and the disembodied heads, the basal panel is composed of glyphs and graphemic shapes, including the striated projection often seen in front of the broad-beaked bird. An upside-down serpent snout just below and to the right of the main figure's foot suggests that he stood within an open-mouthed serpent, again comparable to the arrangement of Stela 6 at Yaxha. If, as it seems likely, the basal panel was carved to wrap around to the sides, it contrasts with the panel above, where the imagery is completely contained within a narrow frame.

While the imagery and composition of the earlier Stela 20 (fig. 52) make no references at all to the radically new plaza images of Tikal, Stela 3 does by representing the three-part vertical hierarchy and the new back shield. Stela 3 is like a compendium of Early Classic plaza imagery—paneled and wraparound fields; the visual hierarchies of both the supernal and basal images, and the three-part vertical display; disembodied, locative heads; and a fancy ceremonial bar with lappets.

Given all the iconographic information that apparently needed to be included, the sculptor(s) nicely conceived of two frames for the figure: a plain frame to contain completely all the imagery, and an "iconographic" frame made up of the supernal bird, the profiled headdress, the serpent heads of the ceremonial bar, the lappets, the back shield, and the two disembodied heads to surround the honored figure. The "iconographic" frame is formally separated from the human body by squared relief cuts to the shadowed background plane. Its outlines and images are clearly visible and comprehensible as are those of the honored figure.

CHAPTER TEN

History of Early Classic Maya Plaza Monuments

INTRODUCTION

THE ACTUALITY OF A STRUCTURAL RELATIONSHIP between the visual arts and contemporary literary traditions, religious and philosophical tenets, or political circumstances is a subject for debate among historians and philosophers.[1] There is no consensus on how these relationships might work, but there is a deep and persistent belief that they exist. This history is reconstructed with just such an assumption: that the works of art standing in the Early Classic plazas give evidence, embedded in their forms and images, about the political, religious, and philosophical ideals and intentions of their sculptors, patrons, and public viewers. That these ideals and intentions reveal efforts to create a plaza space that solicited public interaction and allowed the ambiguities of individual reception is considered a distinct property of the Early Classic plaza.

Just to recount the monuments as they appeared in time would demonstrate that Early Classic plaza art cannot be explained as an evolving tradition: changes in iconography and composition are too rapid and the visible differences between monuments are too obvious not to be historically meaningful. Therefore, this history proceeds from this perception: that individuals and communities acted intentionally as they made their decisions about the production of ancient plaza art, and that, further, these decisive choices can be detected in the artistry of the monuments as well as in their icons.

THE BEGINNINGS: THREE GENERATIONS, 8.12.0.0.0 TO 8.17.0.0.0 (A.D. 278–376)[2]

The emergence of the ancient lowland Maya peoples into what we call the Early Classic period was achieved mostly in their own terms and through their own energies and desires. These terms, however, clearly included a willingness to enter into an exchange, beyond economic advantage, of information, concepts, and ideas with other, "foreign," peoples. During the first years of the Early Classic period, the lowland Maya were open to different points of view, were willing to experiment with these points of view, and while so doing developed a remarkable conception about public participation in the civic plazas, all of which is made evident by the new monuments that came to inhabit these spaces.

The freestanding monuments are such a presence in the plazas of ancient Maya cities that their first appearance is a distinct signal for the "beginnings" of the Early Classic culture. At this time, the ancient Maya redefined and redesigned their plazas by changing the perceived focus from the grand scale of the stucco masks adorning plaza buildings to the human scale of stelae, and by changing their visible themes from god-like timelessness represented in the isotropic stucco compositions to the freestanding monuments representing themes of station about human individuals defined by time and place. These monuments were placed in the plaza and in the way of the people as they moved within its spaces and are interpreted as signals of a important change in how plaza ceremonies were conducted: a shift from ceremony rich in mystery, perhaps, but one organized around a few active participants and many passive witnesses, to ceremonial events designed to engage the active participation of many.

The first public monuments may have been set up in the Ceremonial Astronomical Complexes of Tikal and Uaxactun, plazas for solar ceremonies well established before Early Classic times. Originally, the buildings surrounding these plazas functioned as definers of the ceremonies and were not used for elite burials (Coggins 1983, 52; Laporte and Fialko 1990, 35), which may be why this particular plaza was chosen to be inhabited by the first stelae honoring an actual person, the ruler. The context was a civic ceremonial space with powerful mythic and religious associations, but with no clear associations to elite or dynastic rituals. While the evidence for the Commemorative Astronomical Complex as the first receiver of the new plaza monument is not firm, if the above reconstruction is correct, it leads to the suspicion that the honored figure depicted on the stelae, usually assumed to be the ruler, was not represented as divine.

The freestanding monuments, positive signs of the differently conceived plaza, were carved and composed in ways that solicited an active viewer. While certain traits of monumental composition and many iconographic details found on Early Classic plaza sculpture can be easily traced to Preclassic monuments, important differences in their artistry distinguish the lowland monuments from the Preclassic monuments of the southern highlands and coastal regions. The advent of the Early Classic period is not marked by any technical changes in the carver's craft but by an expressive, experimental vitality. The way stones were quarried and prepared to emphasize their "natural" state, and the manner in which images were carved to bring out the connotative qualities of outline along with descriptive, denotative abilities are subtle but important features of the monuments that begin to inhabit the Early Classic plaza.

Rough-hewn, these monuments display images revealed by the carving process. If the object was achieved through the revelations of process, so was its meaning for the subject or the viewer. Complex, densely interwoven, and engaging images, sometimes placed within compositional fields of multiple planes, required actions of movement and memory, required viewer engagement. The similarities between the image revealed by process and again by engagement equate in some way the actions of the sculptor and the viewer—both participate in the achievement of meaning. Meaning was not ostensibly imposed.

The programmatic theme of the pair was important from the start, as expressed in monument programs and compositions—recto-verso pairs, stela paired to pedestal (human to insigne), and stela paired with stela (human to human). While it is not certain that stelae and pedestals were conceived as pairs during the earliest years of the Early Classic, the other sorts of pairing placed like with like as reversed images of each other. The implications behind such iconographic pairing were probably inspired by ideas about twins (mythic twins) and on a more structural level functioned like semantic parallelisms.

The recto-verso field, first seen on Uaxactun Stela 10 (fig. 10) representing a pair, initiates the functional requirement, or at least the opportunity, for viewer interaction with the plaza monument, thus setting the stage, literally, for a different kind of experience within the plaza. The recto-verso field may not have been the "invention" of the Uaxactun patron/sculptor, but it had never appeared previously with the clear conviction of intent that is evident for its use at Uaxactun and on subsequent monuments erected in other Early Classic plazas.

Used first to represent ideas about pairing and the pair—two things known to be paired because of their concrete connection with one stone but never seen at the same time—the recto-verso field was quickly adopted as a means for visually separating the image of the honored figure from its qualifying text, as seen on Stela 29 of Tikal (fig. 12). Such a strategy enhances the individuality or uniqueness of the honored figure, standing alone within a panel without sacrificing its known, but not seen, connections to time and place. Thus, the plaza came to be a place where interaction occurred and where individuality could be expressed.

The three compositional modes were all established some time in the Preclassic. It is significant, however, that the narrative mode, the Preclassic composition of choice, was absent from the main imagery of Early Classic stelae, having been eclipsed by the stational mode.

Almost any particular icon used in the imagery of the new plaza monuments can also be traced back to some Preclassic monument. Tracing such connections between the southern and lowland areas, suggested by the use of similar icons, is important in terms of the art history of a particular monument, but not as important for defining the more general art history of Early Classic plaza monument. For this, it must be acknowledged that from the start the Early Classic artist/patron consistently transformed and translated the earlier icons, taken from narrative contexts and themes, by using them in the very different compositional context of the stational mode that thematically emphasized one figure, the honored person. It should follow that the meanings adherent in the "borrowed" icon were also translated and transformed, and, indeed, this history shows that during the Early Classic period, several important icons, such as the supplementary bound figures of Uaxactun's Stelae 18 and 19 (fig. 17), the seated figure on "Stela" 36 of Tikal (fig. 11), and the ceremonial bar cradled in the arm of the honored one on the small Seattle Stela, were made to bear greater metaphorical and allegorical burdens of meaning than the more anecdotal and symbolic values they appear to have previously carried in more narrative contexts. The hands of bound figures are tied into the cupped-hand gesture of the ceremonial-bar holder, and disembodied heads are made to represent, in an emblematic and textual fashion, the names of places and people, and to do so for actual as well as for mythical or ancestral names, thus making (on purpose) ambiguous relationships out of the actualities of name and place. In general, the iconographies of hand-held regalia and secondary images are reductions from earlier narrative traditions in the south, and the iconographies of headdresses and costumes, while comparable to southern costumes and headdress, are better explained as restatements of the isotropic, stucco images of the Preclassic lowland plaza (see Freidel and Schele 1988).

Preclassic lowland cities and villages left truly impressive archaeological records, but for reasons not yet understood many of the Preclassic lowland and southern sites underwent ecological, social, or cultural upheavals just before, and at the beginning of, the Early Classic period.[3] Two sites geographically close to one another, Uaxactun and Tikal, are implicated in the realignments of economic and cultural energies that signal the beginnings of the Early Classic period. At Uaxactun and Tikal, the public was drawn into civic life by becoming actors in the ceremonies and dramas of the plaza. They were not a mute audience passively receiving dogma.

Population growth for the Early Classic is a fact determined archaeologically and may have been a factor in the changes for public spaces that appear to be inclusive of people and ideas rather than exclusive. The communities of Tikal and Uaxactun were able to engage the greater numbers of people by offering enfranchisement into the civic and ceremonial life of the city, by engaging individual cooperation and commitment to a large community. Which came first—the desire for a cooperative population on the part of the non-agrarian elites, or the individual's desire for the living advantages offered by Tikal and Uaxactun—is most likely an impossible question to untangle because both could have been true causes at the same time. The effect was an opening up of possibilities for the individual and the community. Perhaps the historical "themes" for Tikal and Uaxactun could be characterized as good ones, for the ancient Maya of this time do not seem to lack teachers, poets, farmers, or those who would "sit straight on their thrones" (Roys 1967, 169).

It has never been clear how the two cities of Tikal and Uaxactun, so close to one another geographically, interrelated in these early and innovative times. The basic question is, if they were separate political entities, as we assume them to have been, why were they so close to one another? As archaeological information about the earliest years of the Early Classic becomes more complete, this question and its assumption of separateness may be altered or clarified. At this time, however, very few sites outside of the primary pair of Uaxactun and Tikal are known to have erected freestanding monuments before 8.17.0.0.0 (A.D. 376).[4]

Only one hypothetical ruler's name is known from these earliest times, Scroll-Ahau-Jaguar, possibly the name of the honored figure on Stela 29 of Tikal (fig. 12), who stood as the first ruler of the Jaguar Paw dynasty. We do not know his deeds, other than that he had a freestanding monument dedicated to himself. The only hint (and it is very slim) of a connection between this dynasty of Tikal and the rulers of Uaxactun can be found in the costuming of the honored figures, and especially in the long jointed-bead necklace, associated later with the Jaguar Paw dynasty but now worn by the figure on Stela 9 of Uaxactun (fig. 15). Given our archaeological knowledge at this time, Uaxactun was able to erect more monuments than Tikal, and quickly established the conventional set of imagery seen repeated on Stelae 9, 18, and 19 (figs. 15 and 17), and on the pedestals of Stelae 18 and

19. Tikal's monuments consisted of Stela 36 (fig. 11), which may not have been a plaza monument, Stela 29 (fig. 12), and Pedestal 13 (fig. 13), and certainly no clear evidence for a set of conventions dictating the imagery of freestanding monuments exists here. This lack of conventional regularity in monumental imagery and carving style continues at Tikal throughout the 8th baktun.

FOREIGN IMAGES: TWO GENERATIONS,
8.17.0.0.0 TO THE TURN OF
THE BAKTUN (A.D. 376–435)

The dynamic ideals, established by the earlier generations, for public participation in plaza events and ceremonies did not necessarily predict or cause the profound changes in plaza imagery that are evident for these years, but they certainly set the stage for them to happen. The plaza images now display a remarkable diversity because of an apparent willingness to use foreign iconographies and to attempt foreign "looks" by trying different carving techniques. New to monumental imagery, and of foreign origin, are the extroverted and offering gestures, the warrior pair wearing its distinctive inter-regional costume, and which, with another new gesture, grasps weapons. Also new, and of possible foreign origin, is a system of carving that defines a background plane and thereby gives visual precedence to the image over its monumental bearing form. Local innovations for plaza imagery are the use of the seated pose at Tikal, and the representation of the staff and bag as hand-held regalia along with the portrayal of women as honored figures at El Zapote.

The plaza image becomes more bellicose. The warrior pair is directly complemented by the appearance, at the same time, of the extroverted gesture. Stelae depicting the main figure enacting the extroverted gesture show him wearing a traditional costume, accompanied by familiar supplementary images, and carved by traditional techniques that worked between the image and the stone to maintain the visual ambiguities characteristic of the earlier plaza monuments (see fig. 19). The opposite can be seen in the concurrent willingness or desire to illustrate the honored figure dressed in the foreign costume of the warrior, which was simpler, or at least was represented as simpler to contrast with the traditional costumes (see fig. 20). On these stelae the human figure itself, unburdened by weighty and complex costuming,

becomes a more important part of the paneled image and stands out even more by the reduction of supplementary images. For these reasons a figure-field relationship, however tentatively at this time, begins to be established. Where previously the image had been carved *from* the stone, imagery depicting the main figure in foreign costume looks more as if it had been carved *on* the stone.

While Tikal and Uaxactun remain the apparent focus of Early Classic cultural and economic energies, it is at this time that we can clearly record several other sites whose plazas were "entered" by the freestanding monuments dedicated to individuals.[5] Because of the number of its monuments dating to these times, and the suggestiveness of their innovative qualities in carving style and iconography, El Zapote plays an important part in the history of this period.

Stelae 4 (fig. 24), 7, and 3 (fig. 27) of El Zapote illustrate that, at this time, the critical interest in things foreign being demonstrated by the Maya patrons of the plaza monument, was more widely focused than just in the Mexican or southern highlands. The clear comparisons that can be drawn with the stelae carved at Cerro de las Mesas do not suggest the one-way movement of imposed influence, but they do suggest the possibility of direct and reciprocal contacts. At Cerro de las Mesas there was an apparent interest in certain traditional icons of Maya costuming, and at El Zapote there was an interest in the (relatively) severe carving style of Cerro de las Mesas and in the use of the offering gesture for monumental purposes.

The monuments of El Zapote, however, are strikingly innovative within the Maya realm. On its plaza monuments were introduced the important iconographies of the staff holder, the offering gesture, and the representation of women as honored figures (if not on Stela 4 [fig. 24], then on Stela 5 [fig. 35], forty or sixty years later). Furthermore, a speculative case could be made for El Zapote introducing the extroverted gesture, which becomes used as a critical counterpart to the iconography of the warrior pair.[6]

The theme of the pair, important to the earlier monuments of the Early Classic plaza, becomes decisive in plaza displays of foreign iconographies. The inter-regional warrior pair was composed by the recto-verso field on Stela 5 of Uaxactun (fig. 20) and carved by the new and simpler manner, which in turn was paired with Stela 4 (fig. 23) displaying the main figure in traditional costume but making the new and foreign extroverted gesture. Stelae 4 (fig. 24) and 7 of El Zapote each exhibit new iconographies and carving styles that are related to the same warrior figure, and they, in turn, are paired with the extroverted gesture depicted on Stela 3 (fig. 27). Both sets of monuments from Uaxactun and El Zapote prefigure the iconographic theme of the later Stela 31 of Tikal (fig. 33): foreign figures in attendance to, or somehow connected with, the extrovert wearing traditional dynastic costuming. Such juxtapositioning of plaza monuments suggests efforts to explain publicly, rationalize, or integrate things foreign within prevailing and popularly held traditional ideals.

The willingness to entertain difference and foreignness as themes proper for plaza monuments had something to do with what is now interpreted as some kind of civic stress between Tikal and Uaxactun. In broad summary, the interpretations are as follows: imposition of Teotihuacano power at Tikal either directly or indirectly from Kaminaljuyu in the south (see Coggins [1975, 146ff.] for the first and most persuasive interpretation, and Adams [1991, 195–96] for a recent and concise restatement); a marriage alliance or warfare between Tikal and Uaxactun (Mathews 1985, 44–45); intrasite and intersite rivalries between clans and/or ruling dynasties (Laporte and Fialko 1990, 35ff.); and warfare between the two sites (Schele and Freidel 1990, 130ff.) wherein they understand Tikal, under the leadership of the war captain, Smoking Frog, to be the winner. Evidence for these interpretations comes from the glyphic texts carved on the monuments dedicated to Curl Snout (Stelae 4 and 18 of Tikal [figs. 21 and 22]) and Smoking Frog (Stelae 5 and 4 of Uaxactun [figs. 20 and 23]), which describe events important enough to be mentioned also in the long historical text of the later Stela 31 at Tikal (fig. 33). These texts make it very clear that Curl Snout and Smoking Frog, closely implicated and/or related to one another, are central characters in the events taking place during the 17th and 18th katuns before the turn of the baktun, events that were defined through the appearance of foreignness in the plazas of Tikal, Uaxactun, and El Zapote. That all three sites use the Tikal emblem glyph in their monumental inscriptions suggests strong political ties between these cities.

The differences in how the foreignness was portrayed are historically important. At Uaxactun, the warrior pair of Stela 5 is directly comparable to the inter-regional warrior pairs or warrior processions: foreign and extra-Maya themes and motifs associated with Monte Alban

and Teotihuacan. The monuments of Curl Snout, Stelae 4 and 18, while depicting certain foreign icons of costume and regalia drawn from the representations of the inter-regional warrior, do not appropriate its full thematic definitions as does the stela of Smoking Frog. It is as if Curl Snout is trying to reconstruct, or reinterpret, the meanings of the foreign iconographies. His stelae represent foreignness within the context of the throne and seated pose, evocative icons with ancient mythic and/or emblematic references to caves and underworld energies, and within the supernal context of the "ancestral" head, which on Stela 4, at least, is depicted not as a human ancestor but as the deity known as God K. At Uaxactun, Smoking Frog, if he is the patron of Stela 5, understands the plaza as a place to display the appropriation of the foreign image and theme; at Tikal, Curl Snout understands the plaza as a place in which to recontextualize the foreign. It is possible to suggest that the programmatic strategy behind Curl Snout's monuments was to illustrate how the meanings of the foreign imagery were connected to, and, in fact, embedded in, the traditional knowledge of the peoples coming into the plaza. However, the fact is, his monuments also recontextualize the traditional by representing on stelae that which was "normally" represented on pedestals, the seated figure and its burden of connotations mentioned above.

Whether Curl Snout was an actual foreigner or from a rival lineage, he clearly patronized monuments that placed him outside the normative expectations previously established for plaza sculpture and image. The frontal faces, the seated poses, and the oddly shaped stelae, along with the foreign icons, make his pair of monuments truly outstanding in the corpus of Early Classic plaza sculpture. Missing, however, is his image of the extroverted gesture. While the extroverted gesture was as new and potentially as foreign as the warrior pair, it was performed by a figure dressed in traditional costuming, and at Uaxactun (Stela 4) and El Zapote (Stela 3) its implied thematic meanings were somehow necessary for the plaza display of the foreign pair.[7] Would this have been necessary as well for Curl Snout's plaza display?

During these sixty years the plazas of Uaxactun, Tikal, and El Zapote become inhabited by a series of monuments that express foreign images surely burdened with different ideas and meanings from those expressed by earlier plaza monuments. While each site's patron and sculptors seem to have been working within distinctly different agendas for the representation of the foreign image, we know they were somehow intimately interlinked with one another through the constant use of the Tikal emblem glyph at all three sites. Direct appropriation of the foreign icon (Uaxactun), its recontextualization (Tikal), or its presence implied only through representations of related imagery (El Zapote), all seem to point to a shared event, or events, made momentous by inter-regional connections or, at least, the suggestions of them. This event (or events) could have been intersite and intrasite warfare, dynastic coupling or uncoupling, or contact and trade with others— their merchants, their artists, their poets, their warriors. These plaza displays of connections, juxtapositions, and synthesizing were taking place within the shadow or the aura of the impending turn of the baktun.

THE TURN OF THE BAKTUN:
9.0.0.0.0 TO 9.1.0.0.0 (A.D. 435–55)

The turn of the baktun must have been perceived as an extraordinary happening by the Early Classic Maya, and yet the structure of their calendar suggests that it was, nonetheless, a known and certainly a predictable event. Clemency Coggins (1990) points out that in contrast to the smaller cycle of time—the turning of the katun, for which many plaza monuments were dedicated—the turning of the baktun is remarkable for how few monuments even mention its date. No plaza monuments displaying the honored human can be surely identified has having been erected at, or dedicated to, the millenial date, 9.0.0.0.0 (A.D. December 8, 435). Instead, the baktun-other was envisioned as the proper plaza image to commemorate the turning of time and the remembered prophesies for the overwhelming histories that could be evoked. In its way, the baktun-other continues to express the Early Classic Maya willingness to entertain difference and foreignness as public subject matter. Nonetheless, the baktun-other, like the holder of the extroverted gesture, was traditionally costumed and was characterized within the contexts of rich supernal and basal imagery.

Two stelae and one pedestal were identified in chapter 5 as most clearly illustrating the baktun-other. The stelae were erected at the so-called provincial centers (Marcus 1976, 32–33) of Xultun (Stela 20 [fig. 30]) and El Zapote (Stela 1 [fig. 29]), while Pedestal 19 of Tikal (fig. 34) represents that major city's participation in commemorating the turn of the baktun. Identifying Stela 35

of Copan (fig. 31) and Stela 26 of Uaxactun (fig. 32) as possible portrayals was a matter of speculative reconstruction. Pedestal 19, in its frontal representation contextualized by the cyclical calendric imagery of its periphery, seems a more understandable representation of the baktun-other than its guise as the honored figure on the stelae. The pedestal seems to "place" the baktun-other in the chthonic realms. If the reconstruction for the imagery of Copan's Stela 35 is correct, it too offers an explanation for the baktun-other by connecting it, through its recto-verso composition, to the concepts associated with the pair or twins: the baktun-other as a complementary character to the figure and status of the human ruler.

Uaxactun's Stela 26 represents a very interesting change or difference in the monumental representation of the ceremonial bar and its contextual associations. Where previously the symmetrical and isotropic gesture was only associated with supplementary and bound figures, and with non-monumental media, such as jade, Stela 26 represents the first time this gesture is associated with an honored figure depicted on a plaza monument. Stela 26 may not have depicted the face of the baktun-other (we will never know), but it certainly depicts a gesture that would have identified the main figure with the other normally represented as the bound figure, the dancer, and the dwarf (see Clancy 1994b).

Whether such speculation about Stela 26 is acceptable or not, the introduction of the isotropic pose for the main figure was innovative and may have been introduced as a strategy for engaging its viewers through a simulation of eye-to-eye contact. In its symmetry, however, the image of the honored figure is rendered as beyond the consensual realities of place and time. Because of this, Stela 26 could be seen as a mistaken, or at best a paradoxical, conception. The public viewer is engaged with an image, but the image, in its symmetries, does not refer to experiential realities.

Stormy Sky of Tikal had Stela 31 and Pedestal 19 (figs. 33 and 34) carved within the aura of the turning of the baktun, and at the same time Stela 26 of Uaxactun was erected. Regardless of the enormous artifactual information that can be read in its texts and gleaned from its abundant imagery, Stela 31 represents a phenomenal integration of conception, intelligence, imagination, and technical mastery. It presents a visual juxtaposition and conceptual interweaving of the old dynastic image with the new iconographies of the warrior pair. The wraparound field is either reinvented or revived and is interwoven with the recto-verso field to represent imagery that is purposefully equivocal. It can be seen as a three-figure scene, a central and main image attended by the warrior pair wrapped around the shaft of the stela, or it can be seen as a recto-verso representation of one warrior attendant, rendered from both his left and right side and to be perceived as standing behind the paneled front figure. However the compositional field of Stela 31 may be understood, its clear rendering of the differences in costume iconography, context, and regalia shows them placed together in a hierarchical relationship: the warrior stands in attendance to the traditional dynastic image of Stormy Sky wearing the costumes of his predecessors, presumably the Jaguar Paws depicted on Stelae 29 and 39 (figs. 12 and 18). The delectation of intricate, evocative visual detail in the main image is countered, but somehow not polemicized, by the clarity of the warrior pair on the sides. There is a conviction of unity and totality in the imagery of Stela 31 that eludes such descriptions as synthesis, encyclopedic, or polemic.

While Stela 31 was dedicated ten years *after* the turn of the baktun (9.0.10.0.0 [A.D. 445]), its glyphic text, after a long recitation of key events from the preceding 8th baktun, describes the turning of the baktun by a full Long Count expression (G10-H14) followed by a statement wherein Stormy Sky claims that this millenial event took place, or was celebrated, in "his lands" (G15-G17). With the baktun-other at his feet and in its proper place (Pedestal 19), and with the foreign warrior pair in their proper place as attendants, Stormy Sky seemingly places himself and Tikal as the rulers (perhaps even the originators) of the new baktun.

THE WRAPAROUND FIELDS:
THE NEXT GENERATION, 9.1.0.0.0 TO
9.2.0.0.0 (A.D. 455–75)

Casually observed, the first plaza monuments of the new baktun do not reflect what we might expect for a time of new beginnings because traditional iconographies for costuming are maintained and continue to signal old dynastic ties to the earliest years of the Early Classic period. However, the item of regalia held in the hands of the main figure is now the ceremonial bar, and this signals a different emphasis in the role of the honored figure. The warrior pair reappears at Tres Islas, a small and

perhaps provincial site, but this will be its last occurrence on plaza monuments. The extroverted gesture also disappears from plaza displays at this time, not to be seen again for at least sixty years at the beginning of the Middle Classic period (Stelae 10 and 12 of Tikal).

The programmatic use of the pair and/or the triad is employed at this time at Tikal and Tres Islas, and the wraparound field becomes the common choice for stelae composition at these sites as well as at Quirigua. In the 8th baktun, the triads of monument images seem to have developed sequentially, and it is not clear whether, for example, the triad of images made up from Uaxactun's Stela 5 recto-verso and the panel figure of the later Stela 4 was the result of a pre-planned strategy or an ad hoc decision arising from some perceived necessity for representing the honored figure in the plaza. In contrast, there can be no question that the three wraparound stelae of Tikal (figs. 36, 37, and 38) were carved to be close reflections of one another.

It was suggested in chapter 7 that the triad was the result of "expanding" the ancient program of a pair by following the precedent of Tikal's Stela 31, wherein a pair of figures was used to flank the honored image. The interpretations given for the triadic programs appearing in the plazas of Tikal and Tres Islas (and possibly Quirigua) were necessarily speculative, but they arose from an effort to account for an apparent change of focus within the general themes of the plaza monument. Empirically, this change is evident in the greater visual complexity of the monumental display. Costumes and regalia were elaborated and rendered in complete detail, and the visual roles of supplementary and marginal imagery were maintained and often heightened, and all this was composed within a wraparound field. The usual objectifying functions of frame and background were intentionally minimized. Where one can see the background, it is carefully smoothed and even, but because of the density of imagery, the background is seldom a strong visual factor. The frames carved on the wraparound stelae of Tikal are so overlapped by imagery that they are virtually invisible, and the frames carved on Stela 2 of Tres Islas (fig. 40) were made to bear two functions—as non-mimetic frames and/or as iconic references to architectural forms.

That this visual complexity and formal ambiguity should be duplicated or made in triplicate indicates, at least, that the patrons and sculptors of these monuments wanted their plaza images to be iconographically inclusive as they actively sought to engage their viewers by using the wraparound composition. The general content or message embodied by the honored figure does not seem to have changed so much as it was refocused to stress the importance of costume, regalia, and context.

These elaborated costumes and contexts iconographically referred to traditional forms recognizable from Preclassic monuments and those of the earliest years of the Early Classic period. Depicted as monumental pairs, it was suggested in chapter 6 that these monuments referred to mythic pairs from the deep histories surrounding the origins of the present world—the Creator Couple and the Hero Twins. Here, maybe, we can get a sense of new beginnings. The honored figure was shown to be in the company of, was attended by, and was related to, the originating deities recalled by the turning of the baktun. While such connections for the honored figure could have been implied through costuming and context before, now, if I am correct, they are more explicitly represented.

INSIGNIA: ONE GENERATION, 9.2.0.0.0 TO CA. 9.3.0.0.0 (A.D. 475–495)

The appearance of insignia as the main image on plaza stelae was probably contemporaneous with the advent of the wraparound stelae of Tikal, Tres Islas, and Quirigua, and can be associated with the same apparent effort on the part of patrons and their sculptors to refocus the themes of the plaza. The insignia, redrawn from hand-held regalia, performed the same refocusing of significant meaning onto regalia that the wraparound stelae achieved through more formal means. The representation of insignia on plaza stelae was a short-lived phenomenon, but it more clearly illustrates the same concerns that found it necessary or desirable to duplicate or triplicate the stela image.

The use of insignia as a main image is known for the sites of Yaxha (figs. 43 and 45), Tikal (fig. 44), and the Tikal-affiliated site of Corozál (fig. 46). While such a geographic restriction could change with future archaeological investigations, as far as we know now, these images only occur in the central area of the ancient Maya realm, and Tikal actively participated in, perhaps even initiated, the upright imagery of insignia. At Tikal and Yaxha, at least, they were erected concurrently with other stelae displaying the more usual subject matter of the honored figure. Thus, the insignia did not replace the usual plaza imagery, but were additions to the plaza experience—and at only a few sites.

Our current knowledge of the history for these years is not detailed. At this time, it is possible that the Tikal dynasty held political and/or dynastic sway over the city of Uaxactun, if the reconstructions of a war or dynastic marriage occurring during the reigns of Curl Snout and Smoking Frog (8.17.0.0.0 [A.D. 376]) are correct. We have no clue, however, why the city of Yaxha figured so prominently in the appearance of the insignia. While no monument from Uaxactun illustrating an insigne was discussed in chapter 8, it was noted that the aberrant Stela 17 depicting a bound figure as a main image may belong to this rather limited corpus of emblematic stelae. If so, however, Uaxactun did not participate in the prevailing theme of insignia extrapolated from hand-held regalia. The few readable glyphs in the hieroglyphic texts dating from these years do not help us (yet) to understand historical events or the unique appearance of the insignia. What follows, then, is more impressionistic and inductively argued.

Because the insignia were drawn from the hand-held regalia of both the ancient ceremonial bar and the relatively new and certainly foreign shield, I sense that they reflect, in some meaningful way, a "debate," with philosophical, political, and perhaps religious dimensions, about appropriate functions for plaza sculpture and how it should represent plaza ceremony. Because the insignia can be structurally linked, in their difference from the usual image of the plaza monument, to the baktun-other, it may be that they were conceptually linked to this millenial image of the other as well. Thus, the "debate" could have been fueled by the sorts of basic and existential questions, and assumptions, that surely arose in the minds of all people during the turning of the baktun. Whether or not this was true, the appearance of the insigne represents the willingness to entertain differences that has characterized Early Classic plaza sculpture from its very beginnings.

Because the insignia appear at the same time as the wraparound stelae and similarly (and clearly) focus on hand-held regalia for their subject matter, it is logical, but not necessarily correct, to suggest they carried similar intentions by referring to the ancient pairs of creation: the Hero Twins evoked by the shield of warrior pair, and the Creator Couple evoked through the ceremonial bar.[8] The observation that regalia was the object of focus and not the person who wears or holds it suggests that it was the office or status of the honored figure, justified through ancient and mythic connections, that took on greater importance in the plaza imagery.

THE NEW IMAGE: ONE GENERATION,
9.2.0.0.0 TO 9.3.13.0.0 (A.D. 475–507)

In the 2nd katun, the monuments dedicated to or by Kan Boar of Tikal display imagery that is radically reduced from the complexities of the wraparound stelae. Changes occur in the size of the monument, in the descriptive outline and connotative edges of imagery, in the scale of costume motif to the human figure, and in the iconography of costume and regalia. No secondary images are included; no interactive compositional fields are used. The stelae of Kan Boar and his supposed son, Jaguar-Paw-Skull, look iconoclastic in comparison to the previous corpus of Early Classic monuments, and perhaps they were, because they take as their model the attendant figure of the warrior, and the plaza figure is represented as an attendant rather than as the traditional honored figure (see fig. 49).

In making this change, new regalia was acquired or required: the bag and the staff. While the new stela image certainly bears reflections from the warrior pair attendants, there is nothing in its imagery that directly refers to the foreign pairs depicted by Stormy Sky or Smoking Frog of Uaxactun. At Tikal, the plaza displayed a very different image of the honored figure, one that may have bordered on iconoclasm, and one that, for whatever reasons, transcends, or at least eliminates, the polemic between the old and new iconographies that had characterized plaza sculpture since the advent of the warrior pair a hundred years previously.[9]

Information we have from archaeological or epigraphic studies still does not permit any firm characterization for a history of these two katuns. Given Christopher Jones' (1991, 112–14) outline of the building projects at Tikal for these years, it is possible that Kan Boar and/or his son had something to do with the construction of the beautifully stuccoed building, Structure 5D-33-2nd, centered in the North Acropolis and marking the burial place of Stormy Sky (Burial 48). It is equally possible, given Jones' matching of archaeological evidence to reign, that this building was planned, if not constructed, before 9.2.0.0.0 (A.D. 475), when the wraparound stelae were being carved, as I am more inclined to believe. The twin, radially staired, pyramids constructed in the East Plaza, however, could have been conceived and built by Kan Boar or Jaguar-Paw-Skull because they represent a strikingly similar kind of revisioning in architecture (no great height, four equal stairways rising to a bare platform) to that just described for the new imagery of the plaza stelae. Still, we have little information with which to explain why such fundamental changes took place in the plazas of Tikal. An equally vexing question is why these monumental traces of change are not evident at Uaxactun—especially if Uaxactun, as supposed in some historical reconstructions, still lacks independence from the political hegemony of Tikal.

For a long time while writing this history my sympathies were with Uaxactun in that I sensed a kind of valiant effort in its maintenance of the traditional plaza display (see figs. 52 and 56), and I saw this as a deliberate and rebellious contrast to the program established at powerful Tikal under Kan Boar, and followed by his son, Jaguar-Paw-Skull, that promoted aesthetically awkward and redundant plaza imagery. Now, however, I wonder if perhaps the traditional image, and the various ways it had changed for over two hundred years, was no longer an effective plaza image, that it no longer "engaged" the peoples in the plaza. I also sense that the brilliant conceptions about pairing the old and the new, juxtaposed and carved onto Tikal's Stela 31, were reused in an academic manner for the excesses of compositional ploys and imagistic displays represented on the triads of wraparound monuments. Perhaps Kan Boar was trying to revalidate the plaza's public function and to reclaim the engagement of the peoples coming within it. Perhaps this was the reason for ridding the honored image of its excessive regalia, its supplementary figures, and its references to esoteric hierarchies—so that the common humanity of the carved image would be visibly dominant.

At the beginning of the 4th katun (ca. A.D. 514), Uaxactun stops erecting plaza monuments, and the plaza projects of Kan Boar and Jaguar-Paw-Skull are rejected, not to be considered again for another two hundred years (with Stela 30, dated at 9.13.0.0.0 [A.D. 692]). Where I had believed Kan Boar's monumental program to exhibit ideals akin to fundamentalist principles (1992), I now think his was the last visionary effort to be framed within the ideals of the Early Classic period. The Early Classic began as a realignment of elite purposes achieved through a plaza redesigned for a public engagement in its civic life and ceremony. The ideals evident in the Early Classic plaza were inclusive, not exclusive. Their monuments publicly illustrated the imagery of foreign things, and presumably the foreign ideas reflected through these images were a proper matter for general public concern. The foreign imagery carved on the public monuments of Curl Snout at Tikal and Smoking Frog at Uaxactun must have raised questions about the basic contradictions inherent in such difference because various rationalizations for these differences, and this is what is surprising, were so obviously illustrated in the compositions and imagery of succeeding plaza monuments throughout the Maya realm. Regardless of how the political history of the Early Classic period is eventually understood, the plaza monuments, through their compositions and images, tell of a "debate," or a polemic, which existed between the traditional dynast and the more recent foreign warrior pair—a polemic that will never again be so obviously or publicly displayed in the central plazas of ancient Maya cities.

Notes

1. The edition published in 1994, no longer bears Morley's name as an author (see Sharer 1994).
2. Michael Coe (1992, 272–73) raises these issues as he reports on the 1989 Symposium, *On the Eve of the Collapse: Ancient Maya Societies in the Eighth Century A.D.*, held at Dumbarton Oaks in Washington, D.C. He vividly describes a closing of ranks among field archaeologists against the onslaught of new information brought by the epigraphers and iconographers to Maya studies.

    The clear demand made by Jeremy Sabloff as he introduced the symposium was to recognize and work with, not against, the variety and differences that now make up our present data and ideas about the ancient Maya, but unfortunately this was not adhered to in the discussions that followed the presentation of the papers.
3. See Michael Coe's Preface for the exhibit catalog, *The Blood of Kings* by Linda Schele and Miller (1986, 3).
4. Edward Casey (1987, 30, 320 n. 8). Casey is discussing the importance of the contexts in which acts of remembering take place. I think this is largely analogous to what is studied in this book—those aspects of an image that are not usually acknowledged as the focus of its meaning but nonetheless affect how its meaning is achieved.

5. Pertinent to this discussion is James Clifford's analysis of such critiques in *The Predicament of Culture* (1988). The critical issues are real ones raised in an effort to stem modern efforts to characterize, and thus to control, the world and its various peoples and histories through Eurocentric paradigms of time, space, and aesthetics. It is not so much that one's imagination is, in fact, limited by one's own culture and time, but that it *ought not* to exceed these limits.
6. See Linda Schele's (1985a) very useful survey of painted architecture and monuments. She points out that paint on relief-carved monuments is more commonly found in the western regions of the Maya realm, and, in fact, the only polychromed examples she cites are architectural sculptures, such as lintels, not the freestanding monuments in the plazas which, if painted, are painted with one color.
7. The term "stela" is the Greek word for a similar form, but the public function performed by the Greek stela is not precisely that of the Maya stela. Both commemorated individuals and events, but the funerary associations of the Greek stela do not belong to the Maya monument.
8. See Schele and Freidel's (1990, 71–72) discussion of Maya ritual space replicating features of a "sacred geography": the forest is represented by tree-stones or stelae, the mountains by the pyramids, and the cave by the temples atop the "mountains."

For Schele and Freidel, ritual and political life were inseparable, and while they discuss public art and mention its political function (159), their perception of ancient Maya life is a more integrated phenomenon than I have understood it. Because the compositions and themes of architectural sculpture are so different from that of plaza sculpture, I argue that the Maya did make some kind of distinction between public plaza ceremonies and the more reclusive rituals held in architectural spaces.

9. See Thompson (1950, 17ff.), I. Graham (1975, 1: 25), and Mayer (1978, 8–9) for typological lists of monument types. These lists are *ad hoc*, and as far as I know there has been no systematic effort to classify ancient Maya arts by type. It is a project that may, in the near future, be a meaningful one because as Houston and Taube (1987) have shown, the ancient Maya named and labeled their goods and monuments. See also Schele (1990) and M. Coe (1992, 244–48).

10. The intercalation between the ancient Maya and Christian dates used in this text is the Goodman, Martinez, Thompson Correlation (commonly referred to as the GMT). Most scholars have accepted it as valid (but see Kelley 1976). For determining this intercalation, I use a program designed by my brother, Ethan A. Simmons, which gives dates that are three days earlier in the Christian, Gregorian calendar than the dates used by Schele and Freidel (1990). This difference is not the result of inaccuracy on either part, but a matter of interpreting the history and inconsistencies of the Christian calendar (see Aveni 1989).

11. Several other cultures are known to have used the twenty-count system, including the early Germans, and because of this there are traces of this ancient system still in modern English usage, such as a "score" of years or a "string" of ponies. See Karl Menninger (1977, 64–68).

12. Thompson (1972, 78–80, 113) reconstructs the meanings of the ancient katun prophesies given in the *Dresden Codex* as being equally dire.

13. Compare Whitrow's (1988) description of various conceptions of time within history and Trompf's (1979) portrayal of Euro-western ideas about historical recurrences which relies very little on conceptions about the workings of time.

14. A similar assumption is the supposed connection between a linear reality and literacy (see Farriss 1987, 567–69). Both ought to take into account the verbal structure of the language used to describe these assumed realities. As Michael Coe (1992, 51–52)

reminds us, verbal tenses "really don't exist in Mayan languages like Yucatec, or at least there are no past, present, and future of the kind familiar to us. In their place are *aspect* words or [deictic] particles, and inflections; these indicate whether an action has been completed or not, whether it is just beginning or ending, or has been in progress for a while." I am reminded of Benjamin Whorf's (1956) analyses of the Hopi verbal structures.

The current philosophical debate between tensed and tenseless theories of time (see Oaklander and Smith 1994) could, perhaps, benefit by considering the realities in a cyclical description of time.

15. One could imagine, within this logic of history, that an astute individual could "insert" himself or herself into a known historical theme by assessing its cyclic life and managing properly (in terms of the community) to assume one of its known roles or to give a convincing reinterpretation to one of its known effects. We might call such a person a usurper whose actions could be perceived as trying to "rewrite" history (Marcus 1992, 235). However, within a cyclical sense of time, why couldn't someone assume a history and a lineage, say, that wasn't theirs by birth, and in so doing be considered astute and/or lucky and not be perceived negatively as a creator of falsehoods or a usurper?

16. Literacy among the ancient Maya is a matter of debate. Some scholars consider that true literacy belonged only to scholarly priests and certain elites (Marcus 1992, 224). However, like Michael Coe (1992, 269–70) and Houston and Stuart (1992), I think, especially after working on the evidence presented in this book, that a kind of general literacy did exist where some "common" people knew and could read the dates, names, and deeds inscribed on the public monuments. Whether they were aware of the more esoteric connotations that were embedded in the texts is more difficult to deduce. Nonetheless, the very fact that plaza monuments displayed text as well as image argues that the text was for public "consumption."

17. Evidence for long-distance and local trade of necessities, such as salt, obsidian, and basalt is well documented in most archaeological site reports. Robert Santley's (1983) article on obsidian trade in conjunction with the rise of the great Classic city, Teotihuacan, is important for its efforts at synthesizing and explaining the effects of trade. See also Flannery (1976, chap. 10), Diehl and Berlo (1989) and Culbert (1988, 1991).

CHAPTER 2

1. A succinct description of the history of the history of art is given by Christopher Wood in the Introduction to his translation of Erwin Panofsky's, *Perspective as Symbolic Form* (1991, 7–24); for the present discussion, see especially pages 8 and 11.

   One of the first examples of the turning from aesthetics and style to the structural and iconographic aspects of pre-Columbian art is, of course, the great work of Eduard Seler (1902–23, 1977). Herbert Spinden's (1913) *A Study of Maya Art* is a curious mix of the "old" formal analysis and the newer structural analyses of that time, and perhaps his work more closely resembles my present work, even though his philosophies differ from mine.

2. For other efforts to understand ancient Maya art and architecture through its delineated forms and styles, see especially Donald Robertson (1963, 1974) and Terence Grieder (1964). See also Kubler (1975); Cohodas (1979); Schele and Miller (1986, 33–40); Tate (1992, 29–49); Reents-Budet (1994, 7–29).

3. Meyer Schapiro (1969) used the term, non-mimetic, to refer to those aspects or traits of an image sign that are not imagistic, such as its field, format, frame, compositional gestalt, and so forth. Whether the non-mimetic arises from arbitrary (given or natural) conditions or is the result of conventional habits, both are worthy of analysis because of how they "affect our sense of the sign" (229).

   I consider compositions more like diagrams, that is, representations of spatial and/or temporal relationships, and therefore do not include compositions within the realm of the non-mimetic.

4. Bassie-Sweet (1991, 35–37) discusses relief-carved planes as being analogous to linguistic methods of foregrounding. Thus, the foremost plane would present the focus of content or "peak event" (ibid., 47). It seems likely that the ancient sculptors could and did intermingle conceptual and visual logics when using the technique of planar recession, but not consistently and not as a rule.

5. Silhouetting is very similar to what has been described as the technique of the "Cookie Cutter Master" of Yaxchilan (M. Miller 1985).

6. One only has to recall Spinden's (1913) or Morley's (1937–38) positivistic assessments of progress in Maya relief carving that assumed a stylistic path from early-crude, to later-advanced, to late-decadent. Vestiges of positivistic assumptions remain today, Copan's Late Classic sculpture is almost always praised for its sculptural techniques, its veristic imagery, and its near attainment of sculpture in the round. In 1988, I characterized Copan's deep relief carving as transcendent relief.

7. Monuments carved with wraparound, recto-verso, or multi-paneled fields are often illustrated as "rollouts" (see fig. 36, this study; Jones and Satterthwaite 1982, fig. 1a), and as such are substantially changed from their original conception and form, which utilizes different spatial planes, to a form that can be seen in the same way as paneled fields were intended to be seen. I believe this can make a real difference in the way these monuments are understood by a modern audience.

8. Although only one example is known at this time, Stela 5 of El Zapote (fig. 35), I suspect such a pairing was more common than the evidence we have would suggest. The variety of pairs represented through the recto-verso field becomes more varied in the Late Classic period. It is not until the Late Classic period that the recto-verso field is used to suggest the front and back of a figure (see Copan Stela H).

9. The Preclassic Monument 2 from Cerro de las Mesas (Clancy 1990, 25, 27) and Stela 2 from the Preclassic Maya site of El Mirador are good examples of possible reuse or recarving. The Olmec-style stela discussed by Maria Cervantes (1967) is the most convincing Preclassic example for a clear intention behind the use of the recto-verso field.

10. Stela 40 was recently discovered in 1996 on the edge of the North Acropolis, just north of Temple 1. The text of this book was already at press when Stela 40 was published by Valdés, Fahsen and Muñoz Cosme (1997).

11. That the ancient Maya sustained and formally trained their memory seems undeniable, especially given the compositional fields that call for the use of memory. Although a brilliant history of memory training in European cultures is charted by Frances Yates (1966), little is known about how memory functioned in non-Western cultures. A recent book, *Images of Memory*, edited by Kuchler and Melion (1991), calls for such studies, and Edward Casey's (1987) efforts, by expanding the study of memory beyond the visual into a more complex sensual, phenomenological arena, suggest certain ways by which this may be accomplished. As Walter Ong (1982) reminds us, however, literacy profoundly affects cognition and memory.

12. The word "mode" was first suggested to me by George Kubler (personal communication 1988), and I use it similarly to the way in which Ernst Kitzinger

(1977, 19, 71) discusses differing stylistic events (modes) that take place within a larger but coherent stylistic unit: for example, the differing stylistic modes identifiable within the larger stylistic unit of Byzantine art.

13. The use of the isotropic mode distinguishes the Late Classic public monuments carved in the southeastern Maya area at the sites of Copan and Quirigua. In other ancient Maya areas, it is a rarely chosen mode for representation and, except for the three Early Classic examples, it is a Late Classic mode.

14. This is still a speculative proposition. For other reconstructions of ancient Mesoamerican geometries, see de la Fuente (1984), Norman (1986), and Harrison (1994).

15. In this regard see Schapiro's (1973, 37–49) analysis of frontal and profile figural representations. For a careful analysis of frontal images in ancient Mesoamerica and their connection to the representation of deities, see Klein (1976, especially 241ff.).

16. As quoted by Arnheim (1988, 275). Visual narratives have been the subject of several studies of ancient Western traditions—for example, see Weitzmann (1970), Brilliant (1984), and Kessler and Simpson (1985); a few scholars have studied narrative in ancient Mesoamerican arts—Kubler (1969), Clancy (1985), and Reents-Budet (1989). Mostly the latter have been done as assessments of image and text, that is, the visual narrative as analog for literary narrative. What I am proposing here are the formal "necessities" that would allow narrative to be illustrated. I have, in the last six years, challenged students in the studio arts to illustrate a story by using a symmetrical composition. As far as I know, it cannot be done. The difference between illustrating, and making reference to, a narrative is important. Emblems and symbols can *refer* to a story without illustrating it.

17. I regret modern "adjustments" in orientation made for the display of ancient pedestals. Late Classic Pedestals 5 and 8 of Tikal are now vertically oriented, I suppose to better see their imagery, but this denies the authentic affiliation and orientation with their stela-mate as well as with the world.

18. Tres Islas Stelae 1 and 3 may have flanked Stela 2 from that site (see below, chapter 7), thus forming a triad of stelae. Similarly, Stela 31 of Tikal (see below, chapter 6) represents a recto-verso warrior pair on its lateral sides, which flank a central image of the front panel, and all together form a trinity of figures.

19. The three tablets from the Cross Group at Palenque are a good example of the Late Classic use of the triad. It can be speculated that a similar relationship between the central figure and those flanking it existed for the Early Classic period.

Three was a symbolic number in ancient Mesoamerica, used to structure the descriptive levels—celestial, terrestrial, and chthonic—of the perceptible world (see Coggins 1979a, 1985); the more recondite iconographies of certain deities, such as the Palenque Triad (Berlin 1963; and see Schele 1976); the compositions of certain Late Classic monumental programs (Clancy 1986); as well as the formal composition of the *Popol Vuh* (Hendrickson 1989).

20. At Tikal (A. Miller 1986; Jones 1991) and at Uaxactun (Ricketson and Ricketson 1937; Valdés 1986, 1987) the stucco masks and the stelae were, for a while, simultaneous productions of different types of plaza monuments. This supports the perception that the function of the masks was not transferred to the stela, and it supports the idea that the divinity expressed by the stucco masks was not directly associated with rulership, if, in fact, stelae portray rulers.

21. Carolyn Tate (1986) characterizes the Late Classic recto-verso stelae of Yaxchilan as presenting a public face and a more esoteric, private face. Since the pairing on these monuments consists of different compositional modes, narrative paired with stational, her perception has merit for this particular situation.

22. While the ancient Maya "general" public may not have looked any more closely at their plaza monuments than we look at public statues in our civic plazas, the fact remains that they could have.

23. David Pendergast (1992, 62–63) understands the difference between the Early and Late Classic architectural designs of certain structures at Altun Ha (Structure B-4) and Lamanai (Structure A-1) as, "an expression in stone of an ever widening gulf between rulers and ruled." That is, Early Classic design was more open, allowing a "linkage" between ceremony and onlookers, while the Late Classic design was more "claustral."

CHAPTER 3

1. The known monuments displaying this figure type are from Abaj Takalik, Stelae 2 and 5; the Seattle Stela; the Leiden Plaque; Uaxactun, Stelae 18?, 4, and 3; Xultun Stela 12; El Zapote Stela 3?; Uolantun Stela 1; Uxbenka Stela 11; the Bodega Stela (Tikal); the Río Azul Plaques; Tikal Stelae 31 (front), 1, 2, 40, and most likely 28; and La Sufricaya Stela 1.

2. The Late Classic Monuments 1 and 3 (Stelae A and C) from Quirigua are carved recto-verso and display verso images of a similar "other" in a posture thought to denote dancing. As main images represented in a public plaza, they may refer to the millenial, baktun-other. In fact, in their glyphic texts, the date for the beginning of the present baktun cycle, 4 Ahau 8 Cumhu (13.0.0.0.0), is given.

3. The Preclassic sculptures in the round, known as pedestal sculptures, or "bench figures" (see Parsons 1986, 22–24 and figs. 31–34 and 38) from the highlands of Guatemala may have been prototypes for the Classic seated figure carved as a main image on the Tikal stelae, as suggested by Coggins (1983, 56). Also, there is the possibility that the Late Preclassic Monument 1 from Chalchuapa, El Salvador (see Morley, Brainerd, and Sharer 1983, fig. 3.12) showing a squatting figure holding a disembodied head is somehow iconographically connected to the Tikal imagery. The context for the image of Monument 1 is glyphic (not readable), and no throne can be seen in what remains of the image.

   The argument presented here is that the seated figure, as it is used in Early Classic Maya imagery, seems to have been associated with a broader and more ancient iconography than just the fact of its pose or regalia.

4. The best examples are the Middle Preclassic Altar 5 from La Venta and the Las Limas figure, illustrated by Milbrath (1979, fig. 32) and M. Coe (1984, 65), respectively.

5. At Teotihuacan the gesture is also rendered emblematically as a large disembodied hand or hands from which jadeite beads, shells, and liquid issue. The liquid is thought to be water with the connotation of fertility (Millon 1988, 122–23). In terms of Early Classic imagery, the offering gesture has much greater currency at Teotihuacan than anywhere else.

6. Emblem glyphs are hieroglyphic signs specifically associated with a city, a polity, or a dynasty (see Houston 1989; Stuart and Houston 1994).

   The "cruller" is depicted as a fillet running from ear to ear, under the eyes, and over the nose, where it is twisted like a cruller. This particular head appears several times on Stela 29 of Tikal (fig. 12).

7. For the supernal disembodied head as ancestor, see Coggins (1975, 126ff.); for disembodied heads as place signs in the basal areas, see Quirarte (1973, 33), Clancy (1976; 1980, 60–61), Schele and Freidel (1990, 146), and Stuart and Houston (1994).

8. Marcus (1976, 39) suggests that the scroll-baby glyph supported by the female on the verso face of Stela 5

of El Zapote is a family emblem, but does not discuss the appended 12.

9. A scenic depiction of a warrior with the same weapon can be found on so-called Stela 10 (most likely a pedestal or wall panel) of Kaminaljuyu (C. Jones 1988). Here the warrior brandishes the axe with the extroverted gesture in the presence of a kneeling woman. The context, supplied by glyphs and disembodied heads, suggests a mythical or religious narrative.

10. "Thick" is an apt description for the complexities of these ancient insignia, and is taken directly from Clifford Geertz's (1973) essay wherein he uses "thick" to connote the dimensions of meaning as well as the difficult passages taken by the student in an effort to understand a particular meaning.

11. Unfortunately the earliest pedestals are only fragments, and the total context of their imagery cannot be reclaimed. Much of this present interpretation relies on the Pedestal of Stela 18 from Uaxactun of ca. 8.16.0.0.0 (A.D. 357), and Pedestal 12 of Tikal (fig. 47), here given the date of ca. 9.2.0.0.0 (A.D. 475), towards the end of the Early Classic period.

12. It may be that the rectangular block pedestals L' and K' of Copan belong to this group of monuments that present insignia drawn from the ceremonial bar by representing manikin figures (or marginal figures) associated either with the serpent jaws or the serpent pole. Peter Mathews (1985) reports style dates of 9.2.10.0.0 ±? (A.D. 485?).

13. Nicholas Hellmuth (1987, advertising brochure) illustrated a "warrior panel," supposedly from the Selva Lacandon, the western Maya region. If this is an authentic piece, it is more closely related to the isotropic images of Teotihuacan than to the emblematic shield images of Tikal and Yaxha.

14. My thinking on this has been helped by Uspensky's (1973) analysis of "representation within a representation constructed in an artistic system which is different from the one applied to the rest of the painting" (158). "What takes place here is an enhancement of the semiotic quality of the representation: the description is not a sign of represented reality, as it is in the case of the central figures, but a sign of a sign of this reality" (162–63). In his analyses of semiotic and non-mimetic signs, Uspensky is using for the most part his considerable knowledge of Byzantine icons.

15. Ever since the Morleys' (1939) convincing essay showing the closeness of the Leiden Plaque's iconography to that of Early Classic Tikal, the celt-like, jade plaque has been thought to be from Tikal or near

Tikal, even though it was found near Puerto Barrios, Guatemala's only port on the Caribbean Sea.

16. The serpent wears a headdress with the glyphs "6 Sky" and this might specify the place as, say, the sixth celestial level. However, 6 Sky occurs with some frequency as a non-calendrical glyph associated with name phrases and Stuart and Houston (1994, fig. 104) illustrate but do not discuss its possible use as a name for a building at Palenque. Freidel, Schele, and Parker (1993, 53, 57, 73) understand 6 Sky as a name for the world tree or *axis mundi*.

17. One wonders if the Uaxactun example, at least, referred to an ancestor, such as the Lady-Bird-Claw mentioned on Stelae 8 and 13 of Tikal, the mother of Kan Boar. Her name glyph is similarly composed.

18. Kubler (1969, 6–7) discusses the difficulty of determining the sign value for certain images. His term, "figural allograph," was meant to indicate the same ambivalence about "correct reading" as my term "graphemic emblem."

19. *Marginalia*, as a term, traditionally indicates notes written in the margins of texts as well as imagery placed in the margins of texts or pictures. In the Introduction to her study of marginal images in Gothic manuscripts, Lillian Randall (1966, 3) says that a careful, structural study of the iconography of marginalia is a daunting, almost unmanageable task, because they are unpredictable in relation to the texts or pictures they surround. Michael Camille (1992) makes a social comparison between marginal events and central events, wherein the *Image on the Edge* (the title of his book) opposes and, at the same time, legitimizes its center (127, 143). Camille (ibid., 41) emphasizes the punning and word-play qualities of marginalia and demonstrates that these little images often deliberately "misread" the central text.

20. There are logical reasons for the hypothesis that the ancient Maya picked out constellations similar to the ones with which Westerners are familiar (see Freidel, Schele, and Parker 1993, 99ff.; Aveni 1980, 199–204). I consider the dedicatory date of the Seattle Stela to be 8.15.7.5.4 (July 22, A.D. 344) (see below, chapter 4), 147 years later than Schele's date.

21. Not all the images found in the jaws of the ceremonial- bar serpents are marginalia. The criteria used is narrative posturing.

22. Randall (1966, 14) found that Gothic illuminated marginalia contrasted with the central text and illuminations, but not necessarily as conflict. While liturgical texts could be surrounded by profane marginalia, the reverse was seldom the case. That is, secular texts were not embroidered by little images of sacred meanings.

Contrasting imagery, but not necessarily as a duality of opposites, was part of the intention. This is clearly illustrated by Camille (1992, chap. 4).

CHAPTER 4

1. A series of unpublished drawings of the Uaxactun monuments by Karen L. Copeland (1974) is housed at the University Museum in Philadelphia. Copeland's drawings for the recto-verso Stela 10 differ from Ian Graham's (1986, 5: 159) and suggest these figures held disembodied heads.

2. Jones and Satterthwaite (1982, 126), however, also suggest Stela 36 belongs to the monuments of Curl Snout because of its resemblance to the seated figures on Stelae 4 and 18 (8.17.0.0.0 and 8.18.0.0.0 [A.D. 376 and 396]).

3. In fact, Jones and Satterthwaite (1982, 76) report, "[Dennis] Puleston speculated that [Stela 36] stood originally in the room of the structure and had fallen backward when the rear wall collapsed."

4. That the JC head is also common at this time in Oaxaca, at Monte Alban, should be a factor in the reconstruction of Early Classic histories. In 1980 I suggested that the direct association between this emblematic head, perhaps originating in Oaxaca, and the Tikal emblem glyph, as seen on Stela 36, suggested dynastic ties between the two sites. This is still an interesting idea, at least to me, but it will have to remain speculative for now. See Coggins' (1983) criticism and assessment of this matter.

5. In 1980, I reconstructed this image as a seated figure, so as to explain the leg-like form at the bottom-right corner of the panel. This placed Stela 29 within Tikal's tradition of carving seated figures during the 8th baktun, given the earlier Stela 36 and two later monuments, Stelae 4 and 18 (figs. 21 and 22), carved about one hundred years after Stela 29. However, I now think my reconstruction was incorrect. The leg form is puny and there seems little room for a foot (despite my efforts to make it fit). I think this shape is what remains of a pendant from a fancy ceremonial bar.

6. For ethnographic and ethnohistoric studies of Maya community structures, see Vogt (1969), Gossen (1974), Farriss (1984), G. Jones (1989), and Hill and Monagham (1987). Tate's (1992, 16–28) perceptive analysis of such ideals for Late Classic Yaxchilan is a welcome recognition of how community may have been defined by the ancient Maya. I think the very idea of a ruler may have been an anathema for many Preclassic and Early Classic Maya people, and Schele

and Freidel's (1990, chap. 3) description of (divine) kingship as being an "invention" of the Late Preclassic Maya is close to the mark here. Indeed, for very different reasons they come to similar conclusions about Scroll-Ahau-Jaguar when they state in a biblical way that, "He is the kingdom made flesh" (141). I am not convinced that in the Early Classic period the ruler was perceived as divine, but certainly he/she did hold extraordinary power.

7. Federico Fahsen O. (1987, 48) believes that Moon-Zero-Bird's name (from the Leiden Plaque) appears in the cartouched glyph labeled 2a in fig. 13, and thus he would place the carving of Pedestal 13 in the 14th katun, at least twenty-five years after the carving of Stela 29.

8. Many pedestals of Copan display binding motifs carved around their perimeters (Clancy 1976). The Early Classic examples are blocks of stone (J', K', L', and M'), while cylindrical pedestals are more common for the Middle and Late Classic periods (see Morley 1920). This intriguing iconographic connection between Early Classic Tikal and Copan has yet to be explored.

9. For a good summary of the scholarship pertaining to Aztec year-bundles (xiuhmolpilli), see Nicholson (1983, 43–45), and for a concise description of the Aztec calendar, see Townsend (1993, 122–28).

10. Recently, however, Stuart and Houston (1994, 49) have suggested that the glyph compound, Moon-Zero-Bird, is a place name rather than a person's name. The ritual or ceremony that took place at the time of the Long Count date 8.14.3.1.12 would then be read as enacted *at* the Moon-Zero-Bird place, rather than *by* the Moon-Zero-Bird person.

11. Schele (Schele and Miller 1986, 121) expresses some doubt about this argument and in a later publication (Schele and Freidel 1990, 143) does not mention it. I am not convinced this is an emblem glyph, as it may be an early title. The main sign of the Tikal emblem glyph has been used in the imagery of Tikal since the production of Stela 36. However, there may have been two emblem glyphs.

12. The jade plaque in the Dumbarton Oaks collection (see Schele and Miller 1986, 82–83) and the two plaques thought to have come from Río Azul (Berjonneau and Sonnery 1985, pls. 330–33) are pertinent to this discussion. Schele and Miller (1986, 82–83) consider the Dumbarton Oaks plaque to be very early, possibly 8.4.0.0.0, based on their stylistic assessment of the glyphs. The costume of the figure, however, argues for the other suggested date of 9.4.0.0.0. The verso texts on the Rio Azul pieces refer to dates in the first years after the turn of the baktun.

13. Morley (1937–38, 1: 155, 156) considers 15 *kin* the best reading, saying that though it looks like "16," the perceived circle added to the three bars is really a lumpy part of the frame. Morley's photographs (ibid., 5: pl. 54a, 54b) look like they were taken from a cast and differ from the photographs published by Ian Graham (1986, 5: 156–57), especially at the edges and in the appearance of the irregular frame. The photograph of the back published by Graham does not indicate any frame around the glyphs, and his drawing clearly shows the kin number to be 16. Thus, the Long Count date could be 8.14.10.13.16 9 Cib 9 Kayab, a difference of one day from that put forward by Morley.

14. Karen Copeland's (1974) drawing shows a manikin, which is also suggested by looking at the stereoptic photographs by Ian Graham (1986, 5: 156). Graham's drawing is conservative and only suggests an arrangement of a head and serpent jaw.

15. I am not suggesting that this piece of jewelry means that the Jaguar Paw clan originated in Uaxactun, but that this particular item becomes strongly associated with the clan at the same time the warrior appears at Uaxactun (Stela 5) (fig. 20) and at the time the Jaguar Paw clan is thought to have been deposed to Uolantun some fifty years later (Coggins 1975, 146–47; Laporte and Fialko 1990). The figure on Uolantun Stela 1 (fig. 28) makes the extroverted gesture and wears the tubular necklace. This history will be resumed again when these later monuments are discussed.

16. I suggested in a recent paper (1994a) that the ancient Maya would distinguish representations of "others" by marking them with odd proportions and representing them by a different (usually smaller) scale than that used for portraits of humans. The small almost miniature size of the stela may have been considered proper for representing a non-human "other" (if the figure is not wearing a mask). The Seattle Stela, however, is early enough in the corpus of ancient Maya imagery to allow for doubt as to whether such conventional distinctions were in place by then.

17. Mary Miller (1985) discusses the use of glyphs to form architectonic forms at Yaxchilan during the Late Classic. See also Karen Bassie-Sweet (1991) and Carolyn Tate (1992). Usually, however, the "niche" is formed by a vertical column attached to supernal glyphs rather than to basal ones as on this piece. Such a difference may have something to do with the unusual "status" of the figure portrayed.

18. M. Charlotte Arnauld (1990) has called this the "Motagua-Caribe route" in her study of obsidian trade between the highlands and the lowlands, and

she suggests that the sea route was preferred to the overland one.

19. Clemency Coggins (1979a, 45) suggests that the recording of period endings rather than unique (uneven) Long Count dates is a Mexican trait. Both I (1980, 29) and Schele and Freidel (1990, 144) have questioned this reconstruction because there is no record of Long Count dating or any kind of dating at contemporary Teotihuacan. Coggins (1983) later suggested that the hegemony of Teotihuacan influence extended to Monte Alban in Oaxaca, where, in fact, there is good evidence of early calendrical recordings, but not with Long Count precision.

In the same (1983) article, Coggins perceptively notes (52) that the change from uneven Long Count dates to even ones expressing period endings signals a change of ritual focus. She suggests a change from dynastic ritual to rituals centered within the calendar itself, while I am arguing that ancient Maya rituals changed in the Early Classic from being exclusive dynastic affairs to inclusive public affairs.

20. Boulder-like pedestals were found in association with Stelae 18 and 19. The pedestal of Stela 19 seems to have been carved with a quatrefoil frame, but nothing else can be said about its imagery (Morley 1937–38, 1: 167). The imagery on the pedestal of Stela 18 is still somewhat readable although badly worn in its center. A likely reconstruction for the worn portion is a seated figure depicted within a quatrefoil frame.

CHAPTER 5

1. Von Euw (1978, 5: 39) is conservative in his drawing of this area. Looking at the photograph there are suggestions of more motifs in the belt-hanging area than drawn, even the possibility of a jaguar paw, but without the actual monument to refer to, I think von Euw's conservativism is proper.

2. An "Olmecoid" appearance is really not a good trait for stylistic dating. Its use by many peoples, especially those living in what Parsons (1978) calls the Peripheral Coastal Lowlands, continues for a long time, up to, and probably into, the Early Classic period. It is a graphic style that had strong and evocative meanings and, perhaps, was used to refer to things ancient and traditional, or to evoke a mytho-historical time. Like the colonnaded Greek temple, the Olmec graphic style never really disappeared, and was often recalled to fulfill more "modern" agendas.

3. Thompson (1941), Stirling (1943, 42), and Bernal (1976, 145) all compare Stela 9 to a similarly posed figure carved on a boulder at Abaj Takalik (San Isidro Piedra Parada). Mary Miller (1991, 30, 31) suggests its Olmecoid features may have been archaistic revivals, but still considers it to be "early".

4. Jade heirlooms from Olmec times were found in a large cache of jade objects placed in a structure on the main plaza of Cerro de las Mesas. The objects ranged in style from the Late Preclassic to the Early Classic (see Stirling 1941).

5. It is interesting that most Mexican examples also lack this piece of imagery, and in fact the goggle-eyed face is more often associated with this costume in Maya iconography. This particular costume has been the object of a great deal of comment (Bailey 1972, 10; Millon 1973, 1988; Coggins 1979b; Pasztory 1976, 1988; Sanders 1977, 406–8; Clancy 1980, 44ff.; Schele 1986; Stone 1989; and Schele and Freidel 1990, 145–46). Authors have different purposes for their discussions, but they agree on the pervasiveness of the costume and the warrior status of its wearers. The major controversies are what this costume means for reconstructing the history of Early Classic Mesoamerica, and where it originated. While, in the time period under discussion, the other aspects of the warrior's costume are also new and unique for Maya plaza imagery, it is the "tlaloc," goggled-eyed image and the atlatl that are understood as patently indicative of Mexican iconography and are prominent in the reconstructions that see the source and origins of the costume in the great city of Teotihuacan (see especially Millon 1973; Coggins 1975; Sanders 1977; and Schele and Freidel 1990).

6. The trilobed eye and the ovoid form in front of the beaked face are iconographic clues. The contextual history of the trilobe is not known at this time, but its earliest appearances are on Stela 10 from Kaminaljuyu, where it is in the face or mask of the central figure brandishing an axe with the extroverted gesture, and on the Seattle Stela, where it emerges from the jaws of the undulating serpent and is associated with the glyph "6 Sky" in the supernal imagery. The fact that it is found in supernal, main, and basal panels suggests it *qualifies* rather than names a place. Stuart and Houston (1994, 13) suggest that the ovoid element, as seen in other examples, reads as the possessive pronoun *u* (hers, his, its), and thus the bird head would read something like, "his/its (adjectival qualifier) place." For other examples, see Uaxactun Stela 4 (fig. 23), Uxbenka Stela 11, and Uolantun Stela 1 (fig. 28).

7. On Stela 67 of Izapa, the head is clearly a broad-beaked bird, while on Stelae 1, 3, and 22, the heads have scrolls designed as their top half, sometimes looking like eyes (Stelae 1 and 23) and sometimes not (Stela 3). See Norman (1973, pls. 2, 6, 36, 54) and Stuart and Houston (1994, 60, 64). Schele and Freidel (1990, 146, figs. 4 and 15) call the scrolled head on Stela 5 an incensario or a censer but do not explain why. On Kaminaljuyu Stela 11, braziers are placed at the feet of a warrior and are the same design as those depicted on the fragmentary Stela 24 of Izapa. Whether this head on Stela 5 was also intended to denote a brazier is not clear from its depiction. The scrolls could denote water, steam, or smoke.

8. Two heads, similar to the Uaxactun example, can be seen at the feet of a figure carved on a stela from Cahal Xux (or Actuncan) (photograph on file at the Peabody Museum, Cambridge). Unfortunately, the piece is a fragment and it cannot be determined if anything else is comparable to Stela 5.

9. A. Miller (1986, 42–43 n. 31) questions whether the "founder of a dynasty," as Curl Snout is thought to be, would be buried in a tomb that is not axially aligned within the North Acropolis. He assigns Curl Snout to Burial 48 within Structure 5D-33-3rd, a tomb more generally thought to be the tomb of Stormy Sky, the son of Curl Snout. Miller suggests that Stormy Sky's tomb was lost in the various re-building projects evident within Structure 5D-33.

10. In 1998, David Stuart reconstructed the dynastic succession of Tikal for this time as follows: Curl Snout was the son of a ruler of Teotihuacan (in Central Mexico) and was placed on Tikal's throne as a young child under the aegis of Smoking Frog, likely to have originated from Teotihuacan himself. In this reconstruction Smoking Frog, the warrior, is implicated in the death of the previous ruler of Tikal, a Jaguar Paw.

11. Schele and Freidel (1990, 154) label this and the throne on Stela 18 as Curl Snout's name glyph. In the discussion of Stela 18 to follow, the representation of the throne is thought to be better understood as a place name.

12. Clemency Coggins (1975, 145) first noted that Curl Snout used a deity rather than a human head for his supernal image. Her interpretation is that, as a for-eigner, Curl Snout had no "local" ancestors and chose to display his foreign storm deity translated into the Maya God K. I think Curl Snout is deliberately alluding to himself as other (Clancy 1994a). In this regard, see Haviland and Moholy-Nagy (1992, 59) and Freidel (1985a).

13. Because of careful archaeological observations (see A. L. Smith 1950, 52, 101), we know that Stela 4 was erected after Stela 5, and while Stela 5 has the primary position in front of Structure B-VIII, it had no sub-stela cache. Stela 4 was dedicated with a cache and surrounded by a pedestal-like coping. Schele and Freidel (1990, 447–48 n. 51) suggest that the burial (Burial 1) found within Structure B-VIII, consisting of women and children (A. L. Smith 1950, 52, 101) was, in fact, the family of the king of Uaxactun who lost in the battle with Tikal that they believe is commemorated by Stela 5.

14. Marcus (1976, 41) considers both stelae to be portraits of women. My judgment is based on the length of the skirt, which is longer on Stela 4 than it is on Stela 7. However, skirt length may not be a valid gender marker.

15. As mentioned in the discussion of the warrior costume of Stela 5 at Uaxactun, this iconographic complex has received a lot of attention because of its importance to the reconstruction of Mesoamerican history and the role of Teotihuacan. Part of its complexity arises, I think, from the fact that though the notion of an inter-regional sect or solidarity explains the widespread use of the costume and regalia (see Millon 1988), it fails to explain the differences that exist in its use. It seems easier to understand if the similarities were seen as not the result of the imposition of an idea, but as the local acceptance of the idea. The iconographic differences, then, would be the result of local refinements that particularize and integrate the idea into local requirements. Such a reconstruction would explain the proliferation, and apparent confusion, of iconographic associations with the costume. I am thinking here of the long, tubular necklace usually associated with the extroverted gesture. If its appearance on Stela 4 is not a provincial misunderstanding, then it can only be explained by a complex sequence of associations: the warrior conceptually related to extrovert in the Maya area; the warrior costume related to offering gesture outside the Maya area; thus, the offering gesture and extrovert iconography can be put together as they are at El Zapote and Cerro de las Mesas—whew! See Nagao (1989) for a discussion about why certain foreign traits and styles are accepted or not accepted into local art productions.

16. Our archaeological knowledge of El Zapote is no better than our knowledge of the Classic period in Veracruz (see Arnold (1994). That there was always trade of some kind between Veracruz and the low-land Maya seems almost certain (Krotser 1977;

Santley 1983). Mary Miller (1991, 35) considers that during the Protoclassic period (the late Late Pre-classic) the peoples of Cerro de las Mesas contributed more, in terms of "imagery and mythology," to the contemporary Maya than it received in return.

17. It is unfortunate that the numbering of the Cerro de las Mesas monuments is consistently confused, starting with Stirling (1943). In his publication, several of the captions labeling the drawings and photographs of the monuments are not consistent with the numbers assigned in the textual description. Thus, his description of Stela 5 (35) matches his drawing labeled Stela 3 (36, fig. 10c), and vice versa, Stela 3 as described (33–34) matches figure 10a labeled as Stela 5. Mary Miller (1991, fig. 2.10) uses the numbers assigned to the drawings of these two stelae, while for Stelae 4 and 15, she "corrects" the numbers assigned in figure 14 (40). I have used the numbers given by Stirling in his descriptions, believing that captioning is more easily susceptible to typographic mistakes.

18. Given what can be read of the text on the back panel, and the iconography of costume and regalia, the idea that the stela honors a member of the Jaguar Paw dynasty of Tikal is probably correct. The last clause of the text (A25, B25) states of whatever is mentioned above it, "it took place at Tikal," perhaps meaning the "Sky Tikal Place" mentioned on Stela 39 of Tikal (fig. 18).

19. One wonders if this aberrant use of a place sign is an iconographic strategy telling of the fortunes of the Jaguar Paw dynasty thought to have been deposed to Uolantun. Also, this aberrance may explain why the supernal portion was recut into a pedestal and placed where a locative with potentially political meanings would be more acceptable.

CHAPTER 6

1. It might also refer to 6 Sky, a place associated with cosmic metaphors, and in several texts specifically with the Jaguar Paw dynasty of Tikal. See the cache pot (Cache 198) found in Structure 5D-46 of the Central Acropolis (Harrison 1970, 262; Coggins 1975, 203–8; and Freidel, Schele, and Parker 1993, 73–74).

2. Fash and Stuart (1991, 151, 153) see a close stylistic relationship to the recently discovered Stela 63 of Copan, carved only with glyphs but bearing a stylistic resemblance to the imagery carved on Stela 35. The glyphic stela begins with an Initial Series date of 9.0.0.0.0 and mentions an important early ruler of Copan, Yax-K'uk-Mo'. Fash and Stuart (ibid.) consider that Stela 35, too, was patronized by Yax-K'uk-Mo' and agree with Baudez in his assessment of southern affinities. Fash (1991, 81) later states that although Stela 63 bears the millenial Long Count, it was dedicated by the son of Yax-K'uk-Mo', and therefore the Initial Series date was retrospective and not the dedicatory date.

3. The comparison with Stela 5 is somewhat awkward because there is no direct evidence that there was any similar concern for the turning of the baktun behind this later pairing of a human with an anthropomorph. I have previously suggested (1988, 203) that Stela 5 might represent the same person at different times of his life, essentially alive and "other" or dead.

4. Circled knees occur on Stelae A, B, D, F, I, N, 4, 6, and possibly 2. They are also a feature given the male figure carved on the Late Classic wall panel now in the New Orleans Museum of Art and thought to belong to the Piedras Negras polity sphere (Montgomery 1992). See as well, Stelae 15 and 16 and Lintel 4 of Piedras Negras.

5. Because Morley's (1937–38, 1: 179–81) discussion of the Uaxactun monuments preceded the publication of the archaeological report (A. L. Smith 1950, 23–24) by twelve years, his designations for the separate buildings of Structure A-V differ from Smith's. Morley's Shrine I, that housed Stela 22, is Smith's Construction H, while Construction G, designated Shrine II by Morley, was built over Stela 26 and the earlier stairs to the main court of Structure A-V. Unfortunately, these stairs contained a small, ill-defined structure called Shrine 1 by Smith, which was matched by a similar structure in front of Stela 26 called Shrine 2 (see A. L. Smith 1950, fig. 63).

6. The symmetrical ceremonial-bar gesture has a long history (see chapter 3 above). Depicted on non-monumental jade pieces carved during the Early Classic period, this gesture signifies dance (Clancy 1994b).

7. The isotropic composition occurs only rarely during the Classic period, but for reasons that may have been structurally or historically similar to the carving of Stela 26, it was very important, during the Late Classic, in the southeast at Copan and Quirigua and in the southwest at Toniná, Chiapas. When it was used at Piedras Negras, during the Late Classic, it was part of a series of monuments dedicated by/to one ruler (see Proskouriakoff 1960) and therefore shown as an aspect of rulership along with the more usual stational compositions.

Interestingly, A. L. Smith (1950, 23) suggests that since Stela 26 represents "one of the earliest attempts at a full-face figure on a stela," it had been awkwardly and poorly carved, and was, finally, unacceptable. This, Smith believes, would explain its defacement and the remains of paint, which was used to replace the image.

8. Miscellaneous Stone 110, published by Jones and Satterthwaite (1982, 93, fig. 66t), depicts this chain. The fragment is so small that neither its monument type nor the context of the chain can be reconstructed. MS 110 was found in the fill of Structure 5D-32-2nd and may have belonged to a monument carved earlier than Stela 31 or Pedestal 19.

9. Otherwise, the tassle headdress and goggle eyes seldomly occur together. The stucco-painted back of a pyrite plaque from Tomb B-V at Kaminaljuyu, however, exceptionally shows just this image (see Kidder, Jennings, and Shook 1946, fig. 175a).

   During the Late Classic, the tassle headdress is dropped in favor of a large, round turban, while the goggle eyes persist along with the "Mexican year sign" as part of the costume, now supposedly associated with war timed by the movements of the planet Venus (see Schele and Freidel 1990, 146–48).

10. Besides Stela 31 of Tikal, pairs of different heights include the figures that flank the great emblems on the tablets of the Cross Group at Palenque, and, similarly, the pair of figures that flank the ball on the Ballcourt Markers of Copan (Clancy 1986). Several Late Classic recto-verso pairs carved on stelae are either of different heights or clearly of different ages (Kubler 1969; Clancy 1988).

11. The question here is whether the wraparound Stelae 1, 2, or 28, from Tikal (figs. 36, 37, and 38) were carved before or after Stela 31. Most scholars consider they were carved after Stela 31, but see Bailey (1972, 65) where she argues Stelae 1, 2, and 28 were carved before, and Fahsen (1987) who thinks Stela 28 was carved before Stela 31. Also, Stela 1 of La Sufricaya was carved with a wraparound field. Stylistically, Mathews (1985, 8) places it in the 8th baktun, but it is a fragment, and no glyphs can be detected (at least on the photographs I have seen).

12. The ceramic assemblage known as the Becan cache, although not monumental, participates in the theme of juxtaposition in a way that echoes the complexities of Stela 31 from Tikal and the explicitness of the El Zapote stelae (4 and 7). (See Ball 1974; Clancy 1985, 118–19.)

13. The various iconographic interpretations for the little reclining figure are confused. It is also thought to represent a variant of God III in the Palenque Triad (Freidel and Schele 1988, 70–72; Schele and Miller 1986, 51), but until 1980, at least, this little figure was associated with God II of the Palenque Triad (Schele 1976; Lounsbury 1980). The little reclining figure also has a formal affinity to the Postclassic sculptural form of a semi-reclining figure known as the Chacmool.

14. I have used Clara Millon's (1972) stylistic descriptions to determine when the trapeze and ray sign appears at Teotihuacan. Its use during the later Xolalpan and Metepec periods is as a border emblem for murals and appended to speech scrolls (see Berrin 1988, 192). An iconographic history of the trapeze and ray has been sketched out by Doris Heyden (1977) who sees its origins in Chavin (ancient Peru) imagery, and its basic meaning having to do with fertility and ancestors. As discussed below, the insigne was connected in ancient Maya ideology to the warrior sodality introduced around 8.17.0.0.0. Coggins (1983) makes this connection as well.

CHAPTER 7

1. Proskouriakoff (1950, 195) gives the style date for Stela 1 as 9.0.0.0.0 ± 2 katuns, for Stela 2 as 9.3.10.0.0 ± 2 katuns, and for Stela 28, reported by Jones and Satterthwaite (1982, 60), as 8.19.0.0.0 ± 3 katuns. Bailey (1972, 65) suggested that the wraparound stelae were carved before Stela 31 with Stela 28 being the last of the triad to be carved. Coggins (1975, 186) considers them to be posthumous portraits of Stormy Sky carved after 9.1.1.10.0, the date painted on the wall of Stormy Sky's Tomb, 48. She does not speculate on the order in which they were carved. Fahsen (1987, 48–49) believes that Stela 28 is of 8th-baktun date and depicts the same Jaguar Paw as does Stela 39 (fig. 18), basing his identification on the beautifully rendered jaguar paw carved at the bottom of the left-hand serpent pole.

2. Stormy Sky's name is part of a statement that includes the *way* glyph, interpreted by Houston and Stuart (1989) as meaning "co-essence." This phrase is given at Az6-Bz8, and it seems to suggest that Stormy Sky, himself, was the *way* or co-essence of Tikal. Such a statement could make sense, given the following descriptive analysis for these stelae, because they place the main figure in an intricate contextual association with what we could call a mythical pair.

3. In 1997 Valdés, Fahsen and Muñoz Cosme published the new Stela 40 from Tikal, dated 9.1.13.0.0 (A.D. 468). It is a multi-panel composition carved on three sides of the monument. While echoing Stela 31's program, the two figures carved on the sides wear male and female costumes that have strong iconographic similarities to Stela 5 of El Zapote. The patron of Stela 40, was Kan Boar (see below) who with his next monument, Stela 9 (Fig. 48), drastically changed the Tikal plaza image of rulership. Valdés et. al. (ibid.) suggest the lateral figures represent Stormy Sky, the father of Kan Boar, and Curl Snout, his grandfather, as the Maize Diety twins.

4. This is the same kind of cape worn by the kneeling warriors wearing beaded helmets depicted on the Late Classic panel (Lintel 12) from Piedras Negras. Note especially the last kneeling figure on the left where his back ornament is visible (see Maler 1901, 2(1): pl. 31).

5. However, birds are beautifully carved on the cylindrical Pedestals 3 and 20 of Izapa.

6. Because the Early Classic warrior pair costume compares positively to the Late Classic costumes worn by ballplayers depicted on ballcourt reliefs at El Tajín, Veracruz and Chichen Itza in the Yucatan, I have previously (1980, 52–53) suggested that while the evidence for a ballgame connection is unclear during the Early Classic, it may, nonetheless, have existed wherein the warrior pair were conceptually linked to the Hero Twins of the *Popol Vuh*.

7. I do not wish to imply by this comparison that the sculptors of Stela 4 were unable to "solve" this source of tension. The tension brought about by the frontal face may have been intentional and, indeed, was underscored by the carvers of Stela 4 as they created concentric circles around the frontal face with the headdress and necklace.

8. Another stela at Quirigua, Monument 21 (Stela U), is also dated to the 2nd katun. Just enough of the imagery remains on its sides to indicate a wraparound composition (Sharer 1990, 70–71, fig. 45). The possibility exists that Monuments 26 and 21 were originally carved to be a pair, and I wonder if there might not be a third stela yet to be unearthed.

CHAPTER 8

1. This combination of motifs is directly comparable to the headdress worn by the figure engraved on Plaque 1 from Río Azul, where its major components are the animal skull with the snake coming from its nose, and a twisted vertical bar with an earflare and ahau bone tied to it (see Berjonneau and Sonnery 1985, figs. 330–31). This plaque is paired with another (Plaque 2), and, because they display texts with dates, we know they were carved around 9.1.0.0.0 (A.D. 455).

2. Just after the marking of the 4th katun, starting at 9.4.3.0.0, the public image of Tikal returns to the wraparound composition of Stela 31 (Stelae 23 and 25) and the display of the extroverted gesture (Stelae 10 and 12).

3. Stela 17 from Group D of Uaxactun may belong in this collection of monuments bearing insignia as a main image. Its imagery is in ruinous condition, but it may be construed as representing in profile a kneeling bound figure as its main image (see Ian Graham 1986, 5: 171–72). In determining the possible emblematic character of this bound figure, it may or may not be significant that all other examples of insignia discussed in this chapter were derived from hand-held regalia. Morley (1937–38, 1: 172–75) is fairly certain that Stela 17 is properly dated at 8.19.0.0.0 (A.D. 416), but I see telling resemblances to the carving style and iconography of Stela 20 of Uaxactun (9.3.0.0.0 [A.D. 495]).

CHAPTER 9

1. While Stela 9 cannot be understood as a wraparound composition, certainly not in comparison with Stelae 1, 2, and 28 (or Monument 26 from Quirigua), it does seem to make an intentional allusion to this field.

2. Coggins (1979a) has suggested that the day sign read as 2 Ahau by Jones and Satterthwaite (1982, 24–25) is, instead, 4 Ahau, and she, therefore, considers Stela 9 to date to 9.3.0.0.0 (A.D. 495).

3. As Joyce Bailey (1972, 152) points out, there are no diagnostic stylistic differences between the stelae of Kan Boar and Jaguar-Paw-Skull. Context, iconography and dates are the only means of trying to group these stelae.

4. Stelae 3, 7, 15, and 27 were almost surely dedicated to or by Jaguar-Paw-Skull. He may also have had Stela 6 (9.4.0.0.0) carved. For stylistic reasons, I add to this series Pedestal 12, but claiming this monument as belonging to Jaguar-Paw-Skull's corpus is debatable because it has no text or date.

5. Neither Maler (1903, 2(2): 69–70) nor Morley (1937–38, 1: 302) mention the basal image. William Coe (1990, 733–34) describes Stela 3's resetting as having concealed the basal image.

6. See Coggins (1979a) for an alternative understanding of these monuments. She suggests this was a time of joint rule, shared between Kan Boar and Jaguar-Paw-Skull. She pairs the stelae with Long Counts (15 and 27) with those that bear Short Counts (9 and 7), respectively.

7. The ceremonial bar of Stela 3 predicts in fairly specific ways the same feature depicted on the first stelae carved at the site of Caracol (Stelae 5 and 16, especially) during the Middle Classic period (see Beetz and Satterthwaite 1981, figs. 6 and 15). It may be worth noting, as well, that the lappet is similar to the apron worn by the honored figure carved on Stelae 6 and 8 of Cerro de las Mesas (fig. 26).

CHAPTER 10

1. See Alastair Fowler (1972) and W. J. T. Mitchell (1980; 1986, especially the first chapter). Mario Praz's (1970) effort is a classic, but for me, Uspensky's (1973) work is valuable because it focuses on the formal rather than the symbolic level.

   Barbara and Dennis Tedlock's (1985) exploration of such structural connections existing between Quiche image and language is more pertinent to ancient Mesoamerican studies, as is Tzvetan Todorov's (1985) essential use of these assumptions for his history of the conquest. However, in my understanding, the insistence on the primacy of language, spoken and/or written, to explain various cultural constructions of reality weakens the validity of most arguments for structural inter-affiliations between the visual arts and other cultural endeavors, especially literature (see Mitchell 1994, 83 ff.).

2. Generations are given as abstract durations, which, nonetheless, has assisted me, and so perhaps others, in realizing more concretely (or existentially) the actual passage of time being described here.

3. See Sheets (1979); Morley, Brainerd, and Sharer (1983); Parsons (1988, 41–41); and Bove (1991).

4. Sites that may possibly have done so are Yaxha (Stela 5?), Bejucal (Mathews 1985, 31), El Palmar (near Xpuhil), and Calakmul, and perhaps the site from which the Seattle Stela originated. As archaeological work progresses at Calakmul, however, we may find ourselves dealing with a different political configuration in the lowlands than the one we now envision as centered around Tikal and Uaxactun at the beginning of the Early Classic. (See Martin and Grube 1994).

   It is impossible to suppress the idea, given the importance of the pair as a programmatic theme, that the two sites of Uaxactun and Tikal were somehow anciently conceived as a pair of civic and ceremonial entities, that they were not separate political entities, and that their existences were interwoven on this more ideological level.

5. The sites of El Zapote and Uolantun, are known to have erected stelae at this time. Stela 12 of Xultun is placed in this period, but it displays no clear dates. It seems fairly certain that Yaxha and Calakmul were also erecting stelae, but, again, no sure dates can be assigned.

6. Stela 6 of El Zapote (not discussed in chapter 4 because of its poor condition) is an early monument that displays its main figure making the extroverted gesture. While little else may be said about this stela, it was carved at a site with almost certain connections with Cerro de las Mesas, and this might economically explain how the extroverted gesture, depicted on the early Stela 9 of Cerro de las Mesas, came into the Maya lowlands. In chapter 5, Stela 9 of Cerro de las Mesas was compared with Stela 12 of Xultun (fig. 19). However, like El Zapote, little archaeological exploration has been performed or published for Xultun.

7. Speculatively, it is worth considering that Uolantun Stela 1 (fig. 28) might be the "missing" monument in Curl Snout's plaza display. Certainly, a strong stylistic comparison can be made between it and the carving on Stela 18, and Stela 1 depicts the supernal ancestral head as God K, repeating the imagery of Stela 4. However, such a reconstruction would require that Curl Snout was somehow directly related to the Jaguar Paw dynasty because there can be little doubt that Stela 1 of Uolantun is dedicated to a Jaguar Paw, or more generally to the Jaguar Paw clan/dynasty. This would actually fit with Schele and Freidel's (1990, 155–57) description of Curl Snout's parentage. The last known Jaguar Paw at Tikal was represented on Stela 39 (fig. 18), which, as reconstructed in chapter 4, would have depicted much the same imagery as the Uolantun stela. Coggins (1975, 142–47) suggests, on the basis of the text on Stela 31 of Tikal, that Curl Snout married this Jaguar Paw's daughter and ousted his son, who was deposed to Uolantun. The historical events of these few and seemingly crucial years are still unclear, and Uolantun's Stela 1 needs to be taken into greater account.

8. I wonder if there is an analogy with the Postclassic, Mexican pairing of an ancient fertility deity, Tlaloc, with the newer warrior hero/god, Huitzilopochtli, so

prominently expressed in the two-templed Templo Mayor of Tenochtitlan (Townsend 1982). It has long been assumed that the "conditions" of the pair and duality are profound aspects of ancient Mesoamerican thought, and so, if such an analogy is proper, it demonstrates an interesting historical difference. In both cases, the warrior represents the newer half of the pair, but the Early Classic version has the goggle eyes associated with the warrior, while the Postclassic version uses the goggle eyes to signify the ancient half of the pair.

9. I have previously speculated (1992) that Kan Boar rejected his father's (Stormy Sky) efforts at connecting the iconographies of the warrior and the traditional dynast (without giving up the hierarchical differences between them) because he fully accepted what I termed the fundamental and populist tenets of the inter-regional warrior sodality. In being the first Maya ruler to do so, he was thought to have set the stage for another, but Middle and Late Classic "debate" about how rulers were to be properly portrayed in the plaza.

References

Adams, Richard E. W., ed.

1977   *The Origins of Maya Civilization.* A School of
American Research Book. Albuquerque:
University of New Mexico Press.

1991   *Prehispanic Mesoamerica.* Rev. ed. Norman:
University of Oklahoma Press.

Adams, Richard E. W., and Richard C. Jones

1981   Spatial Patterns and Regional Growth Among
Classic Maya Cities. *American Antiquity*
46(2): 301–22.

Agrinier, Pierre

1960   The Carved Human Femurs from Tomb 1,
Chiapa de Corzo, Chiapas, Mexico. *Papers
of the New World Archaeological Foundation*
6: 1–28.

Anderson, Dana

1978   Monuments [of Chalchuapa]. In *The Prehis-
tory of Chalchuapa*, edited by Robert Sharer.
Vol. 1. Museum Monographs. University
Museum. Philadelphia: University of Pennsylvania.

Andrews, E. Wyllys, V

1986   Olmec Jades and Maya Ceramics. In *Research
and Reflections in Archaeology and History*,
Essays in Honor of Doris Stone, edited by E.
Wyllys Andrews V. Middle American Re-
search Institute, Publication 57. New Orleans:
Tulane University.

Andrews, George F.

1975   *Maya Cities: Placemaking and Urbanization.*
Norman: University of Oklahoma Press.

Angulo V., Jorge

1987   The Chalcatzingo Reliefs: An Iconographic
Analysis. In *Ancient Chalcatzingo*, edited by
David C. Grove. Austin: University of Texas
Press.

Arnauld, M. Charlotte

1990   El Comercio Clasico de Obsidiana: Rutas
entre Tierras Altas y Tierras Bajas en el Area
Maya. *Latin American Antiquity* 1(4): 347–67.

Arnheim, Rudolf

1988   Symmetry and the Organization of Form: A
Review Article. *Leonardo* 21(3): 273–76.

Arnold, Philip J., III

1994   An Overview of Southern Veracruz Archaeology. *Ancient America* 5(2): 215–21.

Ashmore, Wendy

1980   Discovering Early Classic Quirigua. *Expedition* 23(1): 35–44.

Aveni, Anthony

1980   *Sky Watchers of Ancient America.* Austin:
University of Texas Press.

1989   *Empires of Time: Calendars, Clocks, and Cultures.* New York: Basic Books, Inc., Publishers.

Awe, Jaime J., Mark D. Campbell, and Jim Conlon

1991   Preliminary Analysis of the Spatial Configuration of the Site Core at Cahal Pech, Belize, and its Implications for Lowland Maya Social Organization. *Mexicon* 13(2): 25–30.

Ayala Falcón, Maricela

1987 La Estela 39 de Tikal, Mundo Perdido. In *Memorias de Primer Coloquio de Mayistas (August 1985, San Cristobal de las Casas).* Universidad Nacional Autónoma de México, Mexico.

Bailey, Joyce

1972 A Preliminary Investigation of the Formal and Interpretative Histories of Monumental Relief Sculpture from Tikal, Guatemala: Pre-, Early, and Middle Classic Periods. Ph.D. diss., Yale University.

Ball, Joseph W.

1974 A Teotihuacan-Style Cache from the Maya Lowlands. *Archaeology* 27(1): 2–9.

Bardawil, Lawrence W.

1976 The Principal Bird Deity in Maya Art—An Iconographic Study of Form and Meaning. In *The Art, Iconography and Dynastic History of Palenque.* Part 3. Segunda Mesa Redonda de Palenque, 1974. Edited by Merle Greene Robertson. Pebble Beach, CA: Pre-Columbian Art Research, The Robert Louis Stevenson School.

Barthes, Roland

1972 *Mythologies.* Translated by Annette Lavers. New York: Hill and Wang.

Bassie-Sweet, Karen

1991 *From the Mouth of the Dark Cave.* Norman: University of Oklahoma Press.

Bateson, Gregory

1979 *Mind and Nature: A Necessary Unity.* New York: E. P. Dutton.

Baudez, Claude E.

1983 La Estela 35. In *Introducción a la arqueología de Copan,* edited by Claude E. Baudez. Vol. 2. Tegucigalpa, Honduras: Secretaria de Estado en el Despacho de Cultura y Turismo.

Becker, Marshall

1979 Plaza Plans and Settlement Patterns: Regional and Temporal Distributions as Indicators of Cultural Interactions in the Maya Area. Paper presented at "Interdisciplinary Approaches to Maya Studies," 43rd International Congress of Americanists, Vancouver.

Beetz, Carl P., and Linton Satterthwaite

1981 *The Monuments and Inscriptions of Caracol, Belize.* Museum Monograph 45. University Museum. Philadelphia: University of Pennsylvania.

Berjonneau, Gerald, and Jean-Louis Sonnery

1985 *Rediscovered Masterpieces of Mesoamerica.* Boulogne: Editions Arts 135.

Berlin, Heinrich

1958 El Glifo "emblema" en las Inscripciones Mayas. *Journal de la Société des Américanistes* 47: 111–19.

1963 The Palenque Triad. *Journal de la Société des Américanistes,* n.s., 52: 91–99.

Berlo, Janet C.

1984 *Teotihuacan Art Abroad: A Study of Metropolitan Style and Provincial Transformation in Incensario Workshops.* BAR (British Archaeological Reports), International Series 199(i). Oxford, UK: BAR.

Bernal, Ignacio

1976 *The Olmec World.* Translated by Doris Heyden and Fernando Horcasitas. Berkeley: University of California Press.

Berrin, Kathleen, ed.

1988 *Feathered Serpents and Flowering Trees.* San Francisco: The Fine Arts Museums of San Francisco.

Bove, Frederick

1991 The Teotihuacan-Kaminaljuyu-Tikal Connection: A View from the South Coast of Guatemala. In *Sixth Palenque Round Table, 1986.* Edited by Virginia M. Fields. Gen. ed. Merle Greene Robertson. Norman: University of Oklahoma Press.

Brilliant, Richard

1984 *Visual Narratives: Storytelling in Etruscan and Roman Art.* Ithaca: Cornell University Press.

Camille, Michael

1992 *Image on the Edge: The Margins of Medieval Art.* Cambridge: Harvard University Press.

Casey, Edward S.

1987 *Remembering: A Phenomenological Study.* Bloomington: Indiana University Press.

Caso, Alfonso

1965 Zapotec Writing and Calendar. In Archeology of *Southern Mesoamerica.* Edited by Gordon R. Willey. Vol. 3, pt. 2. of *Handbook of Middle American Indians,* edited by Robert Wauchope. Austin: University of Texas Press.

Caso, Alfonso, and Ignacio Bernal

1952 *Urnas de Oaxaca.* Memorias del Instituto Nacional de Antropología e Historia II. Mexico.

Cervantes, María Antonieta

1967 Una estela olmeca de dos caras. *Boletin de Instituto Nacional de Antropología e Historia* 28(June): 32–35.

Clancy, Flora S.

1976 Maya Pedestal Stones. *New Mexico Studies in the Fine Arts* 1: 10–19. (Occasional series published by University of New Mexico Press.)

1980 *A Formal Analysis of the Relief-Carved Monuments at Tikal, Guatemala.* Ph.D. diss., Yale University. Ann Arbor: University Microfilms International.

1983 A Comparison of Highland Zapotec and Lowland Maya Graphic Styles. In *Interdisciplinary Approaches to the Study of Mesoamerican Highland-Lowland Interaction*, edited by Arthur G. Miller. Washington, D.C.: Dumbarton Oaks Center for Pre-Columbian Studies.

1985 Maya Sculpture. In *Maya Treasures of an Ancient Civilization* [exhibition catalog]. New York: Albuquerque Museum and Harry N. Abrams Inc., Publishers.

1986 Text and Image in the Tablets of the Cross Group at Palenque. *RES. Anthropology and Aesthetics* 11 (Spring): 17–32.

1988 The Compositions and Contexts of the Classic Stelae of Copan and Quirigua. In *The Southeastern Classic Maya Zone*, edited by Gordon Willey. Washington, D.C.: Dumbarton Oaks Center for Pre-Columbian Studies.

1990 A Genealogy for Maya Monuments. In *Vision and Revision in Maya Studies*, edited by Flora S. Clancy and Peter D. Harrison. Albuquerque: University of New Mexico Press.

1992 Late Fifth Century Public Monuments in the Maya Lowlands. *RES. Anthropology and Aesthetics* 22: 108–14.

1994a The Ancient Maya and Others. In *Mesoamerican and Chicano Art, Culture, and Identity*, edited by Robert C. Dash. *Willamette Journal of the Liberal Arts.* Supplementary series 6. Salem, OR: Willamette University.

1994b The Classic Maya Ceremonial Bar. *Anales del Instituto de Investigaciones Esteticas* 65: 7–45.

1994c Spatial Geometry and Logic in the Ancient Maya Mind. Part I: Monuments. In *Seventh Palenque Round Table, 1989.* Edited by Merle Greene Robertson and Virginia M. Fields. San Francisco: The Pre-Columbian Art Research Institute.

Clifford, James

1988 *The Predicament of Culture: Twentieth-Century Ethnography, Literature, and Art.* Cambridge: Harvard University Press.

Coe, Michael D.

1957 Cycle 7 Monuments in Middle America: A Reconsideration. *American Anthropologist* 59(4): 597–611.

1973 *The Maya Scribe and His World.* New York: The Grolier Club.

1977 Olmec and Maya: A Study in Relationships. In *The Origins of Maya Civilizations*, edited by Richard E. W. Adams. School of American Research Book. Albuquerque: University of New Mexico Press.

1984 *Mexico.* 3d ed. New York: Thames and Hudson.

1987 *The Maya.* Rev. 4th ed. New York: Thames and Hudson.

1992 *Breaking the Maya Code.* New York: Thames and Hudson.

Coe, William R.

1965 Tikal: Ten Years of Study of a Maya Ruin in the Lowlands of Guatemala. *Expedition* 8(1): 5–56.

1990 *Excavations in the Great Plaza, North Terrace, and North Acropolis of Tikal.* Tikal Report 14. 5 vols. Museum Monograph 61. University Museum. Philadelphia: University of Pennsylvania.

Coggins, Clemency C.

1975 *Painting and Drawing Styles at Tikal: An Historical and Iconographic Reconstruction.* Ph.D. diss., Harvard University. Ann Arbor: University Microfilms International.

1979a A New Order and the Role of the Calendar: Some Characteristics of the Middle Classic Period at Tikal. In *Maya Archaeology and Ethnohistory*, edited by Norman Hammond and Gordon Willey. Austin: University of Texas Press.

1979b Teotihuacan at Tikal in the Early Classic Period. In *Actes du 42nd Congres International de Americanistes 1976.* Vol. 8. Paris.

1983 An Instrument of Expansion: Monte Alban, Teotihuacan, and Tikal. In *Highland-Lowland Interaction in Mesoamerica: Interdisciplinary Approaches*, edited by Arthur G. Miller. Washington, D.C.: Dumbarton Oaks Research Library and Collection.

1985 Maya Iconography. In *Maya Treasures of an Ancient Civilization* [exhibition catalog]. New York: Albuquerque Museum and Harry N. Abrams, Inc., Publishers.

1990 The Birth of the Baktun at Tikal and Seibal. In *Vision and Revision in Maya Studies*, edited by Flora S. Clancy and Peter D. Harrison. Albuquerque: University of New Mexico Press.

Cohodas, Marvin

1979   The Identification of Workshops, Schools, and Hands at Yaxchilan, a Classic Maya Site in Mexico. In *Actes du 42nd Congres International des Americanistes 1976*. Vol. 7. Paris.

Copeland, Karen

1974   Drawings of the Monuments of Uaxactun, Guatemala. Unpublished set. University Museum. University of Pennsylvania, Philadelphia.

Cortez, Constance

1986   The Principal Bird Deity in Preclassic and Early Classic Maya Art. Master's thesis, University of Texas, Austin.

Culbert, T. Patrick, ed.

1973   *The Classic Maya Collapse*. A School of American Research Book. Albuquerque: University of New Mexico Press.

1988   Political History and the Decipherment of Maya Glyphs. *Antiquity* 62(234): 135–52.

1991   *Classic Maya Political History: Hieroglyphic and Archaeological Evidence*. A School of American Research Book. Cambridge: Cambridge University Press.

de la Fuente, Beatriz

1973   *Escultura Monumental Olmeca*. Mexico: Instituto de Investigaciones Esteticas, Universidad Nacional Autónoma de México.

1984   *Los Hombres de Piedra: Escultura Olmeca*. 2d ed. Mexico: Universidad Nacional Autónoma de México.

Diehl, Richard A., and Janet C. Berlo, eds.

1989   *Mesoamerica after the Decline of Teotihuacan A.D. 700–900*. Washington, D.C.: Dumbarton Oaks Research Library and Collection.

Digby, Adrian

1974   Crossed Trapezes: A Pre-Columbian Astronomical Instrument. In *Mesoamerican Archaeology: New Approaches*, edited by Norman Hammond. Austin: University of Texas Press.

Dillon, Brian D.

1982   Bound Prisoners in Maya Art. *Journal of New World Archaeology* 5(1): 24–50.

Drucker, Philip

1943   *Ceramic Sequences at Tres Zapotes, Veracruz, Mexico*. Bureau of American Ethnology. Bulletin 140. Washington, D.C.: Smithsonian Institution.

Easby, Elizabeth K., and John F. Scott

1970   *Before Cortez: Sculpture of Middle America*. New York: The Metropolitan Museum of Art, New York Graphic Society, Ltd.

Edmonson, Munro S.

1973   Semantic Universals and Particulars in Quiche. In *Meaning in Maya Languages*, edited by Munro Edmonson. The Hague: Mouton and Co.

———, annotator and trans.

1986   *Heaven Born Merida and Its Destiny: The Book of Chilam Balam of Chumayel*. Austin: University of Texas Press.

Fahsen O., Federico

1987   Los Personajes de Tikal en el Clasico Temprano: La Evidencia Epigrafica. In *Primer Simposio Mundial sobre Epigrafia Maya*. Asociación Tikal. Guatemala: Serviprensa Centroamericana.

Farriss, Nancy M.

1984   *Maya Society Under Colonial Rule: The Collective Enterprise of Survival*. Princeton: Princeton University Press.

1987   Remembering the Future, Anticipating the Past: History, Time, and Cosmology among the Maya of Yucatan. *Comparative Studies in Society and History* 29: 566–93.

Fash, William L.

1991   *Scribes, Warriors, and Kings: The City of Copan and the Ancient Maya*. New York: Thames and Hudson.

Fash, William L., and David S. Stuart

1991   Dynastic History and Cultural Evolution at Copan, Honduras. In *Classic Maya Political History: Hieroglyphic and Archaeological Evidence*, edited by T. Patrick Culbert. A School of American Research Book. Cambridge: Cambridge University Press.

Fialko C., Vilma

1987   El Marcador de Juego de Pelota de Tikal: Nuevas Referencias Epigraficas para El Clasico Temprano. In *Primer Simposio Mundial sobre Epigrafia Maya*. Asociación Tikal. Guatemala: Serviprensa Centroamericana.

Flannery, Kent V., ed.

1976   *The Early Mesoamerican Village*. Studies in Archaeology. New York: Academic Press.

Fowler, Alastair

1972   Periodization and Interart Analogies. *New Literary History* 3(3): 487–509.

Freidel, David A.

1985a   New Light on the Dark Age: A Summary of Major Themes. In *The Lowland Maya Postclassic*, edited by Arlen F. Chase and Prudence Rice. Austin: University of Texas Press.

1985b   Polychrome Facades of the Lowland Maya
         Preclassic. In *Painted Architecture in Meso-*
         america, edited by Elizabeth H. Boone. Wash-
         ington, D.C.: Dumbarton Oaks Research
         Library and Collection.
1990   The Jester God: The Beginning and End of a
         Maya Royal Symbol. In *Vision and Revision in*
         Maya Studies, edited by Flora S. Clancy and
         Peter D. Harrison. Albuquerque: University
         of New Mexico Press.

Freidel, David A., and Linda Schele
1988   Symbol and Power: A History of the Lowland
         Maya Cosmogram. In *Maya Iconography*,
         edited by Elizabeth P. Benson and Gillett G.
         Griffin. Princeton: Princeton University
         Press.

Freidel, David A., Linda Schele, and Joy Parker
1993   *Maya Cosmos.* New York: William Morrow
         and Company, Inc.

Gardner, John
1978   *On Moral Fiction.* New York: Basic Books,
         Inc., Publishers.

Geertz, Clifford
1973   *The Interpretation of Cultures.* New York:
         Basic Books, Harper Collins Publishers.

Gossen, Gary H.
1974   *Chamulas in the World of the Sun: Time and*
         Space in a Maya Oral Tradition. Cambridge:
         Harvard University Press.

Graham, Ian
1967   *Archaeological Explorations in El Peten, Gua-*
         temala. Publication 33. Middle American
         Research Institute. New Orleans: Tulane
         University.
1975   *Corpus of Maya Hieroglyphic Inscriptions:*
         Introduction. Vol. 1. Peabody Museum of
         Archaeology and Ethnology. Cambridge:
         Harvard University.
1986   *Corpus of Maya Hieroglyphic Inscriptions:*
         Uaxactún. Vol. 5, pt. 3. Peabody Museum of
         Archaeology and Ethnology. Cambridge:
         Harvard University.

Graham, John A., R. F. Heizer, and E. M. Shook
1978   Abaj Takalik 1976: Exploratory Investigations.
         In *Studies in Ancient Mesoamerica III.* Contri-
         butions of the University of California Ar-
         chaeological Research Facility. No. 36. De-
         partment of Anthropology. Berkeley: Univer-
         sity of California.

Greene Robertson, Merle
1974   The Quadripartite Badge—A Badge of Ruler-
         ship. In *Primera Mesa Redonda de Palenque.*

Part 1. Edited by Merle Greene Robertson.
Pebble Beach, CA: Pre-Columbian Art Research, Robert Louis Stevenson School.

Grieder, Terence
1964   Representation of Space and Form in Maya
         Painting on Pottery. *American Antiquity*
         29(4): 442–48.

Grove, David C.
1968   Chalcatzingo, Morelos, Mexico: A Reap-
         praisal of the Olmec Rock Carvings. *Ameri-*
         can Antiquity 33(4): 486–91.
1970   *The Olmec Paintings of Oxtotitlan Cave, Guer-*
         rero, Mexico. Studies in Pre-Columbian Art
         and Archaeology 6. Washington, D.C.: Dum-
         barton Oaks Research Library and Collection.
1973   Olmec Altars and Myths. *Archaeology* 26(2):
         129–35.
1984   *Chalcatzingo: Excavations on the Olmec Fron-*
         tier. London: Thames and Hudson.
———, ed.
1987   *Ancient Chalcatzingo.* Austin: University of
         Texas Press.

Hammond, Norman
1982a   A Late Formative Stela in the Maya Lowlands.
         American Antiquity 47(2): 396–403.
1982b   *Ancient Maya Civilization.* New Brunswick,
         NJ: Rutgers University Press.

Hammond, Norman, and Gordon Willey, eds.
1979   *Maya Archaeology and Ethnohistory.* Austin:
         University of Texas Press.

Harrison, Peter D.
1970   The Central Acropolis, Tikal, Guatemala: A
         Preliminary Study of Functions of its Struc-
         tural Components During the Late Classic
         Period. Ph.D. diss., University of Pennsylva-
         nia, Philadelphia.
1994   Spatial Geometry and Logic in the Ancient
         Maya Mind: Part 2: Architecture. *Seventh*
         Palenque Round Table, 1989. Edited by Merle
         Greene Robertson and Virginia M. Fields. San
         Francisco: The Pre-Columbian Art Research
         Institute.

Hassig, Ross
1992   *War and Society in Ancient Mesoamerica.*
         Berkeley: University of California Press.

Haviland, William A., and Hattula Moholy-Nagy
1992   Distinguishing the High and Mighty from the
         Hoi-Polloi at Tikal, Guatemala. In *Meso-*
         american Elites: An Archaeological Assessment,
         edited by Diane Z. Chase and Arlen F. Chase.
         Norman: University of Oklahoma Press.

Hellmuth, Nicholas M.
1969   Some Notes on First Season Explorations and

Excavations at Yaxha, El Peten, Guatemala. In *Katunob* 7(3): 35–36, 50–50b.

1975 The Esquintla Hoards: Teotihuacan Art in Guatemala. *F.L.A.A.R. Progress Reports* 1(2).

Henderson, John S.

1981 *The World of the Ancient Maya.* Ithaca: Cornell University Press.

Hendrickson, Carol

1989 Twin Gods and Quiche Rulers: The Relation between Divine Power and Lordly Rule in the Popol Vuh. In *Word and Image in Maya Culture: Explorations in Language, Writing, and Representation,* edited by William F. Hanks and Don S. Rice. Salt Lake City: University of Utah Press.

Heyden, Doris

1975 An Interpretation of the Cave Underneath the Pyramid of the Sun in Teotihuacan, Mexico. *American Antiquity* 40(2): 131–47.

1977 The Year Sign in Ancient Mexico: A Hypothesis as to Its Origin and Meaning. In *Pre-Columbian Art History,* edited by Alana Cordy-Collins and Jean Stern. Palo Alto, CA: Peek Publications. Reprinted from *Estudios de Cultura Maya* 3(1970).

Hill, Robert M., II, and John Monagham

1987 *Continuities in Highland Maya Social Organization: Ethnohistory in Sacapulas, Guatemala.* Philadelphia: University of Pennsylvania Press.

Hochberg, Julian

1972 The Representation of Things and People. In *Art, Perception, and Reality: The Alvin and Fanny Blaustein Thaleimer Lectures, 1970,* edited by Maurice Mandelbaum. Baltimore: John Hopkins University Press.

Houston, Stephen D.

1986 Problematic Emblem Glyphs: Examples from Altar de Sacrificios, El Chorro, Rio Azul, and Xultun. In *Research Reports on Ancient Maya Writing* 3. Washington, D.C.: Center for Maya Research.

1988 The Phonetic Decipherment of Mayan Glyphs. In *Antiquity* 62(234): 126–35.

1989 *Maya Glyphs.* Reading the Past. Berkeley: University of California Press and the British Museum.

Houston, Stephen D., and David Stuart

1989 The *Way* Glyph: Evidence for "Co-essences" among the Classic Maya. In *Research Reports on Ancient Maya Writing* 30. Washington, D.C.: Center of Maya Research.

1992 On Maya Hieroglyphic Literacy. *Current Anthropology* 33(5): 589–93.

Houston, Stephen D., and Karl A. Taube

1987 "Name-Tagging" in Classic Mayan Script. *Mexicon* 9(2): 38–41.

Hunt, Eva

1977 *The Transformation of the Hummingbird.* Symbol, Myth, and Ritual Series, edited by Victor Turner. Ithaca: Cornell University Press.

Johnson, Mark

1987 *The Body in the Mind.* Chicago: The University of Chicago Press.

Jones, Christopher

1969 *The Twin Pyramid Group Pattern: A Classic Maya Architectural Assemblage at Tikal, Guatemala.* Ph.D. diss., University of Pennsylvania, Philadelphia. Ann Arbor: University Microfilms International.

1983 Monument 26, Quiriguá, Guatemala. Edited by Edward Shortman and Patricia Urban. Vol. 2 of *Quiriguá Reports.* Museum Monograph 49. University Museum. Philadelphia: University of Pennsylvania.

1988 A Ruler in Triumph: Chocolá Monument 1. *Expedition* 28(3): 3–12.

1991 Cycles of Growth at Tikal. In *Classic Maya Political History: Hieroglyphic and Archaeological Evidence,* edited by T. Patrick Culbert. A School of American Research Book. Cambridge: Cambridge University Press.

Jones, Christopher, and Miguel Orrego C.

1987 Corosál Stela 1 and Tikal Miscellaneous Stone 167: Two New Monuments from the Tikal Vicinity, Guatemala. In *Mexicon* 9(6): 129–33.

Jones, Christopher, and Linton Satterthwaite

1982 *The Monuments and Inscriptions of Tikal: The Carved Monuments.* Tikal Report 33, pt. A. Museum Monograph 44. University Museum. Philadelphia: University of Pennsylvania.

Jones, Christopher, and Robert J. Sharer

1980 Archaeological Investigations in the Site-core of Quirigua. *Expedition* 23(1): 11–19.

Jones, Grant D.

1989 *Maya Resistance to Spanish Rule: Time and History on a Colonial Frontier.* Albuquerque: University of New Mexico Press.

Kelley, David H.

1965 The Birth of the Gods at Palenque. *Estudios de Cultura Maya* 5: 93–134.

1976 *Deciphering the Maya Script.* Austin: University of Texas Press.

Kessler, Herbert L., and Marianna Shreve Simpson, eds.

1985 *Pictorial Narrative in Antiquity and the Middle Ages.* Studies in the History of Art 16. Washington, D.C.: Center for Advanced Study in the Visual Arts, National Gallery of Art.

Kidder, Alfred, Jesse Jennings, and Edwin Shook

1946 *Excavations at Kaminaljuyu, Guatemala.* Publication 561. Washington, D.C.: Carnegie Institution of Washington.

Kitzinger, Ernest

1977 *Byzantine Art in the Making.* Cambridge: Harvard University Press.

Klein, Cecelia

1976 *The Face of the Earth: Frontality in Two-Dimensional Mesoamerican Art.* New York: Garland Publishing, Inc.

Knorosov, Yuri V.

1956 New Data on the Study of Written Maya Language. *Journal de la Société des Américanistes de Paris* 45.

1958 The Problem of the Study of the Maya Hieroglyphic Writing. *American Antiquity* 23(3): 284–91.

Krotser, Paula

1977 Veracruz: Corridor to the Southeast. Paper presented at symposium, Classic Teotihuacan in Mesoamerica. Colgate University, Hamilton, NY.

Kubler, George A.

1962 *Shape of Time.* New Haven: Yale University Press.

1967 *The Iconography of the Art of Teotihuacan.* Studies in Pre-Columbian Art and Archaeology 4. Washington, D.C.: Dumbarton Oaks Research Library and Collection.

1969 *Studies in Classic Maya Iconography.* Memoirs of the Connecticut Academy of Arts and Sciences XVIII. New Haven: Connecticut Academy of Arts and Sciences.

1975 Study of Glyphs at Tikal. Manuscript on file at the University Museum. University of Pennsylvania, Philadelphia.

1984 *The Art and Architecture of Ancient America.* 3d ed. Pelican History of Art. Baltimore: Penguin Books.

1991 *Esthetic Recognition of Ancient Amerindian Art.* New Haven: Yale University Press.

Kuchler, Susanne, and Walter Melion, eds.

1991 *Images of Memory: On Remembering and Representation.* Washington, D.C.: Smithsonian Institution Press.

Laporte, Juan Pedro, and Vilma Fialko C.

1990 New Perspectives on Old Problems: Dynastic References for the Early Classic at Tikal. In *Vision and Revision in Maya Studies*, edited by Flora S. Clancy and Peter D. Harrison. Albuquerque: University of New Mexico Press.

Leemans, C.

1878 Description de quelques antiquités américaines conservées dans le Musée Royal Neerlandais d'Antiquités a Leide. In *International Congress of Americanists 2nd session, 1877.* Vol. 2. Luxembourg.

León-Portilla, Miguel

1963 *Aztec Thought and Culture.* Translated by Jack E. Davis. Norman: University of Oklahoma Press.

Lewis, C. S.

1974 *The Screwtape Letters.* New York: Macmillan Paperbacks Edition.

López Austin, Alfredo

1993 *The Myths of the Opossum: Pathways of Mesoamerican Mythology.* Translated by Bernard R. Ortiz de Montellano and Thelma Ortiz de Montellano. Albuquerque: University of New Mexico Press.

Lounsbury, Floyd

1980 Some Problems in the Interpretation of the Mythological Portion of the Hieroglyphic Text of the Temple of the Cross at Palenque. In *Third Palenque Round Table, 1978.* Part 2. Edited by Merle Greene Robertson. Austin: University of Texas Press.

Love, Bruce

1987 Glyph T93 and Maya "hand-scattering" events. *Research Reports on Ancient Maya Writing* 5: 7–16.

Lowe, Gareth W., Thomas A. Lee, and Eduardo Martínez Espinosa

1982 *Izapa: An Introduction to the Ruins and Monuments.* Papers of the New World Archaeological Foundation 31. Provo, UT: Brigham Young University.

Lundell, C. L.

1934 Ruins of Polol and Other Archaeological Discoveries in the Department of Peten, Guatemala. *Contributions to American Archaeology* 8: 175–86.

Maler, Teobert

1901 Researches in the Central Portion of the Usumatsintla Valley. In *Memoirs.* Vol. 2, no. 1. Cambridge: Peabody Museum, Harvard University.

1903   Researches in the Central Portion of the
        Usumatsintla Valley. In *Memoirs*. Vol. 2, no. 2.
        Cambridge: Peabody Museum, Harvard
        University.

1908   Explorations in the Department of Peten,
        Guatemala, and Adjacent Regions. In *Memoirs*. Vol. 4, nos. 1 and 2. Peabody Museum,
        Harvard University, Cambridge.

Marcus, Joyce

1976   *Emblem and State in the Classic Maya Lowlands*. Washington, D.C.: Dumbarton Oaks
        Research Library and Collection.

1992   Royal Families, Royal Texts: Examples from
        the Zapotec and Maya. In *Mesoamerican
        Elites: An Archaeological Assessment*, edited by
        Diane Z. Chase and Arlen F. Chase. Norman:
        University of Oklahoma Press.

Martin, Simon, and Nikolai Grube

1994   Classic Maya Politics within a Mesoamerican
        Tradition. An Epigraphic Model of "Hegemonic" Political Organization. Paper presented, *Primer Seminario de las Mesas Redondas de Palenque*, 20 September to 1 October,
        Palenque, Chiapas, Mexico.

Mathews, Peter

1985   Maya Early Classic Monuments and Inscriptions. In *A Consideration of the Early Classic
        Period in the Maya Lowlands*, edited by Gordon
        R. Willey and Peter Mathews. Publication 10.
        Institute for Mesoamerican Studies. Albany:
        State University of New York at Albany.

Mayer, Karl H.

1978   *Maya Monuments: Sculptures of Unknown
        Provenance in Europe*. Translated by Sandra L.
        Brizee. Ramona, CA: Acoma Books.

Menninger, Karl

1977   *Number Words and Number Symbols: A Cultural History of Numbers*. Translated by Paul
        Broneer. Cambridge: The M.I.T. Press, Massachusetts Institute of Technology.

Milbrath, Susan

1979   *A Study of Olmec Sculptural Chronology*.
        Studies in Pre-Columbian Art and Archaeology 23. Washington, D.C.: Dumbarton Research Library and Collection.

Miles, Suzanne

1965   Sculpture of the Guatemala-Chiapas Highlands and Pacific Slopes, and Associated
        Hieroglyphs. Edited by Gordon Willey. Vol. 2,
        pt. 1 of *Handbook of Middle American Indians*, edited by Robert Wauchope. Austin:
        University of Texas Press.

Miller, Arthur G.

1973   *The Mural Painting of Teotihuacan*. Washington, D.C.: Dumbarton Oaks Research Library
        and Collection.

1986   *Maya Rulers of Time: A Study of Architectural
        Sculpture at Tikal, Guatemala*. University Museum. Philadelphia: University of Pennsylvania.

Miller, Mary E.

1985   Yaxchilan: Cookie Cutter Master. Paper presented, New Approaches in the Study of Style
        and Aesthetics in Mesoamerican Art. Esther
        Pasztory, organizer. College Art Association
        Meeting (February), Los Angeles.

1991   Rethinking the Classic Sculptures of Cerro de
        las Mesas, Veracruz. In *Settlement Archaeology
        of Cerro de las Mesas Veracruz, Mexico*, edited
        by Barbara L. Stark. Monograph 34. Institute
        of Archaeology, Los Angeles: University of
        California.

Miller, Mary E., and Stephen D. Houston

1987   The Classic Maya Ballgame and its Architectural Setting. In *RES. Anthropology and Aesthetics* 14 (Spring): 46–65.

Millon, Clara

1972   The History of Mural Art at Teotihuacan. In
        Teotihuacan, 11th Mesa Redonda, 1966.
        Mexico: Sociedad Mexicana de Antropología.

1973   Painting, Writing, and Polity in Teotihuacan,
        Mexico. *American Antiquity* 38(3): 294–314.

1988   A Re-examination of the Teotihuacan Tassel
        Headdress Insignia. In *Feathered Serpents and
        Flowering Trees*, edited by Kathleen Berrin.
        San Francisco: The Fine Arts Museum of San
        Francisco.

Mitchell, W. J. T.

1986   *Iconology: Image, Text, Ideology*. Chicago: The
        University of Chicago Press.

1994   *Picture Theory: Essays on Verbal and Visual
        Representation*. Chicago: The University of
        Chicago Press.

———, ed.

1980   *The Language of Images*. Chicago: The University of Chicago Press.

Montgomery, John

1992   Monuments of the Alta Usumacinta River
        Valley: Secondary Centers, Piedras Negras.
        Senior Honors thesis, Department of Art and
        Art History, University of New Mexico, Albuquerque.

Morley, Frances R., and Sylvanus G. Morley

1939   The Age and Provenance of the Leyden Plate.
        In *Contributions to American Anthropology*

and History 24. Publication 509. Washington, D.C.: Carnegie Institution of Washington.

Morley, Sylvanus G.

1920 *The Inscriptions of Copan*. Publication 219. Washington, D.C.: Carnegie Institution of Washington.

1937–38 *The Inscriptions of Peten*. 5 vols. Publication 437. Washington, D.C.: Carnegie Institution of Washington.

1946 *The Ancient Maya*. Stanford: Stanford University Press.

1956 *The Ancient Maya*. 3d ed. Revised by George W. Brainerd. Stanford: Stanford University Press.

Morley, Sylvanus G., George Brainerd, and Robert J. Sharer

1983 *The Ancient Maya*. 4th ed. Revised by Robert J. Sharer. Stanford: Stanford University Press.

Nagao, Debra

1989 Public Proclamation in the Art of Cacaxtla and Xochicalco. In *Mesoamerica After the Decline of Teotihuacan A.D. 700–900*, edited by Richard A. Diehl and Janet C. Berlo. Washington, D.C.: Dumbarton Oaks Research Library and Collection.

Neuenswander, Helen

1987 Reflections of the Concept of Dualism in Maya Hieroglyphic Pairing, Halving, and Inversion. In *Memorias del Primer Coloquio Internacional de Mayistas*. Instituto de Investigaciones Filológicas, Centro de Estudios Mayas. Mexico: Universidad Nacional Autónoma de México.

Nicholson, H. B. (with Eloise Quinones Keber)

1983 *Art of Aztec Mexico: Treasures of Tenochtitlan*. Washington, D.C.: National Gallery of Art.

Nodelman, Sheldon

1966 Structural Analysis in Art and Anthropology. *Yale French Studies* 36/37: 89–103.

Norman, V. Garth

1973 *Izapa Sculpture*. Part 1, Album. Papers of the New World Archaeological Foundation 30(1). Provo, UT: Brigham Young University.

1986 Geometry and Measure in Mesoamerican Monumental Art. Manuscript in possession of author.

Oaklander, L. Nathan, and Quentin Smith, eds.

1994 *The New Theory of Time*. New Haven: Yale University Press.

Ong, Walter J.

1982 *Orality and Literacy: The Technologizing of the Word*. New York: Methuen and Co., Ltd.

Pahl, Gary W.

1982 A Possible Cycle 7 Monument from Polol, El Peten, Guatemala. In *Pre-Columbian Art History*, edited by Alana Cordy-Collins. Palo Alto, CA: Peek Publications.

Panofsky, Erwin

1991 *Perspective as Symbolic Form*. Translated by Christopher Wood. New York: Zone Books. Originally, 1927, Die Perspektive als "symbolishe Form." In *Vortrage der Bibliothek Warburg 1924–1925*. Leipzig and Berlin.

1962 *Studies in Iconology: Humanistic Themes in the Art of the Renaissance*. Harper Torchbook edition. New York: Harper and Row Publishers. Originally, 1939, New York: Oxford University Press.

Parsons, Lee A.

1978 The Peripheral Coastal Lowlands and the Middle Classic Period. In *Middle Classic Mesoamerica: A.D. 400–700*, edited by Esther Pasztory. New York: Columbia University Press.

1986 *The Origins of Maya Art: Monumental Stone Sculpture of Kaminaljuyu, Guatemala and the Southern Pacific Coast*. Studies in Pre-Columbian Art and Archaeology 28. Washington, D.C.: Dumbarton Oaks Research Library and Collection.

1988 Proto-Maya Aspects of Miraflores-Arenal Monumental Stone Sculpture from Kaminaljuyu and the Southern Pacific Coast. In *Maya Iconography*, edited by Elizabeth P. Benson and Gillett G. Griffin. Princeton: Princeton University Press.

Pasztory, Esther

1974 *The Iconography of the Teotihuacan Tlaloc*. Studies Pre-Columbian Art and Archaeology 15. Washington, D.C.: Dumbarton Oaks Research Library and Collection.

1976 *The Murals of Tepantitla, Teotihuacan*. New York: Garland Publishing, Inc.

1977 The Gods of Teotihuacan: A Synthetic Approach to Teotihuacan Iconography. In *Pre-Columbian Art History: Selected Readings*, edited by Alana Cordy-Collins and Jean Stern. Palo Alto, CA: Peek Publications.

1988 A Reinterpretation of Teotihuacan and Its Mural Painting Tradition. In *Feathered Serpents and Flowering Trees*, edited by Kathleen Berrin. San Francisco: The Fine Arts Museum of San Francisco.

———, ed.

1978 *Middle Classic Mesoamerica: A.D. 400–700.* New York: Columbia University Press.

Pendergast, David M.

1992 Noblesse Oblige: The Elites of Altun Ha and Lamanai, Belize. In *Mesoamerican Elites: An Archaeological Assessment*, edited by Diane Z. Chase and Arlen F. Chase. Norman: University of Oklahoma Press.

Potter, Daniel R.

1985 Settlement. In *A Consideration of the Early Classic Period in the Maya Lowlands*, edited by Gordon R. Willey and Peter Mathews. Institute for Mesoamerican Studies. Publication 10. Albany: State University of New York at Albany.

Praz, Mario

1970 *Mnemosyne: The Parallel Between Literature and Visual Arts.* The A. W. Mellon Lectures in the Fine Arts, 1967. Bollingen Series XXXV.16. Princeton: Princeton University Press.

Proskouriakoff, Tatiana

1950 *A Study of Classic Maya Sculpture.* Publication 593. Washington, D.C.: Carnegie Institution of Washington.

1960 Historical Implications of a Pattern of Dates at Piedras Negras, Guatemala. *American Antiquity* 25(4): 454–75.

1961 Portraits of Women in Maya Art. In *Essays in Pre-Columbian Art and Archaeology*, by Samuel Lothrop et al. Cambridge: Harvard University Press.

1993 *Maya History,* edited by Rosemary A. Joyce. Austin, University of Texas Press.

Puleston, Dennis

1979 An Epistemological Pathology and the Collapse, or Why the Maya Kept the Short Count. In *Maya Archaeology and Ethnohistory*, edited by Norman Hammond and Gordon Willey. Austin: University of Texas Press.

Quirarte, Jacinto

1973 *Izapan-Style Art: A Study of Its Form and Meaning.* Studies in Pre-Columbian Art and Archaeology 10. Washington, D.C.: Dumbarton Oaks Research Library and Collection.

1974 Terrestrial/Celestial Polymorphs as Narrative Frames in the Art of Izapa and Palenque. In *Primera Mesa Redonda de Palenque.* Part 1. Edited by Merle Greene Robertson. Pebble Beach, CA: Pre-Columbian Art Research, Robert Louis Stevenson School.

1977 Early Art Styles of Mesoamerica and Early Classic Maya Art. In *The Origins of Maya Civilization*, edited by Richard E. W. Adams. School of American Research Book. Albuquerque: University of New Mexico Press.

Randall, Lillian M. C.

1966 *Images in the Margins of Gothic Manuscripts.* California Studies in the History of Art 4. Berkeley: University of California Press.

Reents-Budet, Dorie.

1989 Narrative in Classic Maya Art. In *Word and Image in Maya Culture: Explorations in Language, Writing, and Representation*, edited by William F. Hanks and Don S. Rice. Salt Lake City: University of Utah Press.

1994 *Painting the Maya Universe: Royal Ceramics of the Classic Period.* Duke University Museum of Art. Durham, NC: Duke University Press.

Ricketson, Oliver, and Edith B. Ricketson, Jr.

1937 *Uaxactun, Guatemala: Group E—1926–1931: Excavations and Artifacts.* Publication 477. Washington, D.C.: Carnegie Institution of Washington.

Robertson, Donald

1963 *Pre-Columbian Architecture.* The Great Ages of World Architecture. New York: George Braziller.

1974 Some Remarks on Stone Relief Sculpture at Palenque. In *Primera Mesa Redonda de Palenque.* Part 2. Edited by Merle Greene Robertson. Pebble Beach, CA: Pre-Columbian Art Research, Robert Louis Stevenson School.

Roys, Ralph

1960 The Maya Katun Prophesies of the Books of Chilam Balam, Series I. In *Contributions to American Anthropology and History.* Vol. 12, no. 57. Washington, D.C.: Carnegie Institution of Washington.

1967 *The Book of the Chilam Balam of Chumayel.* Norman: University of Oklahoma Press. Publication 438. Washington, D.C.: Carnegie Institution of Washington.

Ruppert, Karl

1977 A Special Assemblage of Maya Structure. In *Essays on Middle American Anthropology and Archaeology,* edited by Clarence L. Hay, et. al. New York: Dover Publications. (Reprinted from Appleton-Century, New York. 1940.)

Ruz Lhuillier, Alberto

1963 *La Civilizacion de los Antiguos Mayas.* Mexico: Instituto Nacional de Antropología e Historia.

Sabloff, Jeremy

1989 *The Cities of Ancient Mexico: Reconstructing a Lost World.* London: Thames and Hudson.

Sanders, William T.

1977   Ethnographic Analogy and the Teotihuacan Horizon Style. In *Teotihuacan and Kaminaljuyu: A Study in Prehistoric Culture Contact*, edited by William T. Sanders and Joseph W. Michels. Monograph Series on Kaminaljuyu. University Park: The Pennsylvania State University Press.

Santley, Robert S.

1983   Obsidian Trade and Teotihuacan Influence in Mesoamerica. In *Highland-Lowland Interaction in Mesoamerica. Interdisciplinary Approaches*, edited by Arthur Miller. Washington, D.C.: Dumbarton Oaks Center for Pre-Columbian Studies.

Satterthwaite, Linton

1958   The Problem of Abnormal Stelae Placements at Tikal and Elsewhere. Tikal Report 3. Museum Monographs. University Museum. Philadelphia: University of Pennsylvania.

Schapiro, Meyer

1969   On Some Problems in the Semiotics of Visual Art: Field and Vehicle in Image Signs. *Semiotica* 1(3): 223–42.

1973   *Words and Pictures: On the Literal and the Symbolic in the Illustrations of a Text*. Approaches to Semiotics 11. The Hague: Mouton and Co.

Schavelzon, Daniel

1980   Temples, Caves, or Monsters? Notes on Zoomorphic Facades in Pre-Hispanic Architecture. In *Third Palenque Round Table, 1978*. Part 2. Edited by Merle Greene Robertson. Austin: University of Texas Press.

Schele, Linda

1976   Accession Iconography of Chan-Bahlum in the Cross Group at Palenque. In *The Art, Iconography and Dynastic History of Palenque*. Part 3. Segunda Mesa Redonda de Palenque, 1974. Edited by Merle Greene Robertson. Pebble Beach, CA: Pre-Columbian Art Research, Robert Louis Stevenson School.

1979   Genealogical Documentation on the Tri-figure Panels at Palenque. In *Tercera Mesa Redonda de Palenque*. Vol. 4. Edited by Merle Greene Robertson. Palenque, Chiapas, Mexico: Pre-Columbian Art Research Center.

1985a   Color on Classic Architecture and Monumental Sculpture of the Southern Maya Lowlands. In *Painted Architecture and Polychrome Monumental Sculpture in Mesoamerica*, edited by Elizabeth H. Boone. Washington, D.C.: Dumbarton Oaks Research Library and Collection.

1985b   The Hauberg Stela: Bloodletting and the Mythos of Maya Rulership. In *Fifth Palenque Round Table, 1983*. Edited by Merle Greene Robertson and Virginia M. Fields. San Francisco: The Pre-Columbian Art Research Institute.

1986   The Tlaloc Complex in the Classic Period: War and the Interaction between the Lowland Maya and Teotihuacan. Paper presented at symposium, *The New Dynamics*. Kimbell Art Museum, Fort Worth, TX.

1990   House Names and Dedication Rituals at Palenque. In *Vision and Revision in Maya Studies*, edited by Flora S. Clancy and Peter D. Harrison. Albuquerque: University of New Mexico Press.

Schele, Linda, and David Freidel

1990   *A Forest of Kings: The Untold Story of the Ancient Maya*. New York: William Morrow and Company, Inc.

Schele, Linda, and Mary E. Miller

1986   *The Blood of Kings* [exhibition catalog]. Fort Worth: Kimbell Art Museum.

Seler, Eduard

1902–23   *Gesammelte Abhandlungen zur amerikanishen Sprach-und Alterthumskunde*. 5 vols. Berlin: n.p.

1977   *Observations and Studies in the Ruins of Palenque*. Translated by Gisela Morganer. Pebble Beach, CA: Robert Louis Stevenson School.

Sharer, Robert S.

1990   *Quirigua: A Classic Maya Center and its Sculpture*. Durham, NC: Carolina Academic Press.

1991   Diversity and Continuity in Maya Civilization: Quirigua as a Case Study. In *Classic Maya Political History*, edited by T. Patrick Culbert. A School of American Research Book. Cambridge: Cambridge University Press.

1994   *The Ancient Maya*. Stanford: Stanford University Press.

Sheets, Payson D.

1979   Environmental and Cultural Effects of the Ilopango Eruption in Central America. In *Volcanic Activity and Human Ecology*, edited by Payson D. Sheets and D. K. Grayson. New York: Academic Press.

Smith, A. Ledyard

1950   *Uaxactun, Guatemala: Excavations of 1931–1937*. Publication 588. Washington, D.C.: Carnegie Institution of Washington.

Smith, Virginia G.

1984 *Izapa Relief Carving.* Studies in Pre-Columbian Art and Archaeology 27. Washington, D.C.: Dumbarton Oaks Research Library and Collection.

Spinden, Herbert J.

1913 A Study of Maya Art. In *Memoirs.* Vol. 6. Peabody Museum. Cambridge: Harvard University.

Stark, Barbara, and L. Antonio Curet

1994 The Development of the Classic-Period Mixtequilla in South-Central Veracruz, Mexico. *Ancient Mesoamerica* 5(2): 267–87.

Stirling, Matthew

1941 Expedition Unearths Buried Masterpieces. *National Geographic Magazine* 80(3): 277–302.

1943 *Stone Monuments of Southern Mexico.* Bulletin 138. Bureau of American Ethnology. Cambridge: Smithsonian Institution.

Stone, Andrea J.

1983 *The Zoomorphs of Quirigua.* Ph.D. diss., University of Texas, Austin. Ann Arbor: University Microfilms International.

1989 Disconnection, Foreign Insignia, and Political Expansion: Teotihuacan and the Warrior Stelae of Piedras Negras. In *Mesoamerica After the Decline of Teotihuacan A.D. 700–900,* edited by Richard A. Diehl and Janet C. Berlo. Washington, D.C.: Dumbarton Oaks Research Library and Collection.

Stuart, David

1984 Royal Auto-Sacrifice Among the Maya: A Study of Image and Meaning. In *RES. Anthropology and Aesthetics* 7/8: 6–20.

1988 Blood Symbolism in Maya Iconography. In *Maya Iconography,* edited by Elizabeth P. Benson and Gillett G. Griffin. Princeton: Princeton University Press.

1996 Kings of Stone. In *RES. Anthropology and Aesthetics* 29/30: 148–71.

1998 Arrival of Strangers. In Pre-Columbian Art Research Institute, Newsletter 25, July [excerpt from paper delivered in Austin, Texas].

Stuart, David, and Stephen Houston

1994 *Classic Maya Place Names.* Studies in Pre-Columbian Art and Archaeology 33. Washington, D.C.: Dumbarton Oaks Research Library and Collection.

Stuart, George

1987 A Carved Shell from the Northeastern Maya Lowlands. *Research Reports on Ancient Maya Writing* 13: 13–19.

Tate, Carolyn

1980 The Maya Cauac Monster: Formal Development and Dynastic Implications. Master's thesis, University of Texas, Austin.

1982 The Maya Cauac Monster's Formal Development and Dynastic Contexts. In *Pre-Columbian Art History: Selected Readings,* edited by Alana Cordy-Collins. Palo Alto, CA: Peek Publications.

1986 *The Language of Symbols in the Ritual Environment of Yaxchilan, Chiapas, Mexico.* Ph.D. diss., University of Texas Press. Ann Arbor: University Microfilms International.

1992 *Yaxchilan: The Design of a Maya Ceremonial City.* Austin: University of Texas Press.

Taube, Karl A.

1985 The Classic Maya Maize God: A Reappraisal. In *Fifth Palenque Round Table, 1983.* Edited by Merle Greene Robertson and Virginia M. Fields. San Francisco: The Pre-Columbian Art Institute.

1988 A Prehispanic Maya Katun Wheel. *Journal of Anthropological Research* 44(2): 183–203.

Taylor, Dicey

1979 The Cauac Monster. In *Tercera Mesa Redonda de Palenque.* Vol. 4. Edited by Merle Greene Robertson. Palenque, Chiapas, Mexico: Pre-Columbian Art Research Center.

Tedlock, Barbara

1982 *Time and the Highland Maya.* Albuquerque: University of New Mexico Press.

1983 Quichean Time Philosophy. In *Calendars in Mesoamerican and Peru: Native American Computations of Time,* edited by Anthony F. Aveni and Gordon Brotherson. BAR, International Series 174, Oxford, UK: BAR.

Tedlock, Barbara, and Dennis Tedlock

1985 Text and Textile: Language and Technology in the Arts of the Quiche Maya. *Journal of Anthropological Research* 41(2): 121–46.

Tedlock, Dennis

1985 *Popol Vuh (translation and commentary).* New York: Simon and Schuster.

Thompson, J. Eric. S.

1941 Dating of Certain Inscriptions of non-Maya Origin. In *Theoretical Approaches to Problems.* No. 1. Cambridge, MA: Carnegie Institution of Washington.

1950 *Maya Hieroglyphic Writing: An Introduction.* Publication 589. Washington, D.C.: Carnegie Institution of Washington. Reissued, 1960, Norman: University of Oklahoma Press.

1962   *A Catalog of Maya Hieroglyphs*. Norman: University of Oklahoma Press.

1966   *The Rise and Fall of Maya Civilization*. Enlarged 2d ed. Norman: University of Oklahoma Press.

1970   *Maya History and Religion*. Norman: University of Oklahoma Press.

1972   *A Commentary on the Dresden Codex*. Philadelphia: American Philosophical Society.

Todorov, Tzvetan

1985   *The Conquest of America*. Translated by Richard Howard. Perennial Library. New York: Harper and Row, Publishers.

Townsend, Richard F.

1982   Pyramid and Sacred Mountain. In *Ethnoastronomy and Archaeoastronomy in the American Tropics*, edited by Anthony F. Aveni and Gary Urton. Annals of the New York Academy of Sciences 385. New York: The New York Academy of Sciences.

1993   *The Aztecs*. London: Thames and Hudson.

Tozzer, Alfred M., ed.

1941   *Landa's Relación de las Cosas de Yucatán: A Translation*. Papers of the Peabody Museum of American Archaeology and Ethnology XVIII. Cambridge, MA: Harvard University.

Trompf, G. W.

1979   *The Idea of Historical Recurrence in Western Thought*. Berkeley: University of California Press.

Uspensky, Boris

1973   *A Poetics of Composition*. Translated by Valentina Zavarin and Susan Wittig. Berkeley: University of California Press.

Valdés, Juan Antonio

1986   Uaxactún: Recientes Investigaciones. In *Mexicon* 8(6): 125–28.

1987   Estado Actual de las Investigaciones en Uaxactún, Guatemala. In *Memorias de Primer Coloquio Internacional de Mayistas (August 1985, San Cristóbal de las Casas, Chiapas)*. Mexico: Universidad Nacional Autónoma de México.

Valdés, Juan Antonio, Frederico Fahsen and Gaspar Muñoz Cosme

1997   *Estela 40 de Tikal. Hallazgo y lectura*. Instituto de Antropología e Historia de Guatemala, Agencia Española de Cooperación Internacional.

Vogt, Evon Z.

1969   *Zinacantan: A Maya Community in the Highlands of Chiapas*. Cambridge: The Belknap Press of Harvard University.

von Euw, Eric

1978   *Corpus of Maya Hieroglyphic Inscriptions: Xultun*. Vol. 5, pt. 1. Peabody Museum of Archaeology and Ethnology. Cambridge: Harvard University.

von Euw, Eric, and Ian Graham

1984   *Corpus of Maya Hieroglyphic Inscriptions: Xultun, La Honradez, Uaxactun*. Vol. 5, pt. 2. Peabody Museum of Archaeology and Ethnology. Cambridge: Harvard University.

Weitzmann, Kurt

1970   *Illustrations in Roll and Codex: A Study of the Origin and Method of Text Illustration*. Studies in Manuscript Illuminations 2. Princeton: Princeton University Press.

Whitrow, G. J.

1988   *Time in History*. Oxford and New York: Oxford University Press.

Whorf, Benjamin L.

1956   *Language, Thought, and Reality: Selected Writings*. Edited by John B. Carroll. Cambridge: The M.I.T. Press, Massachusetts Institute of Technology.

Willey, Gordon R., and Peter Mathews, eds.

1985   *A Consideration of the Early Classic Period in the Maya Lowlands*. Institute for Mesoamerican Studies. Publication 10. Albany: State University of New York at Albany.

Yates, Frances B.

1966   *The Art of Memory*. Chicago: The University of Chicago Press.

Index

Numbers in bold refer to figures.